Well Logging I—Rock Properties, Borehole Environment, Mud and Temperature Logging

James R. Jorden
Manager, Petroleum Engineering Research
Shell Development Co.

and

Frank L. Campbell
Vice President, Exploration Research
Chevron Oil Field Research Co.

First Printing
Henry L. Doherty Memorial Fund of AIME
Society of Petroleum Engineers of AIME
New York   1984   Dallas

Dedication

This Monograph is dedicated to Gus Archie and John Walstrom who blazed the trail we followed.

SPE Monograph Series

The Monograph Series of the Society of Petroleum Engineers of AIME was established in 1965 by action of the SPE Board of Directors. The Series is intended to provide authoritative, up-to-date treatment of the fundamental principles and state of the art in selected fields of technology. The Series is directed by the Society's Monograph committee, one of more than 50 Society-wide committees. A committee member designated as Monograph Coordinator provides technical evaluation with the aid of the Review Committee. Below is a listing of those who have been most closely involved with the preparation of this monograph.

Monograph Coordinators

Dennis J. Graue, Scientific Software
Robert N. Hart, Bow Valley Petroleum Inc.
Charles E. Konen, Amoco Production Co.
Joseph W. Martinelli, Gulf Oil E&P Co.
Herbert L. Stone, Exxon Production Research Co.
Lawrence W. Thrasher, Consultant

Monograph Review Committee

Robert P. Alger, Consultant
Roy M. Dicharry, J.R. Butler and Co.
Charles E. Konen, Amoco Production Co.
Gary S. Neinast, Sun Production Co.

Acknowledgments

Dr. Samuel Johnson once said: "A man will turn over half a library to make one book." Read we did, but it wasn't enough. Writing this monograph required the talented help and generous support of many people and we want to acknowledge them here.

This monograph had a gestation period longer than any living creature ever created. We outlasted several monograph coordinators and sorely tried the patience of the review committee. All these people are listed on the preceding page, and we gratefully acknowledge their contribution. Among this group we especially salute Chuck Konen, Amoco Production Co., whose gentle yet persistent persuasion did much to bring this project to a successful conclusion. Of all the SPE staff who helped develop this monograph, we particularly thank Pat Pate and Erin Stewart for their guidance as the authors struggled with policy issues on scope, structure, format, and deadlines.

Dresser-Atlas provided the graphics for this monograph. Among the several Dresser management staff who guided the firm's contributions for more than 7 years, Jim Anderson and Barbra Myers deserve special thanks. Most importantly, Debbie Schliesser created all the original illustrations and recreated all figures taken from the literature to provide a consistent nomenclature and format. Her ability to grasp engineering concepts and translate them into artistic images added substantially to this monograph's readability. Thanks go to Susan Burt for help in obtaining the photographs of the Dresser-Atlas tools. Ernie Finklea helped obtain the photographs of the Schlumberger tools.

Dr. Johnson after surveying the English language called it "copious without order, and energetick without rules." This book is much less copious thanks to Charles Everett who applied 25 years of technical editing experience to improving the readability of this book. As the editing process evolved, our goal became: to have written a sentence that Charlie could not shorten and improve; we succeeded only occasionally. The order, with a minimum of rules, came from Kathleen Jun, SPE Asst. Editor, who coordinated the publication. Her thoroughness certainly improved the consistency of the highly interrelated components of this book.

We wish to thank Chevron Oil Field Research Co. and Shell Oil Co. for their many unheralded contributions to this monograph. Foremost among these is the technical insight we have gained through discussions with knowledgeable coworkers and access to proprietary technology. These opportunities have definitely improved the coherence of our review of the open literature. Whatever quality this monograph has as a comprehensive treatment of existing technology results in large part from the cooperation of the library science staff of both organizations. Aphrodite Mamoulides, Bernice Melde, and the other staff at Shell's Bellaire Research Center library were always willing to find "just one more paper." Special thanks also to Elaine Spencer, Chevron.

In addition to the regular review process, we have asked numerous colleagues to challenge the scope, accuracy, and clarity of various chapters.

Chap. 1 contains log usage data furnished by Schlumberger. The project to gather these data turned out to be a larger task than originally expected. Nonetheless, Schlumberger stuck with it and produced log usage data available nowhere else in the well logging literature. In particular, Adam Perez and Bud Griswold devoted many of their own weekend hours to this chore.

Chap. 2 contains much geologic information outside the bounds of traditional petroleum engineering technology; Bob Sneider, consultant, and Don Harris, Exxon Production Research Co., brought a geologist's perspectives to their review. Bert Thomeer, Shell Oil Co., helped clarify several discussions of pore space properties and fluid distribution. E.C. Thomas, also with Shell, added a teacher's insight to the review.

Chap. 3 was built on an AAPG-sponsored short course presented by Ray Campbell of Schlumberger, Turk Timur of Chevron, and the authors. Many of the examples and explanations are from the notes of that course, especially Ray and Turk's sections on geometry, stress, and tool performance. Paul Hull, Al Brown, Bob Davis, and Chuck Haskin reviewed Chap. 3 and, as Chevron colleagues can, made many constructive suggestions. Jim Klotz, Union Oil Co. of California, reviewed this chapter and provided useful insights. Together their contributions significantly improved this chapter, which was fun but difficult to write because we tried to deal with real boreholes rather than the ideal world of test pits, computer models, and chart books.

Chap. 4 on mud logging was first reviewed by Fritz Reuter and Alun Whittaker of Exlog Inc. and John Spangler, Chevron. Their suggestions encouraged expanding the scope and revising the balance of the contents. Rich Mercer, EGG Continental Laboratories, shared his considerable experience and understanding by making many suggestions, which are now incorporated into the text. Carl Buchholz, Francis Crofton, Bill Zoeller, and Henry Potts of The Analysts were very helpful in clarifying some issues and obtaining some hard-to-find examples. Special thanks go to Exlog for the use of many examples from their fine training manuals. Mark Zetter, Delphian Corp., was an important source of information about gas detectors. The dialog with these experts raised Chap. 4 from what could have been simply an authors' perspective to an industry statement. Not to be forgotten when acknowledging contributions are those from the many dedicated logging crews with people like the late Al Lipphardt, whose patient teachings and strong convictions about the value of mud logging have influenced the authors' views that are presented in this chapter.

The long and lonely hours devoted to writing this were shared by Laurene Campbell and Shirley Jorden. They gave up many weekends and vacations needed to make that next deadline. If that wasn't enough, they were always ready to help with the typing, proofing, and editing. Our loving thanks to them.

We are grateful to all!

Foreword

While writing this, we struggled with several issues that eluded alternative solutions that will please everyone. Use of conventional options offered safe refuge from criticism but did not satisfy our objective to make this as readable as possible. Accordingly, we opted for some less conventional alternatives when dealing with scope, style, literature citations, and, especially, units.

The scope of this monograph is confined primarily to formation evaluation. It was tempting to broaden the discussion to include production logging and subsurface modeling applications based on borehole gravity, vertical seismic profiling, ultralong-spaced electric logging, and dipmeters. The role of mud logging in drilling optimization is recognized but not systematically reviewed. These are important subjects but are considered beyond the scope of formation evaluation, as originally defined and from time to time reaffirmed by our review committee.

A single system of units is not always used for very carefully considered reasons. We started writing this using SI. However, our objectives were compromised by loss of visualization, uncertain precision, and difficulties in referring back to the original literature. So we chose to use units that are most commonly used in oilfield practice or, alternatively, are consistent with the particular reference that is being discussed. Equations are developed using units that allow an uncluttered view of the physical/chemical concepts and principles being expressed. Dual units were considered but seemed cumbersome and unenlightening. However, many figures are drafted with dual scales, SPE-preferred SI values for constants used in major equations are provided in the Appendix, and conversion factors for all quantities are presented in the Nomenclature.

The availability of the literature cited in some chapters remains a concern to us. We cited what seemed to be the best references, recognizing that some may not be available in every science library. We did not acknowledge all of the literature. The Selected Reading List on Page 157 contains what we found to be the most significant and helpful references. Computerized search services should provide adequate information about other sources.

We requested and accepted technical editing to make this monograph more readable—especially considering that English is the second language of many SPE members. Moreover, esoteric qualifications and details were omitted for clarity and brevity. We really tried to keep the readers in mind and hope it shows!

Contents

Preface

This monograph is the first of a four-volume set offering a comprehensive treatment of formation evaluation by well logging. The other volumes in this series are *Well Logging II—Electric and Acoustic Logging; Well Logging III—Radiation, Nuclear Magnetism, and Borehole Gravity Logging;* and *Well Logging IV—Formation Evaluation Methods.*

Well logging is one of the most dynamic areas in the oil industry. Data collection methods have been improved significantly by advances in microelectronics, computers, and computer processing methods. The advances over the past 50 years are shown clearly in this volume. At the time of publication, this monograph represents the state of the art. The authors, editor, and review committee have made every effort to eliminate erroneous information; however, it is inevitable that some of the material will be proved inaccurate in the future.

The ultimate objective of well logging is to evaluate subsurface formations. The form of the evaluation depends considerably on the information being sought, whether for hydrocarbon or mineral content, rock characteristics, or correlation. Wireline logging is by its very nature an indirect measurement of fluid and rock characteristics. Thus, the interrelations between rocks, fluids, and physically measurable parameters must be understood if the user of the data is to derive accurate interpretations. Wireline measurements, however, are influenced strongly by the environment of the wellbore even though significant efforts have been made to reduce these factors. This volume provides insight into both these areas.

Log interpretation often requires additional information to resolve discrepancies and conflicts. The required information is available from the mud log in many instances, as the log contains a history of drilling mud properties, hydrocarbon detection, and rock samples. A thorough discussion of mud logging is presented in Chap. 4.

Formation temperatures and temperature profiles are a very important component of modern log interpretation. Temperature logs have been recorded since the very early years of logging and remain an important source of information.

The authors, J.R. Jorden and F.L. Campbell, are well known in the well logging and petroleum industry. J.R. Jorden is manager of the Petroleum Engineering Research Dept. of Shell Development Co. and 1984 President of SPE. F.L. Campbell is vice president of the Exploration Research Dept. of Chevron Oil Field Research Co.

This monograph provides much basic information regarding log interpretation. As such, it is anticipated that the monograph will be used as a primary reference for petroleum engineers and for training purposes. Subsequent volumes will build upon this foundation.

Houston
December 1984

WELL LOGGING
REVIEW COMMITTEE

Chapter 1

Prologue

We made a sonde by connecting four metre-long sections of Bakelite tubing together. . . . The electrodes were wired to the Bakelite tubes. We contrived a weight . . . filling it with lead pellets like those used in duck shooting. . . . The whole assembly looked like a long black snake with five joints. . . . The cable, if you could call it that, was three lengths of rubber-insulated copper wire, like the kind used on spark plugs in cars. . . . We planned to take readings at intervals of one metre. . . . We made our measurements with a standard potentiometer mounted on a tripod like those we used in our surface exploration work ...

from the personal recollections of H.G. Doll,
who participated in recording the first wireline log.

1.0 Introduction. This chapter sets the stage for the monograph set by detailing the earliest history of well logging and well log analysis. Comment is given on the significance of these events to well logging development and to today's log user. The chapter also provides a perspective of how wireline and mud logging have grown. This overview illustrates current logging methods and their use relative to each other and to former methods.

The objective of this monograph set is to review and to summarize those aspects of mud and wireline logging that are pertinent to formation evaluation. It is written for log users interested in knowing what technical options are available as they use log data to evaluate formations. These include both the "generalist" log user and "specialist" log analyst. The monograph is formatted so that new data on logging tools and interpretive techniques can be added by the reader.

Skillful formation evaluation requires an understanding of several interrelated components, from fundamental reservoir properties through evaluation methods. This monograph set includes four books, of which this is the first, to treat these several topics adequately.

1.1 Early History of Well Logging and Log Analysis

For the first 70 years of oilfield development, the only well logs were written records (or logs) of formation cuttings and fluids exposed by the drilling process. The first wireline log of a borehole was obtained in the Pechelbronn oil field, France, on Sept. 5, 1927.[1] This survey, of electrical resistivity only (Fig. 1.1), was obtained by taking point-by-point measurements, essentially by hand. The methods were typical of those then used for surface geophysical prospecting, but ingeniously adapted for borehole surveying.

Similar creative adaptations have led to the automatically recorded, continuously operating, multifunctional tools of modern well logging. The prin-cipal events defining these creative adaptations and the technological evolution of well logging are summarized in numerous histories. The API history[1] traces well logging from its inception through 1958. The Natl. Petroleum Council study[2,3] looks at the growth of and improvements in well-logging technology from 1946 to 1965. Johnson[4] gives a complete chronology of the pioneer developments and improvements in well logging from 1927 through 1960, and also provides detail rich in human interest about the earliest days of wireline logging. Several World Petroleum Congress papers[5-12] review technological improvements in well logging over successive 4-year periods since 1951. Allaud and Martin[13] chronicle the story of the Schlumberger organization's evolution, from its beginning in 1920 to its status in the middle 1970's; they also explain the science-based techniques used in modern well logging.

Fig. 1.2 and Table 1.1 record the growth of wireline logging since 1927. During the decade following, logging was used mainly for picking formation tops and well-to-well correlation. Its use grew dramatically thereafter as analysts came to recognize that the measured parameters are interpretable in terms of useful reservoir properties. Early on, several qualitative correlations were noted among log data and reservoir characteristics,[1] as summarized in Table 1.2.

During the late 1930's, experimental programs were undertaken to define the relationship between electrical resistivity and oil saturation. Although the first results were summarized by Martin *et al.*[14] in 1938, the results reported in 1941 by Archie[15] were especially useful in two ways:

1. They provided the basic principles for quantitatively interpreting the electrical resistivity of rock in terms of oil saturation.

2. They demonstrated that wireline logs can be quantitatively interpreted if a relationship (or model) can be found between the measured log parameters and desired reservoir properties. Such modeling can be through empirical field observations, laboratory experiments, theoretical constructions, etc.

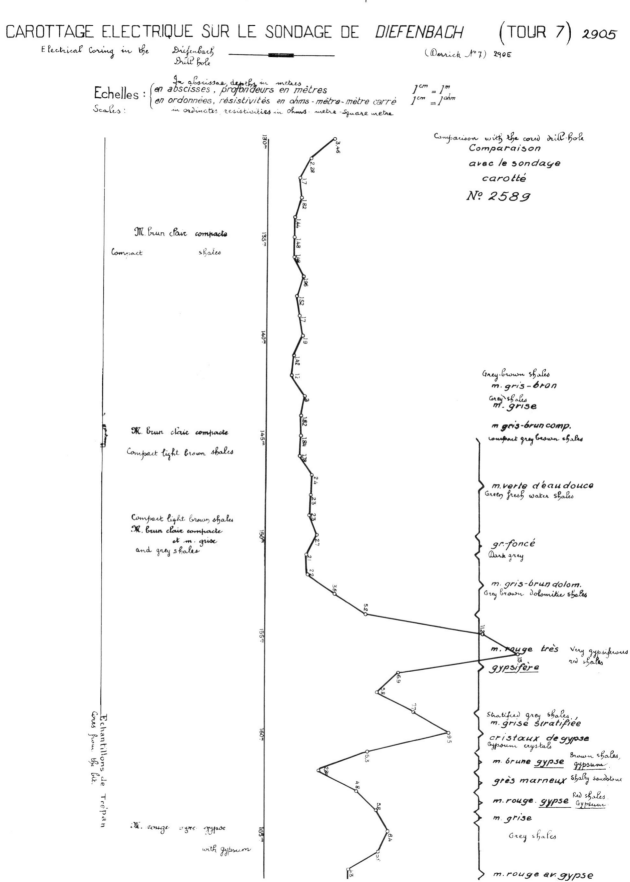

Fig. 1.1—First wireline log of a borehole (courtesy of Schlumberger Well Services).

The second achievement was probably the more important. As is repeatedly emphasized in this monograph set, reliable wireline log analysis and formation evaluation require that models be developed relating measured log data and desired reservoir properties. Archie's research started the industry on an evolving technology that developed interpretive models for wireline log analysis and formation evaluation.

Mud logging (defined in Chap. 4) has been practiced almost since the inception of the petroleum industry; drill-cuttings logs were made during the 1870's.[1] However, the work of J.T. Hayward[16] in the late 1930's marks the beginning of mud logging as a coordinated and coherent tool for formation evaluation. Fig. 1.3 shows an early mud log. Fig. 1.4 shows that, like wireline logging, mud logging has grown steadily, both commercially and technologically.

1.2 Relationship of Well Logging to Formation Evaluation

Formation evaluation, as applied to subsurface petroleum reservoirs, has historically been defined as the practice of determining reservoir thickness, lithology, porosity, hydrocarbon saturation, and permeability, using information obtained from a borehole. This definition probably represents a consensus from the statements in Table 1.3, which is a summary of quotations on the definition, scope, and objectives of formation evaluation from experts on the subject.[3,17-23]

Formation evaluation can be more generally defined as the practice of determining the physical and chemical properties of rocks and their contained fluids.

Four major classes of tools and techniques are available for formation evaluation: (1) *mud logging*, (2) *coring and core analysis,* (3) *drillstem testing*, and (4) *wireline logging.*

To many log users, "well logging" means "wireline logging." Actually, *well logging* is the creating of a record (a log) of some engineering or geologic parameter vs. borehole depth or time. This includes wireline logs, mud logs, core-analysis plots, stratigraphic sample logs, drilling parameter logs, and many others.

This well-logging monograph set deals only with mud logging and wireline logging. Excluded are drillstem testing, coring and core analysis, and production logging (now a sophisticated and widely used branch of wireline logging). Thus, this monograph set is not a complete treatment of either formation evaluation or well logging, except for those aspects of mud and wireline logging pertinent to formation evaluation. To simplify terminology, "well logging" is used synonymously with "wireline logging" and "mud logging."

1.3 Objectives and Scope of This Monograph Set

Well logging has been discussed in many papers and texts. Thus, readers might ask why this monograph set is needed and how it can be useful. The prime objective is to review and to summarize completely those aspects of mud and wireline logging pertinent to formation evaluation. Readers of this monograph are perceived as log users interested in knowing the available technical options in the use of log data to evaluate formations. This publication set should give "generalist" log users, who have not had time to master completely all the details of logging tools and interpretive techniques, a quick yet comprehensive summary of the technology and its applications. At the same time, it should provide "specialist" log analysts with a retrospective overview that will deepen their perception of their profession. This objective is achieved by (1) reviewing as thoroughly as possible the entire body of technical literature, (2) identifying and referencing the truly significant technical work, and (3) unifying and interpreting the current state of technology to achieve a comprehensive treatment of log analysis and formation evaluation. This monograph set is not addressed to beginning students nor to those engaged in research and development of new logging tools or interpretive techniques.

Well logging is based on well-established principles of physics and chemistry. Although these principles are completely developed in other texts and reviews, they are restated and summarized here for ready use on future novel problems.

Log users who apply these principles to well-log interpretation and formation evaluation soon encounter dilemmas created by a rapidly improving technology. There is a continuous stream of improvements in geologic and petrographic concepts, logging-tool electronics, and computer-processing capabilities, as well as the opening of new geologic provinces. All of these combine to add quickly to the knowledge available and required to evaluate formations. How then could any well-logging review, once completed, have any lasting value in such a rapidly changing technological environment?

This monograph set attempts to minimize the problem through a format that can be easily updated. Specifically, existing knowledge is summarized in tables and graphs. Further, preformatted blank tables and graphs are provided for adding new knowledge as it becomes available. These concepts are particularly emphasized in the accompanying loose-bound chart collection. This scheme permits the new to be compared with the old, and allows the various logging tools and interpretive techniques to be put in a time frame.

1.4 Organization of This Monograph Set

Skillful formation evaluation requires an understanding and mastery of several somewhat sequential yet highly interrelated components: (1) the fundamental (primary) properties of reservoirs (i.e., thickness, lithology, porosity, permeability, and fluid distribution) and the relationships among them; (2) the borehole environment; (3) the secondary reservoir properties (such as electrical resistivity and acoustic velocity) and their relationships with the primary reservoir properties; (4) the methods used to measure these properties (i.e., mud logging, coring and core analysis, drillstem testing, and wireline logging); and (5) the interpretation methods used in formation evaluation. The monographs in this set (Table 1.4) present topics in approximately this order.

This first monograph, *Rock Properties, Borehole Environment, Mud and Temperature Logging,* reviews the fundamental properties needed to evaluate a hydrocarbon reservoir. Emphasis is placed on the basic geologic and petrographic characteristics that control these properties,

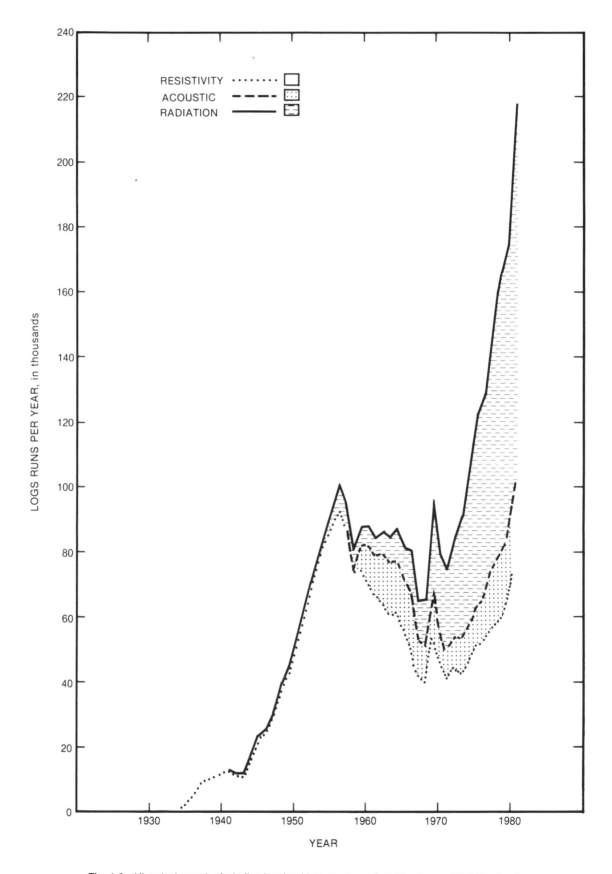

Fig. 1.2—Historical growth of wireline logging (data courtesy of Schlumberger Well Services).

TABLE 1.1—GROWTH OF WIRELINE LOGGING, NUMBER OF LOGS RUN PER YEAR, 1927–1980*

| | Electrical | | | Acoustic | Radiation | | | | |
Year	Conventional	Focused	Micro	Induction	Interval Transit Time	Natural Gamma Ray**	Steady-State Neutron	Pulsed Neutron	Gamma-Gamma Density	Total
1927	10									10
1928	20									20
1929	160									160
1930	216									216
1931	384									384
1932	27									27
1933	243									243
1934	580									580
1935	2,790									2,790
1936	5,180									5,180
1937	8,930									8,930
1938	10,170									10,170
1939	10,810									10,810
1940	11,720					200				11,920
1941	12,470					400	200			13,070
1942	11,100					600	200			11,900
1943	10,960					800	300			12,060
1944	16,730					1,000	400			18,130
1945	22,040	100				1,200	500			23,840
1946	23,490	200				1,400	600			25,690
1947	27,840	300				1,600	700			30,440
1948	35,070	400	500			1,700	800			38,470
1949	38,910	600	2,000			1,500	900			43,910
1950	42,020	1,200	6,000			1,600	1,000			51,820
1951	44,130	1,800	12,000	400		1,800	1,200			61,330
1952	49,060	2,400	16,000	600		2,000	1,400			71,460
1953	53,020	2,600	18,000	1,000		2,200	2,000			78,820
1954	55,030	4,000	20,000	2,500		2,500	3,000			87,030
1955	54,320	5,000	24,400	3,500		2,800	4,000			94,020
1956	52,920	6,000	27,200	6,100		3,000	5,400			100,620
1957	41,160	5,000	26,800	13,750	50	3,000	5,000			94,760
1958	34,430	3,500	22,000	14,000	1,820	1,300	4,800			81,850
1959	29,150	4,600	22,000	18,300	7,760	1,000	4,700		200	87,710
1960	27,630	4,000	19,000	20,000	11,300	1,000	4,500		500	87,930
1961	24,470	4,000	15,000	23,000	12,550	900	4,000		600	84,520
1962	17,310	5,100	14,300	28,000	15,100	800	3,900		2,100	86,610
1963	16,250	4,300	11,200	29,000	16,100	600	4,200		2,950	84,600
1964	15,040	3,700	10,100	32,500	15,800	500	4,500		4,800	86,940
1965	11,550	3,200	8,100	33,100	15,900	500	2,800		6,480	81,630
1966	11,660	2,530	6,100	30,500	16,800	500	3,600		8,810	80,500
1967	5,090	1,820	4,400	30,700	11,300	500	2,900		8,570	65,280
1968	5,540	1,690	3,600	28,800	11,900	500	3,600		10,030	65,660
1969	4,700	2,030	13,000	34,390	13,970	500	9,800	490	15,000	93,880
1970	3,900	1,710	11,000	30,140	9,830	200	9,500	910	13,000	80,190
1971	3,300	1,690	8,000	28,180	9,080	200	9,700	1,330	14,000	75,480
1972	3,000	2,370	8,000	30,810	10,050	200	12,600	1,560	16,000	84,590
1973	2,800	3,290	6,000	30,340	11,050	100	13,700	1,650	22,000	90,930
1974	2,800	3,740	6,000	33,520	11,850	100	20,000	2,020	27,000	107,030
1975	2,500	4,950	6,000	38,060	12,590	100	25,400	2,350	30,000	121,950
1976	2,000	4,120	4,000	41,820	14,370	100	27,560	2,470	31,860	128,300
1977	1,500	5,620	2,000	47,160	18,710	100	34,310	2,490	38,570	150,460
1978	1,000	6,060	1,200	50,220	20,900	200	40,210	2,680	42,930	165,400
1979	700	6,540	1,200	53,380	21,420	300	43,190	2,660	44,400	173,790
1980	500	9,320	1,200	63,670	25,620	100	56,110	3,410	57,600	217,530

*Data for 1927–1931 are worldwide; data for 1932–1980 are North America only. Data courtesy of Schlumberger Well Services.
**Natural gamma ray logs are counted only when run singly; "combination gamma ray" logs began being run in about 1958.

TABLE 1.2—EARLY INTERPRETATION OF WIRELINE LOGS (after Leonardon[1])

Resistivity Log	SP Log	Probable Conclusion
Low resistivity	no SP	shales
Low resistivity	large SP	saltwater sand
High resistivity	low SP	freshwater sand
Good resistivity	moderately large SP	possible oil sand
Very high resistivity	no SP	hard rock; very compact sand with sweet water

and less discussion concerns the diagenetic processes that modify the properties. Perhaps the most important characteristic of a rock is its pore-size distribution, which strongly influences porosity, permeability, and fluid distribution (basic definitions of these are given). Discussion includes the pore-distribution differences for both clastics and carbonates. The use of capillary pressure curves to infer pore-size-distribution characteristics is introduced. The principles of capillarity are used to explain and to quantify further the concepts of fluid distribution. Also presented are the petrophysical relationships that exist among various fundamental rock properties (such as porosity/permeability and porosity/water saturation), and examples are given from the literature. Reviews are given of the chemical nature of subsurface formation waters and methods of measuring and relating water compositions.

This monograph discusses the actual borehole environment for well logging, which can be very different from that in the idealized models used to formulate tool response and formation-evaluation methods. Included are reviews of (1) wellbore geometry; (2) the impregnation and infiltration processes (with their resultant influences on porosity and saturation) during and after drilling; (3) the temperature distribution in the borehole during and after drilling; (4) the stress disturbances induced by drilling; (5) chemical alteration effects; and (6) example tool performance in nonideal environments and recommended practices.

This book also deals with the techniques of mud and temperature logging. The organizational scheme is similar to that described next for the more conventional wireline logging methods.

Chapters in the second and third monographs in the set, *Electric and Acoustic Logging* and *Radiation, Nuclear Magnetism, and Borehole Gravity Logging,* deal with a specific wireline logging method in this order: (1) the relevant principles of physics and chemistry; (2) the use of models to relate measurable secondary reservoir properties to required primary reservoir properties; (3) the instrumentation and operation of the logging tools; (4) the problems that can arise in measuring true secondary properties (i.e., the perturbations caused by the borehole, invaded zone, and thin beds); (5) the limitations of existing logging-tool designs and tool-response models for accurately portraying the heterogeneous and anisotropic properties of natural rock; and (6) the methods of deriving true secondary properties from recorded log responses.

Example logs and pertinent interpretation charts are used. Emphasis is on summarizing, through tables and graphs, the characteristics of past and present logging tools. These books, particularly the companion chart inserts, are formatted so that readers can conveniently update the summaries as new and improved tools become commercially available—which will assuredly happen.

The fourth monograph in this set, *Formation Evaluation Applications,* covers the methods that can be applied through the use of well logging data. The opening chapter reviews principles and general techniques, including crossplots, "quick-look" logs, and digitized well log processing by computer. Subsequent chapters deal with estimating primary formation properties from

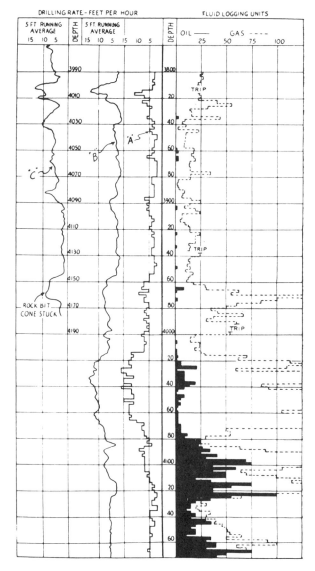

Fig. 1.3—Example of an early mud log of a borehole (after Hayward[16]).

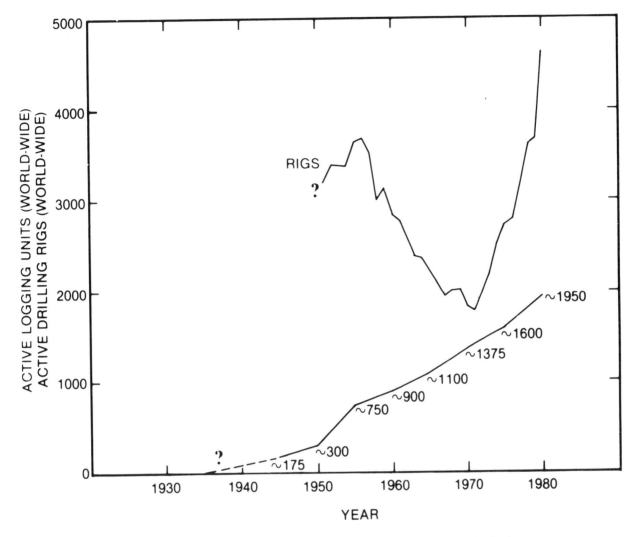

Fig. 1.4—Historical growth of mud logging (data courtesy of Exploration Logging Inc.).

log responses for one or more of those properties: (1) lithology; (2) porosity, permeability, and fractures; (3) water composition; and (4) saturation. Chapters on the use of well log data for correlation and abnormal pressure analysis also are included.

Each of the chapters presents methods for evaluating the major rock types encountered in petroleum reservoir exploration and development. Actual example problems and pertinent interpretation charts are included.

Interpretation charts are included in the monograph texts to illustrate how to correct apparent log responses to true rock properties, or how to derive fundamental (primary) rock properties from secondary rock properties. In addition, a separate, loose-bound chart collection is provided. It contains (1) a complete indexing system providing a framework for organizing a collection of charts into a system compatible with the monograph text discussion and (2) a few actual charts, which illustrate the types of charts intended for each "pigeonhole" in the framework. Generally speaking, these are the universal (or basic) charts necessary for rudimentary log interpretation. Beyond this, readers can add to their chart collection as they wish.

This monograph set presents a cross-reference system within the four books (Fig. 1.5 shows one example of this system). This guide is given in each monograph text and the separate chart collection as an outline of how to use the monograph set and where to find related topics in the four books.

References

1. Leonardon, E.G.: "Logging, Sampling, and Testing," *History of Petroleum Engineering*, API, Dallas (1961) 493.
2. McDonal, F.J.: "Geophysics," *Impact of New Technology on the U.S. Petroleum Industry 1946–1965*, Natl. Pet. Council, Washington, DC (1967) 67–71.
3. Archie, G.E.: "Formation Evaluation," *Impact of New Technology on the U.S. Petroleum Industry 1946–1965*, Natl. Pet. Council, Washington, DC (1967) 150–57.
4. Johnson, H.M.: "A History of Well Logging," *Geophysics* (1962) **27**, 507–27.
5. Wyllie, M.R.J.: "Theoretical Considerations Involved in the Determination of Petroleum Reservoir Parameters from Electric Log Data," *Proc.*, Third World Pet. Cong., The Hague (1951) Sec. II, 378–93.
6. Walstrom, J.E. (ed.), "Symposium on Well Bore Surveys," *Proc.*, Fourth World Pet. Cong., Rome (1955) Sec. II, 155–273.
7. Doll, H.G., Martin, M., and Tixier, M.P.: "Review of the Progress of Well Logging Since the Fourth World Petroleum Congress," *Proc.*, Fifth World Pet. Cong., New York City (1959) Sec. I, 645–66.
8. Doll, H.G., Tixier, M.P., and Segesman, F.: "Recent Developments in Well Logging in the U.S.A.," *Proc.*, Sixth World Pet. Cong., Frankfurt-am-Main (1963) Sec. II, 233–51.

TABLE 1.3—FORMATION EVALUATION—ITS DEFINITION, SCOPE, AND OBJECTIVES

Author(s)	Reference	Definition, Scope, and Objectives
Pirson	17	"... reservoir engineers and ... oil and gas property appraisers ... use logs for the evaluation of structural or stratigraphic closure, effective pay, porosity, fluid saturation, calculation of oil and gas originally in place, expected ultimate recovery, and present reserves .... In the oil and gas industries, the main purpose of well log analysis is the evaluation of reservoir rock properties in situ ...."
Archie	3	"The process of using information obtained from a borehole to determine the physical and chemical properties of the rocks and their fluid content, especially hydrocarbons, is known as formation evaluation. The complexity and importance of formation evaluation have led to the establishment of a new technical position in many companies — the formation analyst or petrophysical engineer .... Evaluation of a reservoir involves defining its areal extent and determining its thickness, porosity, permeability, and oil saturation. Accurate determination of the last four of these parameters at a reasonable cost is the goal of the formation analyst or petrophysical engineer .... Formation evaluation methods can be divided into two categories: ... Analyses of cores, cuttings, and drilling fluids are the methods that constitute the first category. The second category includes drill-stem testing and all the tools run in the hole on wireline to measure natural electrical potential, electrical resistivity, radioactivity, acoustic velocity, and other physical parameters which provide an indirect measure of rock and fluid properties."
Lynch	18	"...the duty of the wellsite geologist or engineer to locate those formations that contain hydrocarbons and to evaluate their commercial significance ... comprises the field known as Formation Evaluation .... Included in the formation evaluation methods are logging from drill returns, coring and core analysis, formation testing, and various wireline services .... The value of an oil reservoir is defined by its areal extent, its thickness and permeability, its fractional porosity, and the fraction of porosity that is saturated with oil. The objective of good formation evaluation is the quantitative determination of these items."
Guyod and Shane	19	"... the objectives of geophysical well logging may be said to be: the location of petroleum reservoirs, the estimation of the ability of a well to produce petroleum, the mapping of the reservoir shape, the estimation of the petroleum reserves, the determination of the best well completion procedure."
Evans and Pickett	20	"... the field of formation evaluation ... includes: estimates of in-place and recoverable hydrocarbon volumes, lithology determination, identification of geological environments, derivation of initial versus residual oil saturation relations, evaluation of water flood feasibility in early wells, location of reservoir fluids contacts, reservoir 'quality' mapping, determination of water salinity, determination of fluid pressures in reservoirs during the drilling of wells, detection of fractures, derivation of parameters required for reservoir engineering studies, prediction of probability of interzone fluid communication in casing-formation annulus, determination of porosity and pore size distribution, monitoring of fluid movement in reservoirs."
Jorden	21	"An intelligent system of formation evaluation requires a complete understanding of the primary reservoir properties and the relationships among them, then an understanding of the secondary reservoir properties and the relationships both among them and with the primary properties. Next the methods used to measure the properties—the data-gathering phase, the core and fluid analysis and well logging aspects of formation evaluation—must be thoroughly understood. Finally, the interpretation methods used in formation evaluation must be mastered."
Walstrom	22	"The evaluation of subsurface formations ... includes all coring, logging, mud logging, testing and sampling procedures. It includes log interpretation methods and laboratory analyses related to subsurface evaluation of the formations including an analysis of their contained fluids. ...The principal objectives of formation evaluation are to evaluate the presence or absence of commercial quantities of hydrocarbons in formations penetrated by, or lying near, the wellbore and to determine the static and dynamic characteristics of productive reservoirs. Another objective of formation evaluation is to detect small quantities of hydrocarbons which nevertheless may be significant from an exploratory standpoint. A further objective is to provide a comparison of an interval in one well to the correlative interval in another well."
Jennings and Timur	23	"In a general sense, formation evaluation can be defined as the science and the art, in that order, of economic evaluation of natural resources occurring in earth formations. For the purposes of this paper, however, the definition will be confined to the evaluation of petroleum reservoirs. In this context, formation evaluation may be considered to include all coring, well logging, mud logging, testing, and sampling."

9. Brown, A.A.: "New Methods of Characterizing Reservoir Rocks by Well Logging," *Proc.*, Seventh World Pet. Cong., Mexico City (1967) **2**, 301-08.

10. Riboud, J. and Schuster, N.A.: "Well Logging Techniques,"

Proc., Eighth World Pet. Cong., Moscow (1971) **3**, 327-37.

11. Rutman, G.: "Progress in Well Logging Methods," *Proc.*, Ninth World Pet. Cong., Tokyo (1975) **3**, 295-305.

12. Evans, C.B. and Gouilloud, M.: "The Changing Role of Well

Logging in Reservoir Evaluation: A Challenge of the 1980s,'' *Proc.*, Tenth World Pet. Cong., Bucharest (1979) **3**, 181–89.

13. Allaud, L. and Martin, M.: *Schlumberger, the History of a Technique*, John Wiley & Sons Inc., New York City (1977).

14. Martin, M., Murray, G.H., and Gillingham, W.J.: ''Determination of the Potential Productivity of Oil Bearing Formations by Resistivity Measurements,'' *Geophysics* (1938) **3**, 258–72.

15. Archie, G.E.: ''The Electrical Resistivity Log as an Aid in Determining Some Reservoir Characteristics,'' *Trans.*, AIME (1942) **146**, 54–62.

16. Hayward, J.T.: ''Continuous Logging at Rotary Drilling Wells,'' *Drill. and Prod. Prac.*, API (1940).

17. Pirson, S.J.: *Handbook of Well Log Analysis for Oil and Gas Formation Evaluation*, Prentice-Hall Inc., Englewood Cliffs, NJ (1963).

18. Lynch, E.J.: *Formation Evaluation*, Harper & Row Publishers Inc., New York City (1962).

19. Guyod, H. and Shane, L.E.: *Geophysical Well Logging*, Guyod, Houston (1969) 9.

20. Evans, H.B. and Pickett, G.R.: ''Status and Development of Formation Analysis,'' paper SPE 2743 presented at the 1969 SPE California Regional Meeting, San Francisco, Nov. 6–7.

21. Jorden, J.R.: ''Goals for Formation Evaluation,'' *J. Pet. Tech.* (Jan. 1971) 55–62.

22. Walstrom, J.E.: ''A Review of Formation Evaluation,'' paper SPE 4187 presented at the 1972 SPE California Regional Meeting, Bakersfield, Nov. 8–10.

23. Jennings, H.Y. Jr. and Timur, A.: ''Significant Contributions in Formation Evaluation and Well Testing,'' *J. Pet. Tech.* (Dec. 1973) 1432–46.

TABLE 1.4—ORGANIZATION OF THE WELL LOGGING MONOGRAPH SET

Book	Topics
I	Fundamental properties of reservoir rocks and waters Borehole environment Mud logging Temperature logging
II	Electric logging Acoustic logging
III	Radiation logging Nuclear magnetism logging Borehole gravity logging
IV	Formation evaluation methods—introduction Lithology evaluation Porosity, permeability, and fracture evaluation Water composition evaluation Saturation evaluation Correlation applications Abnormal pressure analysis

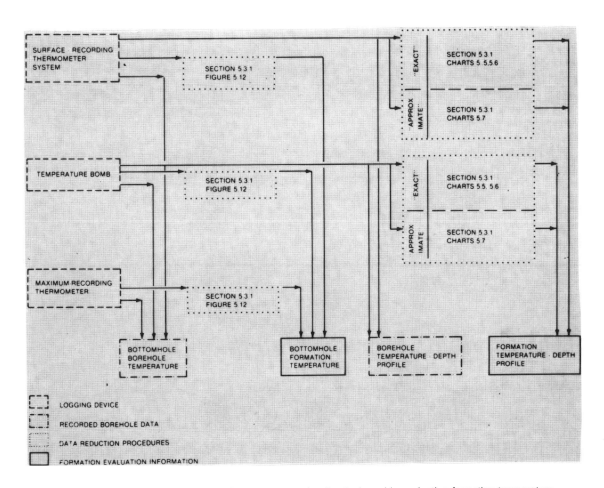

Fig. 1.5 —Options available in selecting temperature logging tools and in evaluating formation temperature.

Chapter 2

Fundamental Properties of Reservoir Rocks and Waters

... a term to express the physics of rocks ... should be related to petrology much as geophysics is related to geology. "Petrophysics" is suggested as the term pertaining to the physics of particular rock types .... This subject is a study of the physical properties of rock which are related to the pore and fluid distribution...

from G.E. Archie,[1] whose understanding of rocks
helped to start the quantification of log analysis
and formation evaluation.

2.0 Introduction. Formation evaluation of a petroleum reservoir is the practice of determining reservoir thickness, lithology, porosity, hydrocarbon saturation, and permeability, using information obtained from a borehole. These fundamental reservoir properties[1] often are derived or interpreted from indirect well log measurements. To understand formation evaluation by use of well logging data, one must first understand the fundamental properties that characterize a reservoir.

Most commercial petroleum reservoirs occur in sedimentary rocks; few occur in metamorphic or igneous rocks. Any sedimentary rock has two components: solids and pore space. The major task in formation evaluation is characterizing the rock pore system and its contained fluids. The solids properties and pore-space properties of most rocks are closely related. Today's well log suite contains some data measurements that are influenced greatly by the solids properties. Hence, formation evaluation requires a clear understanding of both rock solids and pore-space properties.

2.1 Lithology

The American Geological Inst. *Glossary of Geology* defines *lithology* as "the physical character of a rock." This character is influenced mainly by the *mineral composition* and *texture* of the solids. These attributes are discussed next for the major rock classes of (1) clastics and (2) carbonates and evaporites.

2.1.1 Clastic Rocks

Clastic rocks generally are defined as those created by physical sedimentation.[2] Table 2.1 shows the major classes of clastic rocks; in this monograph, discussion is limited to sandstones, siltstones, and claystones and shales.* This monograph uses "sandstones," etc. as synonymous with a particular type of clastic rocks—i.e.,

siliciclastic rocks, those whose mineral composition is primarily quartz. The major parameter defining sandstones, siltstones, and claystones is grain size (Table 2.2). Sandstones are the type most commonly found as petroleum reservoir rock; conglomerates and siltstones are rarer; and shales and claystones normally are not considered reservoir rock. Minor fractions of clay minerals and shale often have a major influence on reservoir-rock properties (e.g., porosity and permeability) and on logging tool response.

Composition

Sandstone is composed of at least 50% sand-size particles. Three mineral components used to define sandstone classes are *quartz*, *feldspar*, and *rock* (or lithic) *fragments* (igneous rocks, chert, limestone, slate, etc.). Table 2.3 outlines a classification scheme of these components and Chart 2.1 gives their physical/chemical properties.[3-5] A very similar classification for arenites only, but one with terms appropriate for practical field use, is illustrated in Fig. 4.41. Chart 2.2 details the physical/chemical properties of accessory minerals, many of which may be present in small amounts in sandstones.

Siltstone is composed of at least 50% silt-size particles that are generally less rich in quartz than is sandstone. *Claystone* is composed of at least 50% clay-size particles, generally *clay minerals* (hydrous aluminum silicates). Common *mudstone* or *shale* is a mixture of clay-size particles (mainly clay minerals), silt-size particles (mainly quartz, occasionally feldspar or calcite), and perhaps some sand-size particles (mainly quartz, occasionally feldspar or calcite).

Table 2.4[6] outlines a classification scheme based on the structure of clay crystal unit layers. Chart 2.3 lists the physical/chemical properties of clay minerals.

The electrical charge properties of clays are of particular interest. In the crystal lattices of many clay minerals, atoms of lower positive valence often replace ones of similar size but higher positive valence. This

---

*These classification schemes consistently use the nomenclature for consolidated rocks. There are often parallel nomenclatures for the unconsolidated and metamorphosed equivalents.

TABLE 2.1—CLASSIFICATION
OF SEDIMENTARY ROCKS (after Pettijohn[2])

I. Exogenetic sediments ("clastic")
  A. Epiclastics
    1. Conglomerates
    2. Sandstones
    3. Siltstones
    4. Claystones and shales
  B. Cataclastics (tills, etc.)
  C. Pyroclastics (tuffs, etc.)
II. Endogenetic sediments ("chemical and biochemical")
  A. Precipitated sediments
    1. Limestones
    2. Dolomites
    3. Evaporites (halites, anhydrites, etc.)
    4. Cherts
    5. Phosphorites
    6. Iron-bearing sediments
  B. Organic residues (coals, etc.)

TABLE 2.2—GRAIN-SIZE BOUNDARIES AND
NOMENCLATURE OF EPICLASTIC ROCKS
(after Pettijohn[2])

Grain Size		Nomenclature	
(μm)	(mm)	Component	Aggregate*
		boulder	boulder conglomerate
256,000	256		
		cobble	cobble conglomerate
64,000	64		
		pebble	pebble conglomerate
4,000	4		
		granule	granule conglomerate
2,000	2		
		sand	sandstone
62.50	1/16		
		silt ⎱	siltstone ⎱
3.906	1/256	⎰ mud	⎰ mudstone (nonlaminated) or
		clay ⎰	claystone ⎰ shale (laminated and fissile)

*As applied to consolidated rocks.

TABLE 2.3—CLASSIFICATION OF CLASTIC ROCKS ACCORDING TO COMPOSITION (after Pettijohn[2])

Nomenclature	Framework Fraction Properties
I. Arenites	less than 15% "interstitial material" of less than 30-μm size
A. Quartz arenites	more than 95% quartz
B. 1. Arkoses	more than 25% feldspar; percent feldspar greater than percent rock fragments
2. Subarkoses	2.5% to 25% feldspar; percent feldspar greater than percent rock fragments
C. 1. Lithic arenites	more than 25% rock fragments, percent rock fragments greater than percent feldspar
2. Sublithic arenites	2.5% to 25% rock fragments; percent rock fragments greater than percent feldspar
II. Wackes	more than 15% "interstitial material" of less than 30-μm size
A. Quartz wacke	more than 95% quartz
B. Feldspathic greywacke	percent feldspar greater than percent rock fragments
C. Lithic greywacke	percent rock fragments greater than percent feldspar

isomorphous substitution produces the various species of clay minerals and also results in a net negative charge at the substitution site. The excess negative charge is "countered" by surface adsorption of hydrated cations too large to fit into the interior of the crystal lattice (hence, the term *counterions*).

When a clay platelet is immersed in an ionic solution, these counterions can exchange with other ions in the solution (hence, the synonymous term *exchange ions*). The *cation exchange capacity* (CEC), or base exchange capacity, is a measure of the amount of such exchangeable cations on the surface of any clay. This laboratory-determined property is commonly expressed in meq/100 g of dry clay (or rock).

The net negative charge on many clay mineral surfaces attracts positive counterions from the surrounding ionic solution, establishing a nonuniform distribution of net positive charge (modeled as an electric double layer). Fig. 2.1a is a simple representation (the Guoy model) of this double layer. For the first few molecular layers away from the clay surface (the fixed layer), the cations are concentrated and relatively immobile. Their concentration decreases with distance from the surface (the diffuse layer), finally equaling the number of anions.

A more sophisticated model (the Stern model, Fig. 2.1b) considers that the counterions are "insulated" from the clay surface by (1) adsorbed water on the clay surface and (2) hydration water around the cations.

Texture

Texture deals with the size, sorting, shape, roundness, and packing (arrangement) of the rock solids.[2]

Grain size measures the approximate diameter. For nonspherical grains, the particular diameter measured depends on the technique used. The most common oilfield laboratory method is sieve analysis, which gives a close estimate of the diameter of the minimum cross-sectional area.

Grain size already has been discussed as the defining parameter for the major clastic rock classes (see Table 2.2). Fig. 2.2 gives a complete grain-size scale, showing both major and subordinate class limits as well as the nomenclature. Also shown is the *phi*, ϕ, scale, where

$$\phi = -\log_2 d_{gr}, \quad \dots\dots\dots\dots\dots\dots\dots (2.1)$$

where d_{gr} is the grain diameter in millimeters.

Also shown, for comparison, are several other commonly used size scales.

TABLE 2.4—CLASSIFICATION OF CLAY MINERALS (after Grim[6])

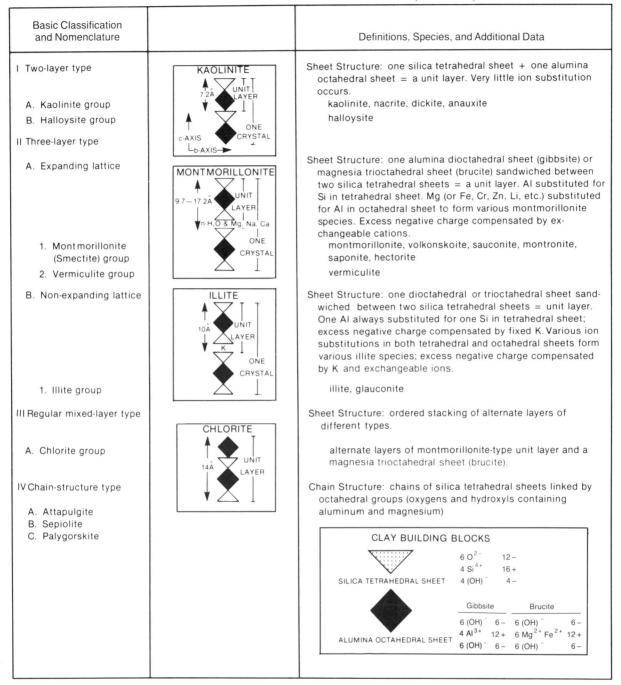

Basic Classification and Nomenclature		Definitions, Species, and Additional Data
I Two-layer type	KAOLINITE	Sheet Structure: one silica tetrahedral sheet + one alumina octahedral sheet = a unit layer. Very little ion substitution occurs.
A. Kaolinite group		kaolinite, nacrite, dickite, anauxite
B. Halloysite group		halloysite
II Three-layer type		
A. Expanding lattice	MONTMORILLONITE	Sheet Structure: one alumina dioctahedral sheet (gibbsite) or magnesia trioctahedral sheet (brucite) sandwiched between two silica tetrahedral sheets = a unit layer. Al substituted for Si in tetrahedral sheet. Mg (or Fe, Cr, Zn, Li, etc.) substituted for Al in octahedral sheet to form various montmorillonite species. Excess negative charge compensated by exchangeable cations.
1. Montmorillonite (Smectite) group		montmorillonite, volkonskoite, sauconite, montronite, saponite, hectorite
2. Vermiculite group		vermiculite
B. Non-expanding lattice	ILLITE	Sheet Structure: one dioctahedral or trioctahedral sheet sandwiched between two silica tetrahedral sheets = unit layer. One Al always substituted for one Si in tetrahedral sheet; excess negative charge compensated by fixed K. Various ion substitutions in both tetrahedral and octahedral sheets form various illite species; excess negative charge compensated by K and exchangeable ions.
1. Illite group		illite, glauconite
III Regular mixed-layer type		Sheet Structure: ordered stacking of alternate layers of different types.
A. Chlorite group	CHLORITE	alternate layers of montmorillonite-type unit layer and a magnesia trioctahedral sheet (brucite).
IV Chain-structure type		Chain Structure: chains of silica tetrahedral sheets linked by octahedral groups (oxygens and hydroxyls containing aluminum and magnesium)
A. Attapulgite B. Sepiolite C. Palygorskite		

The grain-size distribution of any sandstone is represented best by a cumulative distribution curve (Fig. 2.3). Several statistical measures of such a curve have both petrological and petrophysical significance, as summarized in Table 2.5 and Fig. 2.3.

Grain sorting measures how nearly a collection of grains approaches a single size. The Trask sorting coefficient, S_O, a common measure, is defined as

$$S_O = \left(\frac{d_{25}}{d_{75}}\right)^{1/2}, \quad \dots \dots \dots \dots \dots \dots (2.2)$$

where

d_{25} = grain size (mm) of 25 percentile (cumulative wt%) and

d_{75} = grain size (mm) of 75 percentile (cumulative wt%).

Grain shape (sphericity) measures how nearly a particular grain approaches the shape of a perfect sphere, as defined and measured in Chart 2.4.[7] This chart provides projected images of grains of known sphericity for visual comparison against rocks or grains of interest.

Grain roundness (angularity) measures the sharpness

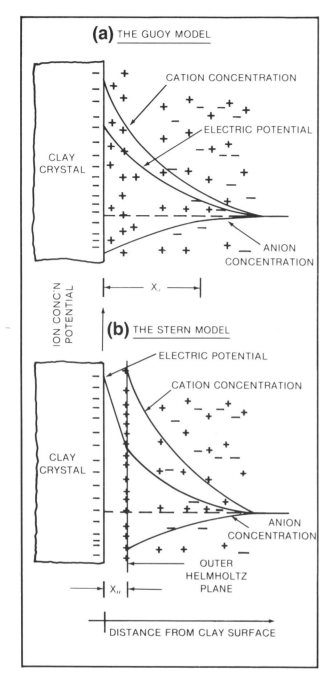

Fig. 2.1—Two models of the electric charge near a clay surface.

of the edges or corners of a grain; it is independent of grain shape. Chart 2.5[8] defines and illustrates the measurement of angularity. This chart provides projected images of grains of known angularity for visual comparison against rocks or grains of interest.

Grain packing describes the spacing (or density) of the grains. Packing is a difficult parameter to measure; the literature contains no significant theoretical definitions or standards of comparison for packing.

2.1.2 Carbonate and Evaporite Rocks

Nonclastic rocks are generally defined as those created by chemical or biochemical precipitation.[2] Table 2.1 shows the major classes of nonclastic rocks; in this monograph, discussion is limited to carbonates (limestones and dolomite rocks) and evaporites. Strictly speaking, many carbonate rocks are clastic in origin; however, this monograph treats all carbonate rocks as a single group.

Most of the numerous classification schemes for carbonate rocks describe their depositional origin. However, that factor has much less influence on pore-size distribution for carbonate rocks than for clastic rocks. This is because carbonate rocks generally undergo much more diagenesis—i.e., compaction, cementation, etc.—than clastic rocks, and are more subject to major changes in their pore-space characteristics. Consequently, discussion of carbonate rock classification systems emphasizes those that describe the final and observable pore-size distribution.

Composition

Limestone is composed of more than 50% carbonates, of which more than half is calcite ($CaCO_3$). *Dolomite rock* is composed of more than 50% carbonates, of which more than half is dolomite [$CaMg(CO_3)_2$]. Table 2.6 lists the names of the end members and mixtures of these rock types.[2]

Chart 2.6 gives the various physical/chemical properties of calcite and dolomite. Chart 2.2 details the physical/chemical properties of accessory minerals, many of which may be present in small amounts in carbonates.

The common *evaporites* encountered in oilfield operations generally are formed by precipitation of salts. Evaporites typically are classified by origin (marine vs. nonmarine) and composition (halite, anhydrite, etc.). Chart 2.7 details the major mineral species (and their physical/chemical properties) found in evaporites. Natural evaporites almost always contain many other minerals in trace amounts.

Texture

Dunham[9] devised a carbonate-rock classification system based on depositional texture (Table 2.7). This system contrasts mud-bearing* vs. mud-free carbonate rocks; emphasis is on (1) the hydraulic environment of origin (still vs. agitated water) and (2) the type pore-size distribution the rock would be apt to have upon lithification. Carbonate rocks containing too little of their depositional texture to be classified in this system are called "crystalline carbonates.[9]"

2.2 Pore-Space Properties

In formation evaluation, the most important characteristics of rocks are their pore-space properties. The geometric arrangement of pore space, commonly called pore- (and pore-throat-) size distribution, controls the well-known reservoir characteristics of porosity, permeability, and fluid distribution.

A pore-space system often is conceptualized as containing both pores and pore throats. *Pores* are local enlargements in a pore-space system (Fig. 2.4) that provide the majority of the porosity available for fluid storage. *Pore throats* are the smaller connecting spaces that link pores (Fig. 2.4) and provide the more significant restrictions to fluid flow. The size distributions of

*Mud is defined here as carbonate particles with a diameter less than 20 μm. A clastic mud can have particles as large as 62.5 μm.

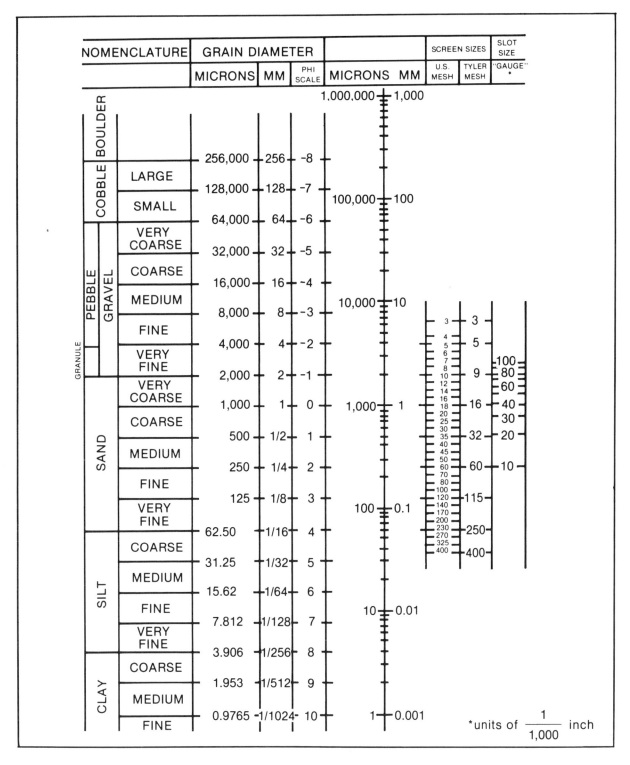

Fig. 2.2—Classification of clastic rocks according to texture.

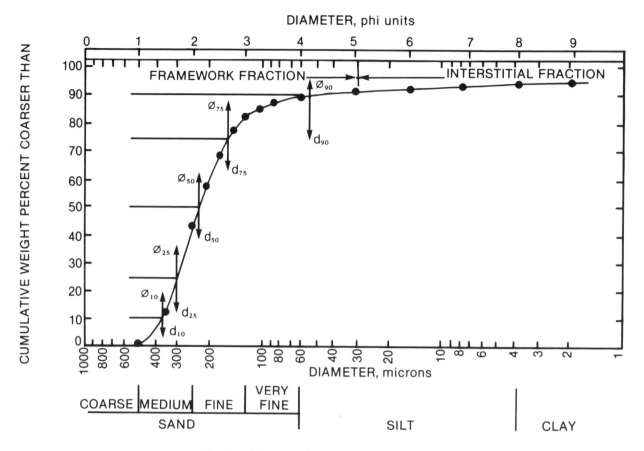

Fig. 2.3—Schematic of grain size-distribution curve.

pore throats and pores control the fluid distribution, transmissibility, and retention properties of reservoir rock.

2.2.1 Pore-Size Distribution

The mercury/air capillary-pressure curve often is used to gain insight into what volume of pore space is accessible through what sizes of pore throats in real rocks. Thomeer[10] characterizes this curve with three parameters (Fig. 2.5):

1. $(V_b)_{P_\infty}$ is the fractional bulk volume occupied by mercury at infinite mercury pressure—i.e., the total interconnected pore volume.

2. P_d is the extrapolated mercury displacement pressure, in psi, indicating the pressure required to enter the largest pore throat.

3. G is the pore geometrical factor, reflecting the distribution of pore throats and their associated pore volumes.

It has been observed repeatedly that these parameters are related through a hyperbolic relationship that can be expressed as

$$\frac{(V_b)_{P_c}}{(V_b)_{P_\infty}} = e^{-G/\log(P_c/P_d)}, \quad\ldots\ldots\ldots\ldots (2.3)$$

where $(V_b)_{P_c}$ is the fractional bulk volume occupied by mercury at some capillary pressure, P_c. Large values of

P_d suggest that the largest pores or pore throats (those first entered by mercury) are small. Large values of G suggest that pore throats are tortuous and/or pore sizes are poorly sorted.

Figs. 2.6 and 2.7, capillary-pressure curves from two different formations, illustrate the variation in Thomeer parameters (hence, inferentially pore-size distribution) within a geologic formation.[1] These figures also inferentially illustrate how the fundamental reservoir property of permeability is controlled by pore-size distribution.

Additional insight into pore-size distributions in rocks can be gained by thinking about (1) the pore-space properties of sediments as deposited and (2) the effects of diagenetic processes on pore space. Table 2.8[11] is a comparison of pore-space properties of clastics and carbonates. Archie defines a *rock type* as a formation that has "... been deposited under similar conditions and ... undergone similar processes of later weathering, cementing, or re-solution...."[1] A given rock type has particular lithologic (especially pore-space) properties and similar and/or related petrophysical and reservoir characteristics.

Clastic sediments have pore systems that originally were almost exclusively intergranular (interparticle). Original pore-size distribution in clastic rocks depends mainly on the textural properties of the solids. Secs. 2.2.2 and 2.2.3 discuss the respective dependencies of porosity and permeability on textural properties.

Once a clastic sediment is deposited, diagenesis begins

TABLE 2.5—STATISTICAL MEASURES OF GRAIN-SIZE DISTRIBUTION (after Pettijohn[2])

Petrological/ Petrophysical Attribute	Statistical Measure	Formulas	
		Diameter (mm)	Diameter (phi units)
Average size	mean		$\bar{d}_{gr\phi} = \dfrac{\phi_{16} + \phi_{84}}{2}$
	median	$\hat{d}_{gr} = d_{50}$	$\hat{d}_{gr\phi} = \phi_{50}$
	mode	$\tilde{d}_{gr} = d_{\text{midpoint of most abundant class}}$	$\tilde{d}_{gr\phi} = \phi_{\text{midpoint of most abundant class}}$
Sorting	dispersion	$S_O = \left\{ \dfrac{d_{25}}{d_{75}} \right\}^{1/2}$	$\sigma_{84\phi} = \dfrac{(\phi_{84} - \phi_{16})}{2}$
			$\sigma_{90\phi} = \dfrac{(\phi_{90} - \phi_{10})}{2}$
Symmetry	skewness	$S_k = \left\{ \dfrac{d_{75} \cdot d_{25}}{\hat{d}_{gr}^2} \right\}^{1/2}$	$S_{k\phi} = \dfrac{\frac{1}{2}(\phi_{95} + \phi_5) - \hat{d}_{gr\phi}}{\sigma_{84\phi}}$
Peakedness	kurtosis	$K = \dfrac{d_{25} - d_{75}}{2(d_{90} - d_{10})}$	$K_\phi = \dfrac{\frac{1}{2}(\phi_{95} - \phi_5) - \sigma_{84\phi}}{\sigma_{84\phi}}$

TABLE 2.6—CLASSIFICATION OF CARBONATE ROCKS ACCORDING TO COMPOSITION (after Pettijohn[2])

Nomenclature	Definition		
	Dolomite (%)	MgO Equivalent (approx. %)	MgCO$_3$ Equivalent (approx. %)
Limestone			
High calcium	0 to 10	0 to 1.1	0 to 2.3
Magnesium	0 to 10	1.1 to 2.1	2.3 to 4.4
Dolomitic limestone	10 to 50	2.1 to 10.8	4.4 to 22.7
Calcitic dolomite	50 to 90	10.8 to 19.5	22.7 to 41.0
Dolomite rock	90 to 100	19.5 to 21.6	41.0 to 45.4

TABLE 2.7—CLASSIFICATION OF CARBONATE ROCKS ACCORDING TO DEPOSITIONAL TEXTURE (after Dunham[9])

Nomenclature	Definition			
Mudstone	Original components *not* bound together during deposition.	contains mud*	mud-supported	< 10% grains
Wackestone		contains mud*	mud-supported	> 10% grains
Packstone		contains mud*	grain-supported	
Grainstone		lacks mud*	grain-supported	
Boundstone	Original components *were* bound together during deposition.			

*Particles of less than 20-μm diameter.

to modify the pore system through compaction, cementation, solution, clay-filling, and fracturing. The resulting pore system can be

1. intergranular,
2. dissolution,
3. micro, or
4. fracture, or any combination of these.[12]

The result is usually a pore geometry with poorer petrophysical/reservoir characteristics than the original.

Figs. 2.8 through 2.10 illustrate scanning electron microscope photomicrographs of pore systems of clastic rocks having the following characteristics.

1. Grain size and sorting vary from lower fine grained, very well sorted to lower very fine grained, moderately to poorly sorted.
2. Little or no cement is present.
3. Little or no clay is present.

Also shown are porosity, permeability, and capillary pressure-curve data representing variations in petrophysical/reservoir characteristics.

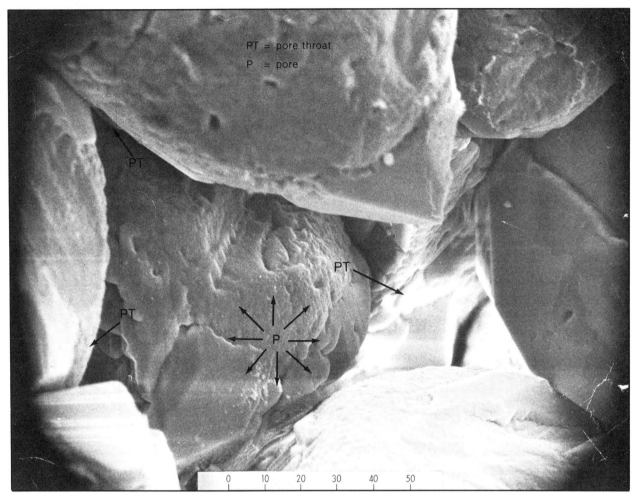

Fig. 2.4—Pores and pore throats in a pore-space system.

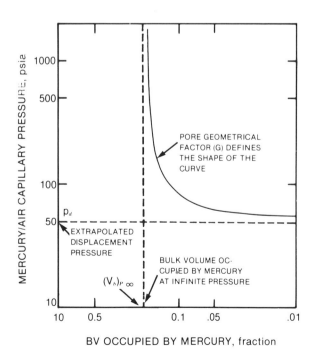

Fig. 2.5—Characterization of capillary-pressure curve with Thomeer parameters (after Thomeer[10]).

Fig. 2.11 shows scanning electron microscope photomicrographs and petrophysical data for a rock having the following characteristics.

1. Grain size and sorting are the same as rock of Fig. 2.8.

2. Significant amounts of cement and clay are present (see photomicrographs).

The poorer petrophysical/reservoir characteristics are caused largely by the cement and clay.

Fig. 2.12[13] shows scanning electron microscope photomicrographs and petrophysical data for rocks having the following characteristics.

1. Grain size and sorting are approximately the same as the rock of Fig. 2.8.

2. Significant amounts of dispersed clay are present in the pores.

3. Different types of dispersed clays are present.

Note that (1) the rocks containing dispersed pore-filling clay have poorer petrophysical/reservoir characteristics than do the "clean" rocks and (2) the different types of dispersed clay have a systematically adverse effect on petrophysical/reservoir characteristics.

Newly deposited carbonate sediments have pore systems that can be interparticle, intercrystal, intraparticle, fenestral, shelter, growth-framework, or a combination of these[11] (Fig. 2.13). Because of the complex

TABLE 2.8—COMPARISON OF PORE-SPACE PROPERTIES IN CLASTIC AND CARBONATE ROCKS
(from Choquette and Pray[11])

Factor	Clastics	Carbonates
Type(s) of original pores	almost exclusively intergranular (interparticle)	interparticle commonly predominates, but intraparticle and other types important
Size(s) of original pores	pore and pore-throat sizes closely related to sedimentary particle size and sorting	pore and pore-throat sizes commonly show little relation to sedimentary particle size or sorting
Shape(s) of pores	strong dependence on particle shape (always a "negative" of particles)	ranges from (1) a strong dependence on particle shape (either a "negative" or "positive" of particles) to (2) complete independence of shapes of depositional or diagenetic components
Uniformity of pore size, shape, and distribution	commonly fairly uniform within a single rock type	ranges from (1) fairly uniform to (2) extremely heterogeneous, even within a single rock type
Influence of diagenesis	often minor, but sometimes major, reduction of original pore spaces; compaction and cementation are important	ranges from (1) minor reduction to (2) complete destruction or modification of original pore spaces or creation of new pores; cementation and solution are important
Type(s) of ultimate pores	almost exclusively intergranular	widely varied because of postdepositional modification

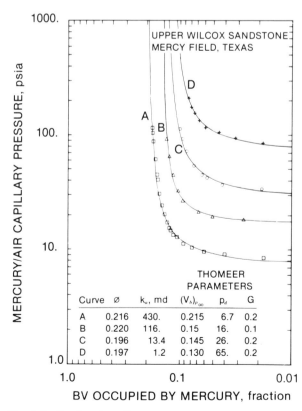

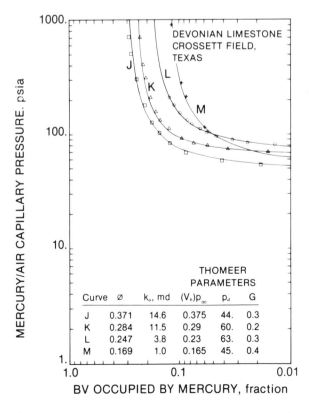

Fig. 2.6—Family of capillary-pressure curves in a sandstone formation (modified after Archie[1]).

Fig. 2.7—Family of capillary-pressure curves in a limestone formation (modified after Archie[1]).

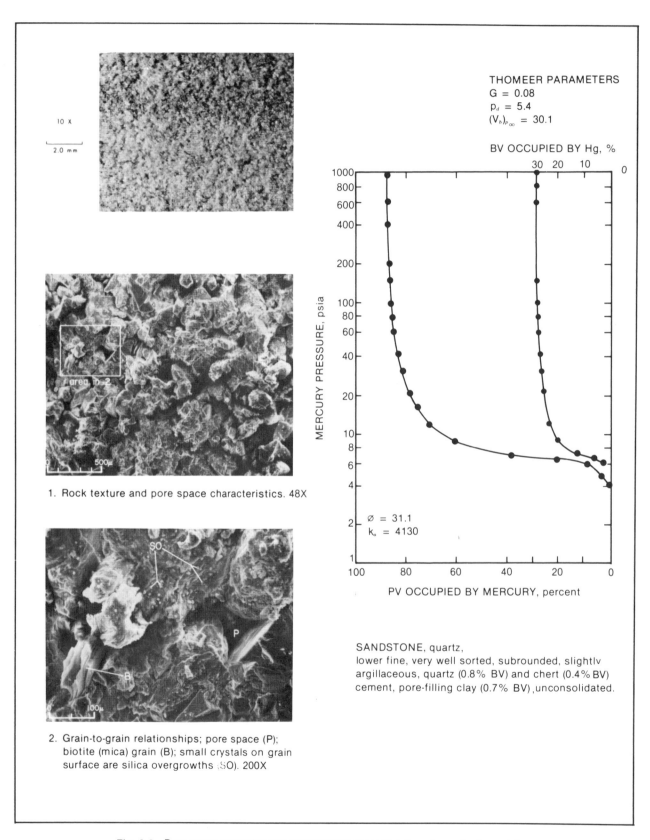

THOMEER PARAMETERS
$G = 0.08$
$p_d = 5.4$
$(V_b)_{P_\infty} = 30.1$

1. Rock texture and pore space characteristics. 48X

$\varnothing = 31.1$
$k_a = 4130$

2. Grain-to-grain relationships; pore space (P);
   biotite (mica) grain (B); small crystals on grain
   surface are silica overgrowths (SO). 200X

SANDSTONE, quartz,
lower fine, very well sorted, subrounded, slightly
argillaceous, quartz (0.8% BV) and chert (0.4% BV)
cement, pore-filling clay (0.7% BV), unconsolidated.

Fig. 2.8—Pore-space properties and petrophysical characteristics of a particular rock type.

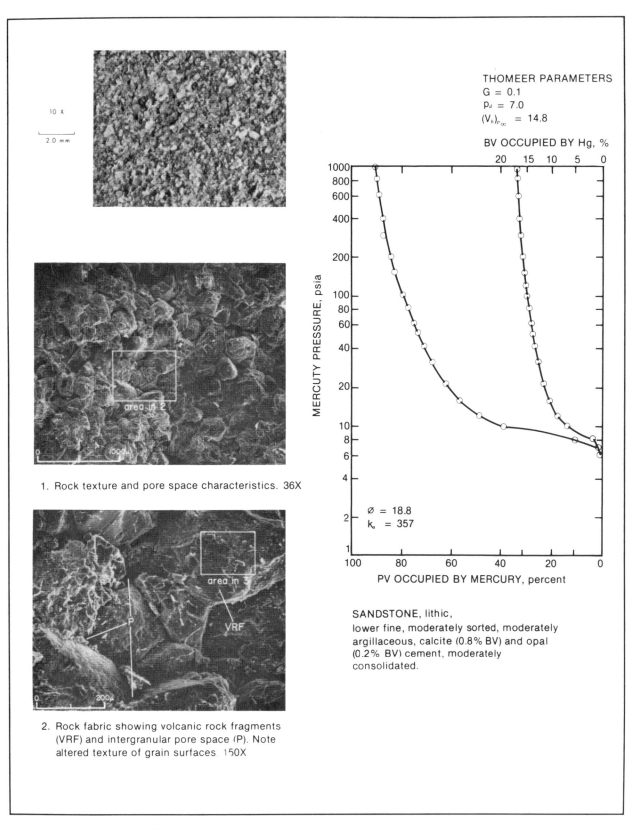

1. Rock texture and pore space characteristics. 36X

2. Rock fabric showing volcanic rock fragments (VRF) and intergranular pore space (P). Note altered texture of grain surfaces. 150X

THOMEER PARAMETERS
G = 0.1
p_d = 7.0
$(V_b)_{P_\infty}$ = 14.8

$\emptyset$ = 18.8
k_a = 357

SANDSTONE, lithic, lower fine, moderately sorted, moderately argillaceous, calcite (0.8% BV) and opal (0.2% BV) cement, moderately consolidated.

Fig. 2.9—Pore-space properties and petrophysical characteristics of a particular rock type.

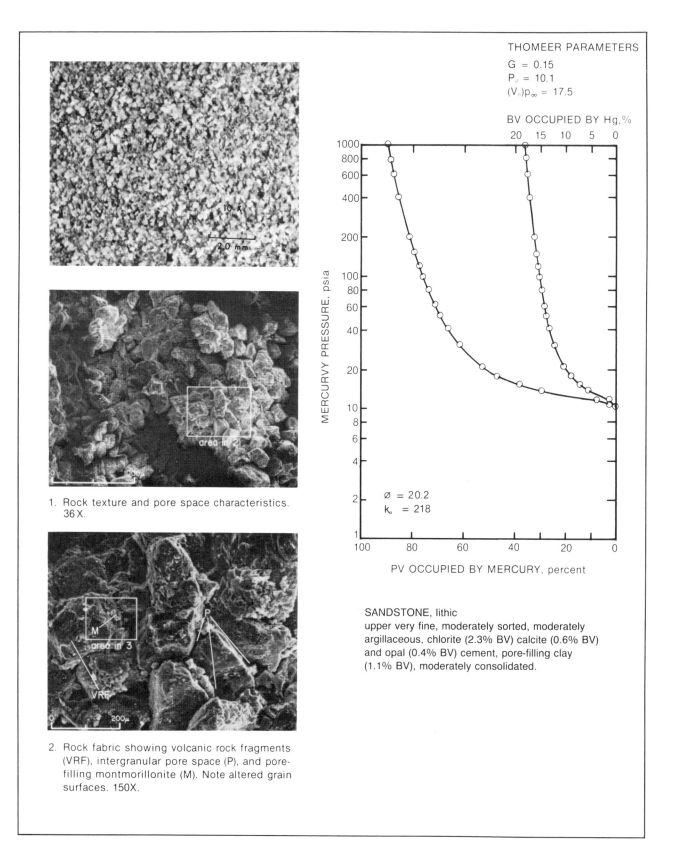

1. Rock texture and pore space characteristics. 36 X.

2. Rock fabric showing volcanic rock fragments (VRF), intergranular pore space (P), and pore-filling montmorillonite (M). Note altered grain surfaces. 150X.

THOMEER PARAMETERS
G = 0.15
P$_d$ = 10.1
(V$_b$)p$_\infty$ = 17.5

SANDSTONE, lithic
upper very fine, moderately sorted, moderately argillaceous, chlorite (2.3% BV) calcite (0.6% BV) and opal (0.4% BV) cement, pore-filling clay (1.1% BV), moderately consolidated.

Fig. 2.10—Pore-space properties and petrophysical characteristics of a particular rock type.

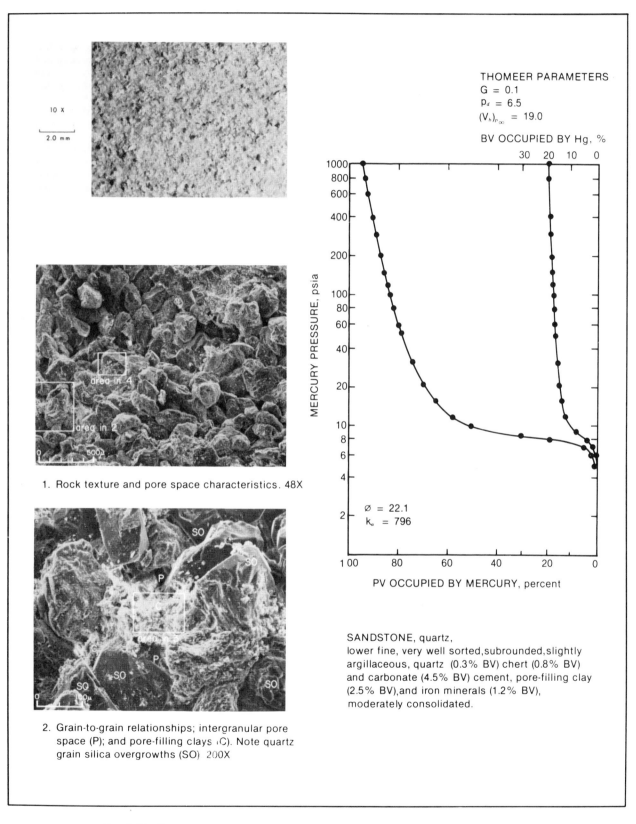

1. Rock texture and pore space characteristics. 48X

2. Grain-to-grain relationships; intergranular pore space (P); and pore-filling clays (C). Note quartz grain silica overgrowths (SO) 200X

THOMEER PARAMETERS
G = 0.1
p_d = 6.5
$(V_b)_{p_\infty}$ = 19.0

BV OCCUPIED BY Hg, %

$\emptyset$ = 22.1
k_a = 796

SANDSTONE, quartz,
lower fine, very well sorted, subrounded, slightly argillaceous, quartz (0.3% BV) chert (0.8% BV) and carbonate (4.5% BV) cement, pore-filling clay (2.5% BV), and iron minerals (1.2% BV), moderately consolidated.

Fig. 2.11—Pore-space properties and petrophysical characteristics of a particular rock type.

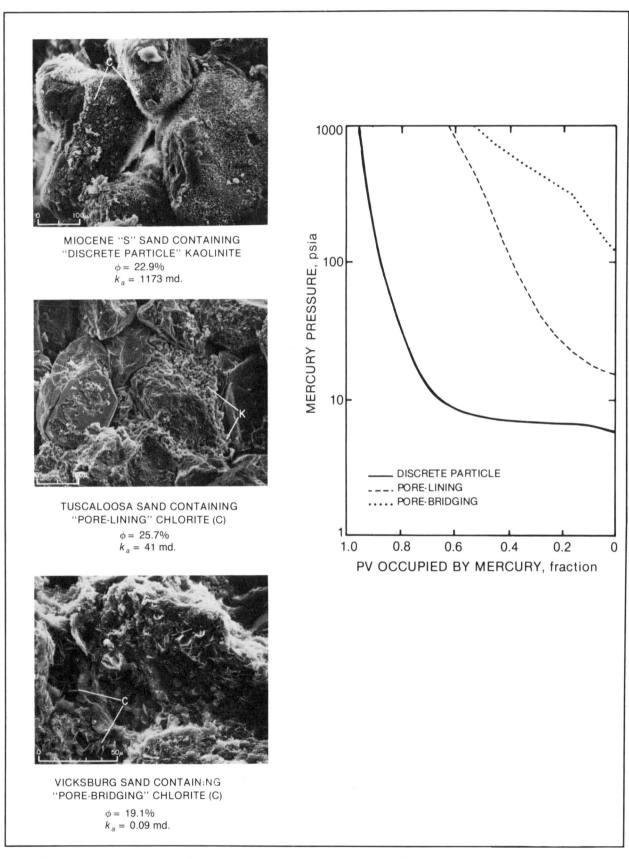

MIOCENE "S" SAND CONTAINING
"DISCRETE PARTICLE" KAOLINITE
$\phi = 22.9\%$
$k_a = 1173$ md.

TUSCALOOSA SAND CONTAINING
"PORE-LINING" CHLORITE (C)
$\phi = 25.7\%$
$k_a = 41$ md.

VICKSBURG SAND CONTAINING
"PORE-BRIDGING" CHLORITE (C)
$\phi = 19.1\%$
$k_a = 0.09$ md.

Fig. 2.12—Scanning electron microscope photomicrographs and petrophysical/reservoir characteristics of sandstones containing dispersed clay-filling material (after Neasham[13]).

nature of carbonate rock solids, the original pore-size distribution is likewise very complex. Analogous to clastics, original pore-size distribution in interparticle and (often) intercrystal carbonate rocks depends on the textural properties of the particles or crystals.

Once a carbonate sediment is deposited, diagenesis begins to modify the pore system through compaction, cementation and cavity filling, solution, grain growth, grain shrinkage, replacement recrystallization, and fracturing. The resulting pore system can be one of many types (Fig. 2.13). The most important are

1. interparticle,
2. intercrystal,
3. intraparticle,
4. channel/vug/cavern, and
5. fracture. [11]

The result of such diagenesis is often a pore geometry with poorer petrophysical/reservoir characteristics than the original. Unlike most clastic rocks, such diagenesis also can result in a pore geometry with better petrophysical/reservoir characteristics than the original.

Since evaporites seldom have significant pore space they are omitted from further discussion of pore-size distribution, porosity, permeability, and fluid distribution.

The preceding discussion and illustrations emphasize the following concepts.

1. Rocks have pore-space properties strongly related to their textural characteristics, unless they have undergone severe diagenesis.

2. Rocks can be classified into lithologic types with similar and/or related petrophysical and reservoir characteristics. Although rock typing is primarily on the basis of pore-space properties, its origins are in the depositional and diagenetic history of the rock.

3. Any rock—clastic or carbonate—can be unique in its pore-space properties (hence unique in its porosity, permeability, and fluid distribution).

4. Rocks have pore-space properties that are very complex. Simple mathematical or experimental models (summarized in Table 2.9 [14-25]) only approximate the pore-space properties of natural rocks.

2.2.2 Porosity

Porosity is the fraction (or percentage) of rock bulk volume occupied by pore space. This definition seems simple enough; however, a family of porosity definitions has evolved to meet various petroleum engineering and well logging conditions. Table 2.10 and Fig. 2.14 summarize the Society of Petroleum Engineers definitions of porosity; these seem most applicable to clastic rocks.

The formation-evaluation specialist determining porosity should know how porosity is related to lithology and the porosity expected for any given rock; the answers and relationships are somewhat different for each major rock class.

Clastic Rocks

Newly deposited clastic sediments are moderately to highly porous. Artificially packed sands have porosities ranging from 0.23 to 0.43 (Table 2.11) and the following relationships between porosity and textural properties. [26]

1. Porosity is independent of grain size for the same sorting.

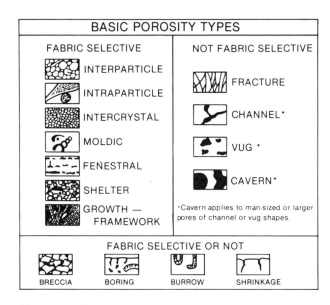

Fig. 2.13—Classification of pores and pore systems in carbonate rocks (after Choquette and Pray[11]).

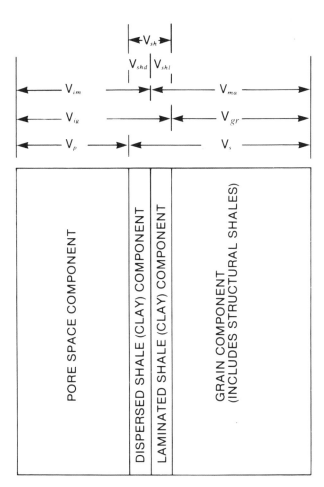

Fig. 2.14—Types of clastic rock volumes.

**TABLE 2.9—MODELS OF PORE-SIZE DISTRIBUTION
AND THEIR APPLICATIONS**

Model	Uses	Reference(s)
Bundle of "tubes"*	permeability	Carmen[14] Purcell[15] Burdine et al.[16]
	relative permeability	Fatt and Dykstra[17] Gates and Tempelaar-Leitz[18]
	electrical resistivity	Wyllie and Spangler[19]
Sphere pack	permeability	Berg[20]
	electrical resistivity	Wyllie and Gregory[21]
Network	capillary pressure	Fatt[22]
	relative permeability	Fatt[22]
	electrical resistivity	Fatt[22]
	fluid displacement processes	Rose[23] Simon and Kelsey[24, 25]

*Parallel, similar channels, not cylindical capillaries.

**TABLE 2.10—DEFINITIONS OF AND RELATIONSHIPS AMONG
ROCK POROSITIES AND VOLUMES**

Rock Property	Definition	Relationships
Porosity	fraction of bulk volume occupied by pore space	$\phi = \dfrac{V_p}{V_b} = \dfrac{V_b - V_s}{V_b}$
Porosity, apparent		ϕ_a
Porosity, effective	fraction of bulk volume occupied by interconnected pore space	$\phi_e = \dfrac{V_{pe}}{V_b}$
Porosity, noneffective	fraction of bulk volume occupied by noninterconnected pore space	$\phi_{ne} = \dfrac{V_{pne}}{V_b}$
"Porosity," intergranular	fraction of bulk volume occupied by fluids and *all* shales	$\phi_{ig} = \dfrac{V_{ig}}{V_b} = \dfrac{V_b - V_{gr}}{V_b}$
"Porosity," intermatrix	fraction of bulk volume occupied by fluids and *dispersed* shales	$\phi_{im} = \dfrac{V_{im}}{V_b} = \dfrac{V_b - V_{ma}}{V_b}$
Volume, solids	volume of *all* formation solids	$V_s = V_b - V_f$
Volume, grain	volume of all formation solids except *all* shales	$V_{gr} = V_s - V_{sh}$
Volume, intergranular	volume of fluids and *all* shales	$V_{ig} = V_f + V_{sh} = V_b - V_{gr}$
Volume, matrix	volume of all formation solids except *dispersed* shales	$V_{ma} = V_s - V_{shd}$
Volume, intermatrix	volume of fluids and *dispersed* shales	$V_{im} = V_f + V_{shd} = V_b - V_{ma}$

Note: The currently accepted terms are (1) "dispersed shale" and (2) "laminated shale." It would be petrographically more correct to use (1) "dispersed clay" and (2) "laminated shale" (or "laminated clay").

2. Porosity decreases as sorting becomes poorer.

3. Porosity increases as grain sphericity (shape) decreases and as grain angularity (roundness) decreases.

The general, though not universal, tendency is for diagenesis to reduce original porosities of clastic rocks.

Carbonate Rocks

At deposition, carbonate sediments are highly to very highly porous. Holocene carbonate sediments have porosities ranging from 0.40 to 0.78 (Table 2.12) and the following relationships between porosity and textural properties.[27]

1. Porosity is not correlated strongly with either median grain size or sorting.

2. Porosity is controlled largely by the amount of fines present—i.e., the larger the percentage fines, the larger the porosity.

Diagenesis of carbonate rocks can result in porosities

TABLE 2.11—POROSITY (FRACTION BULK VOLUME) OF ARTIFICIALLY MIXED AND WET-PACKED SAND
(from Beard and Weyl[26])

	Size									
	Coarse		Medium		Fine		Very Fine		Average	Standard
Sorting	Upper	Lower	Upper	Lower	Upper	Lower	Upper	Lower	Porosity	Deviation
Extremely well sorted	0.431	0.428	0.417	0.413	0.413	0.435	0.423	0.430	0.424	0.008
Very well sorted	0.408	0.415	0.402	0.402	0.398	0.408	0.412	0.418	0.408	0.006
Well sorted	0.380	0.384	0.381	0.388	0.391	0.397	0.402	0.398	0.390	0.008
Moderately sorted	0.324	0.333	0.342	0.349	0.339	0.343	0.356	0.331	0.340	0.010
Poorly sorted	0.271	0.298	0.315	0.313	0.304	0.310	0.305	0.342	0.307	0.018
Very poorly sorted	0.286	0.252	0.258	0.234	0.285	0.290	0.301	0.326	0.279	0.028
Average porosity	0.350	0.352	0.353	0.350	0.355	0.364	0.367	0.374		
Standard deviation	0.060	0.063	0.055	0.062	0.049	0.053	0.050	0.042		

TABLE 2.12—POROSITY AND PERMEABILITY
OF HOLOCENE CARBONATE SEDIMENTS (from Enos and Sawatsky[27])

	Porosity (fraction bulk volume)		Permeability (darcies)	
Depositional Texture	Mean	Range	Mean	Range
Grainstone	0.445	0.40 to 0.53	30.8	15.8 to 56.6
Packstone	0.547	0.45 to 0.67	1.84	0.0315 to 9.30
Wackestone	0.680	0.64 to 0.78	0.228	0.0376 to 6.57
Very fine wackestone	0.705	0.67 to 0.73	0.00087	0.00063 to 0.00137
Supratidal wackestone	0.635	0.61 to 0.66	5.59	0.617 to 24.1

that are either significantly less than or greater than original porosity.

Archie[28] proposed a classification system for carbonate rocks (Table 2.13)[28,29] that strongly emphasizes the pore characteristics (hence the fluid distribution, fluid permeability, and electrical conductivity) of the rock. This system deals with (1) the texture of the matrix* and (2) the character of the visible pore structure.

Lucia[30] proposed a classification system for carbonate rocks (Fig. 2.15) that also emphasizes the pore characteristics. A first-order division is made between interparticle porosity and vuggy porosity. Subdivision of interparticle porosity is based on particle size and porosity; particle size is divided into (1) fine, (2) medium, or (3) large, whereas porosity is qualitatively described as present or absent. Subdivision of vuggy porosity is based on the degree of interconnection of vugs, either separate or touching. Lucia shows that these classification parameters provide a useful insight into carbonate rock pore geometry, and (together with log- or core-derived total porosity) often can be used to estimate petrophysical/reservoir properties such as permeability.

2.2.3 Permeability

Permeability is a measure of the capacity of a rock pore system to transmit fluid. Hubbert[31] gives a basic physical definition of permeability, k, as

$$k \equiv K(L^2) = \frac{\vec{u}\mu}{[-g \; \text{grad} \; Z - (1/\rho)\text{grad} \; p]\rho}, \quad \ldots \ldots (2.4)$$

*Matrix, as defined by Archie, means the entire rock-solids component, as contrasted to the pore-space component. To many geologists, it means that part of the rock solids less than a certain size, usually 30 μm.

where

K = a proportionality constant,

L = a length that characterizes the pore geometry of the rock, m,

$\vec{u}$ = the volume rate of flow per unit cross-sectional area and is a vector quantity, $m^3/s \cdot m^2$,

g = the acceleration of gravity, m/s^2,

Z = the elevation above an arbitrary datum, m,

p = the pressure at the elevation, Pa,

ρ = the density of the transmitted fluid, kg/m^3,

and

μ = the viscosity of the transmitted fluid, $Pa \cdot s$.

Hubbert also shows that Eq. 2.4 can be expressed as

$$k = \frac{u\mu}{\rho g_s - (\partial p/\partial s)}, \quad \ldots \ldots \ldots \ldots \ldots \ldots (2.5)$$

for flow in any direction, s.

Table 2.14 summarizes several SPE definitions of permeability.

For reservoir-rock systems of specified geometry, Eq. 2.5 can be integrated over their boundaries. Chart 2.8 shows the permeability equations for two geometric systems, and the constants required for these equations when both (1) historic and customary units (bbl/day, psi, etc.) and (2) SPE preferred units (m^3/day, kPa, etc.) are used.

Many workers have studied the quantitative relationships between permeability and other properties of models and/or real rocks (Table 2.15).[10,14,15,20,32-35]

Clastic Rocks

Newly deposited clastic sediments are extremely permeable. Artificially packed sands have permeabilities ranging from less than 2.4 to 475 darcies (Table 2.16)

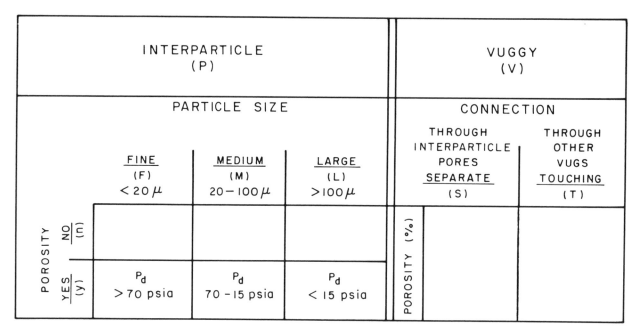

Fig. 2.15—Classification of carbonate pore space (after Lucia[30]).

and the following relationships between permeability and textural properties.[26]

1. Permeability decreases as grain size decreases.

2. Permeability decreases as sorting becomes poorer.

3. Permeability increases as grain sphericity (shape) decreases and as grain angularity (roundness) decreases.

Diagenesis usually decreases the permeabilities of clastics, and the effect (positive or negative) is often greater than on the porosity.

Carbonate Rocks

At deposition, carbonate sediments have extreme variations in permeability. Holocene carbonate sediments have permeabilities ranging from 0.00087 to 57 darcies (Table 2.12) and the following relationships between permeability and textural properties.[27]

1. Permeability is not correlated strongly with either median grain size or sorting.

2. Permeability is controlled largely by the amount of fines present—i.e., the larger the percentage fines, the smaller the permeability.

Diagenesis of carbonate rocks can result in a permeability that is either significantly less than or greater than original permeability.

2.3 Fluid Distribution

This section discusses fluid distributions in petroleum-reservoir rocks under static conditions, where viscous forces have no effect and gravity and capillary forces are in balance. This static system (1) generally defines the original fluid distribution in the reservoir, (2) is the one encountered upon discovery of a petroleum reservoir, and (3) is the one that must be interpreted through the use (in part) of well logging data. Not discussed are dynamic fluid distributions caused by production, such as fluid trapping and residual saturation.

Three factors control a reservoir's static fluid distribution[36]:

1. the geometric configuration of the interstitial spaces—i.e., pore space system—of the rocks;

2. the physical and chemical natures of the interstitial surfaces—i.e., pore walls—of the rocks; and

3. the physical and chemical properties of the fluid phases in contact with the interstitial surfaces and each other.

Fig. 2.16 illustrates static fluid distribution in a petroleum reservoir, by means of a schematic vertical sandstone column in which three regions of saturation are present. In the *saturation region*[37] the rock is 100% saturated with the wetting phase (water, in this case) up to Level A, the *100%-water level*. The 100% water level should not be confused with the free-water level, also shown. The 100% water level is characterized by the displacement pressure,[37] sometimes called the threshold pressure or entry pressure, of the capillary-pressure curve (Fig. 2.16). *Displacement pressure* is that capillary pressure at the top of the saturation zone; the minimum pressure required for the nonwetting phase to displace wetting phase and enter the pore system.

In the *funicular region*,[37] or transition zone, large changes in saturation occur over relatively small changes in reservoir height, and are represented by the plateau of the capillary-pressure curve of Fig. 2.16. This region (between Levels A and B of Fig. 2.16) reflects the most abundant and accessible pore-throat sizes; the steeper the capillary pressure curve in this region, the less uniform the pore throats.

In the *pendular region*,[37] the wetting phase is found mostly in pendular rings around grain-to-grain contacts and filling very small pores. If there is perfect wetting by the wetting phase, it coats the remaining grain surfaces with a very thin (perhaps monomolecular) film. In this region (above Level B in Fig. 2.16) only small changes in saturation occur over large changes in reservoir height, and are represented by the steep slope of the capillary-pressure curve on Fig. 2.16. The wetting-phase

TABLE 2.13—ARCHIE CLASSIFICATION OF CARBONATE ROCKS (from Archie[28] and Jodry[29])

Type	Crystal or Grain Size (μm)	Matrix (rock solids component)		Pore Space			
		Usual Appearance		Approximate Porosity (fraction bulk volume)			
		1X Magnification	10X to 15X Magnification	(not visible)	Size of Visible Pores (μm)		
					< 100	100–2000	> 2000
				A	B	C	D
I Compact	XF 62.5 VF 125 F 250 M 500 C	Crystalline, hard, dense, sharp edges and smooth faces on breaking. Resinous.	Matrix made up of crystals tightly interlocking, allowing no visible pore space between crystals, commonly producing "feather edge" on breaking as a result of fracturing of clusters of crystals in thin flakes.	~0.05 ~0.02	~0.10	~0.15	—
II Chalky	XF <50	Dull, earthy or "chalky." Crystalline appearance absent because small crystals are are less tightly interlocked thus reflecting light in different directions, or made up of extremely fine granules or sea organisms. May be siliceous or argillaceous.	Crystals, less effectively interlocking than the foregoing joining at different angles. Extremely fine texture may still appear "chalky" under this power, but others may begin to appear crystalline.	<0.15	~0.10	~0.15	—
III Sucrose	XF 62.5 VF 125 F 250 M 500 C	Sandy or sugary appearing (sucrose).	Crystals interlocking at different angles, generally allowing space for considerable porosity between crystals. Oolitic and other granular textures fall in this class.	~0.10 ~0.05	~0.10 ~0.10	~0.15 ~0.15	— —

TABLE 2.14—DEFINITIONS OF AND RELATIONS AMONG ROCK PERMEABILITIES

Rock Property	Definition	Relationships
Permeability, absolute	capacity of rock to transmit a fluid when the rock is completely saturated with that fluid	$k = K(L^2) = \dfrac{\vec{u}\,\mu}{[-g\,\text{grad}\,Z - (1/\rho)\text{grad}\,p]\rho}$
Permeability, effective, to gas	capacity of rock to transmit a gas when the rock is partially saturated with that gas	k_g
Permeability, effective, to oil	capacity of rock to transmit an oil when the rock is partially saturated with that oil	k_o
Permeability, effective to water	capacity of rock to transmit a water when the rock is partially saturated with that water	k_w
Permeability, relative, to gas		$k_{rg} = k_g/k$
Permeability, relative, to oil		$k_{ro} = k_o/k$
Permeability, relative, to water		$k_{rw} = k_w/k$

TABLE 2.16—PERMEABILITY (DARCIES) OF ARTIFICIALLY MIXED AND WET-PACKED SAND (from Beard and Weyl[26])

Sorting	Size							
	Coarse		Medium		Fine		Very Fine	
	Upper	Lower	Upper	Lower	Upper	Lower	Upper	Lower
Extremely well sorted	475.	238.	119.	59.	30.	15.	7.4	3.7
Very well sorted	458.	239.	115.	57.	29.	14.	7.2	3.6
Well sorted	302.	151.	76.	38.	19.	9.4	4.7	2.4
Moderately sorted	110.	55.	28.	14.	7.0	3.5		
Poorly sorted	45.	23.	12.	6.0				
Very poorly sorted	14.	7.0	3.5					

TABLE 2.15—SUMMARY OF RELATIONSHIPS BETWEEN PERMEABILITY AND OTHER PETROPHYSICAL PROPERTIES

Basic Model	Reference	Mathematical Relationship	Symbol	Measurement Unit	Assumptions	Limitations
Bundle of "tubes"	Carmen[14]	$k = \dfrac{\phi^3}{C(A_s)^2}$	k A_s C	cm² cm⁻¹ (internal surface per unit bulk volume) Kozeny constant	1. Porous medium is a group of parallel, similar channels. 2. Total internal surface = particle surface; and total internal volume = PV; thus, mean hydraulic radius = ϕ/A_s. 3. Actual fluid velocity = $\dfrac{u/\phi}{L_e/L}$.	$C = 5.0$ for uniformly sorted powder packs.
Bundle of "tubes"	Purcell[15]	$k = \dfrac{F}{2\times10^4}\,\dfrac{(\sigma\cos\theta)^2\,\phi}{1}\displaystyle\int_0^{100}\dfrac{dS_w}{(P_c)^2}$	k σ ϕ S_w P_c F	md dyne/cm % % atm correlation factor	1. Porous medium is bundle of capillary tubes of equal length, of various radii, which are not interconnected.	
Sphere pack	Berg[20]	$k = 5.1\times10^{-6}(\phi)^{5.1}(\bar{d}_{gr})^2\,e^{-1.385\sigma_{90\phi}}$	k ϕ $\bar{d}_{gr}$ $\sigma_{90\phi}$	darcies % mm phi units		Correlation rigorously valid only for well-sorted sphere packs with ϕ = 30 to 40%.
Quartz powder pack	Seevers[32]	$k = A(FFI)\dfrac{(T_l\,T_{lb})^2}{(T_l - T_{lb})^2}$	A T_l T_{lb} FFI	correlation factor seconds (nuclear magnetic relaxation time of rock/fluid system) seconds (nuclear magnetic relaxation time of bulk fluid) (free fluid index)	1. Nuclear magnetism measures part of pore-size distribution in consolidated rocks that is "effective" in fluid flow.	Rigorously valid only for unconsolidated quartz powder packs
Sandpack	Krumbein and Monk[33]	$k = 760(\bar{d}_{gr\phi})^2\,e^{-1.31\sigma_{84\phi}}$	k $\bar{d}_{gr\phi}$ $\sigma_{84\phi}$	darcies phi units phi units		Correlation rigorously valid only for sandpacks with ϕ = 0.40.
Various rocks	Timur[34]	$k = \dfrac{A\phi^B}{(S_{iw})}C$	k ϕ S_{iw} A B C	md % % correlation factor (0.136 general case) correlation factor (4.4 general case) correlation factor (2.0 general case)		Correlation rigorously valid only for formations studied.
Various rocks	Thomeer[10,35]	$k_a = 3.8068\,G^{-1.3334}\left[\dfrac{(V_b)_{P\infty}}{P_d}\right]^2$ (Also see Chart 2.9.)	k_a P_d $(V_b)_{P\infty}$ G	md (air permeability) psia % bulk volume dimensionless		Correlations rigorously valid only for formations studied.

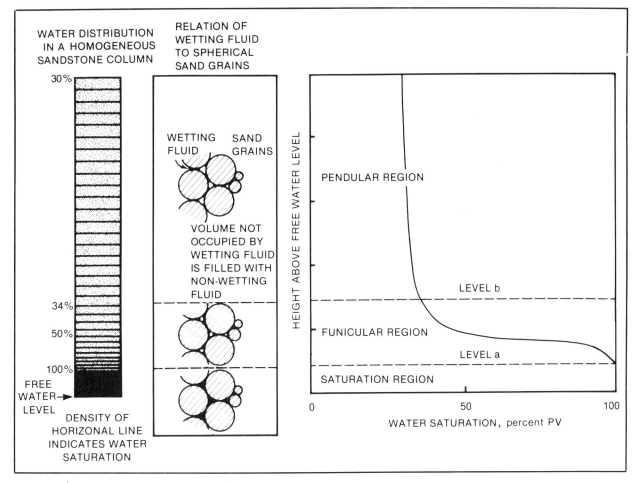

Fig. 2.16—Fluid distribution in a homogeneous reservoir.

saturation in this region is often called the *irreducible wetting-phase saturation.*

These saturation/height relationships occur because under static conditions equilibrium exists between gravity and capillary forces in a reservoir-rock/fluid system.

Capillary pressure, P_c, the pressure difference (pascals) across the curved interface between two immiscible fluids,[37] is related to the curvature of the interface by

$$P_c = \sigma \cos \theta \left(\frac{1}{r_1} + \frac{1}{r_2} \right) , \quad \dotsc\dotsc\dotsc\dotsc (2.6)$$

where σ is the interfacial tension (N/m) and θ is the angle (radians) between the granular solid surface and the fluid interface. The angle θ is measured, by convention, through the wetting phase (Fig. 2.17). The quantities r_1 and r_2 (meters) are defined in Fig. 2.17, which shows enlargements of a fluid interface from the pendular region. By convention, the signs of the vector quantities r_1 and r_2 are taken to be

1. negative if the center of rotation of any r lies within the wetting-phase fluid, or

2. positive if the center of rotation of any r lies within the nonwetting-phase fluid.

Examination of Eq. 2.6 and Fig. 2.17 shows that when $P_c = 0$, then $r_1 = r_2$, and the interface has no curvature and is defined as the free-liquid surface or free-water

level. Fig. 2.18 illustrates a free-water level for a laboratory system. In real subsurface rock, the *free-water level* is a physical impossibility; however, it is a useful concept, being the hypothetical level where capillary pressure is zero.

Leverett[37] shows that the incremental pressure difference, $dp_o - dp_w$, (pascals) caused by gravity difference between two immiscible fluids at some incremental distance, dL, above an arbitrary datum in a reservoir is

$$dp_o - dp_w = \rho_w g dL - \rho_o g dL , \quad \dotsc\dotsc\dotsc\dotsc (2.7)$$

where ρ_w and ρ_o are the densities (kg/m^3) of the two fluids and g is the acceleration of gravity (m/s^2). Because capillary pressure is defined as the pressure difference across the interface between two immiscible fluids, then

$$dP_c = \rho_w g dL - \rho_o g dL . \quad \dotsc\dotsc\dotsc\dotsc (2.8)$$

Conveniently and arbitrarily, $L = 0$ where $P_c = 0$, or at the free-water level. Integrating Eq. 2.8 between the limits of the free-water level and some arbitrary reservoir level, h, (meters) gives

$$P_c = (\rho_w - \rho_o)gh . \quad \dotsc\dotsc\dotsc\dotsc (2.9)$$

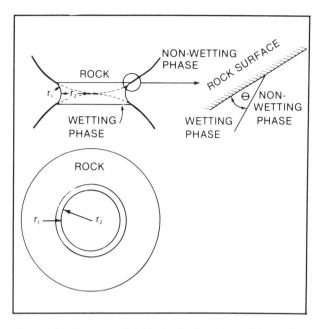

Fig. 2.17—Close-up of fluid distribution in pendular region (modified after Leverett[37]).

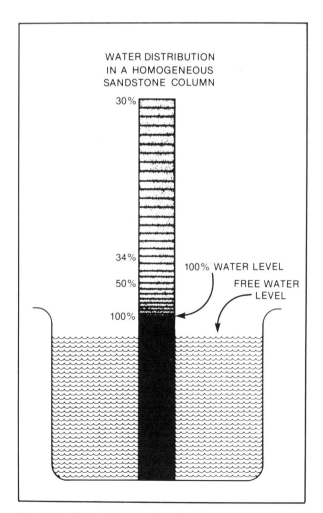

Fig. 2.18—Fluid distribution in a laboratory sandstone column.

Chart 2.10 summarizes typical values for the interfacial tensions and contact angles in several laboratory systems used to measure capillary pressure. Assuming that the pore system behaves as a group of equivalent circular capillary tubes, then magnitudes of capillary pressure made on the same pore system with different fluid systems are proportional to $\sigma \cos \theta$. Eq. 2.6 and Chart 2.10 show that the factor for converting capillary pressure from one fluid system to another is simply the ratio of the respective $\sigma \cos \theta$ values. Obviously, fluid systems with $\sigma \cos \theta$ values different from those tabulated can be used; the fluid systems shown in Chart 2.10 even may exhibit slightly different values of $\sigma \cos \theta$. For instance, Brown[38] reports factors ranging from 5.4 to 8.3 for the $(P_c)_{Hg/A/R}/(P_c)_{A/W/R}$ ratio; he ascribes this variation in ratio to variations in interfacial tension.

Chart 2.11 summarizes several variations of Eq. 2.9 for obtaining elevation above the free-water level. These equations contain the appropriate conversions for using capillary pressure and density difference as measured in common oilfield units.

Fig. 2.19 shows an example of static fluid distribution through a cross section of five wells in an oil reservoir of nonhomogeneous sandstone. The capillary curves used to characterize the rock are the same as shown in Fig. 2.6.

The free-water level is by definition a horizontal plane where $L = 0$. However, the 100% water level is not a horizontal plane, *but its elevation above the free water level varies with pore geometry*, and is quantified by the displacement pressures of the several capillary-pressure curves. Note that a 100% water level is seen in Wells 1 and 3 at widely varying elevations; the difference is caused by different pore geometries. Likewise, the elevation of any other saturation level (for example, the 50% water level) varies with pore geometry as shown. Note that Well 3 penetrates the bottom portion of a very long transition zone. Note also that both Well 2 and Well 4 penetrate reservoir rock at irreducible water saturation; however, the water saturation in Well 4 (the structurally higher well) containing Type D rock is three times greater than the water saturation found in Well 2 containing Type A rock. Note that had Well 2 encountered Type D rock, it probably would have been a noncommercial well.

2.4 Petrophysical Relationships Among Fundamental Reservoir Properties

Rock type is defined (see Sec. 2.2) as a formation (e.g., upper Eocene Wilcox in a particular area) that has been deposited under similar conditions and has undergone similar diagenetic processes. Such a rock type possesses particular lithologic (especially pore-space) properties and has similar and/or related petrophysical and reservoir characteristics. Archie[1] illustrated such interrelationships as shown on Fig. 2.20, observing that a specific rock type has a particular pore-space geometry (pore-/pore-throat-size distribution) that

1. produces a certain family of capillary pressure curves,

2. controls the porosity, and

3. is related to the permeability and water saturation.

Fig. 2.20 suggests a functional relationship between

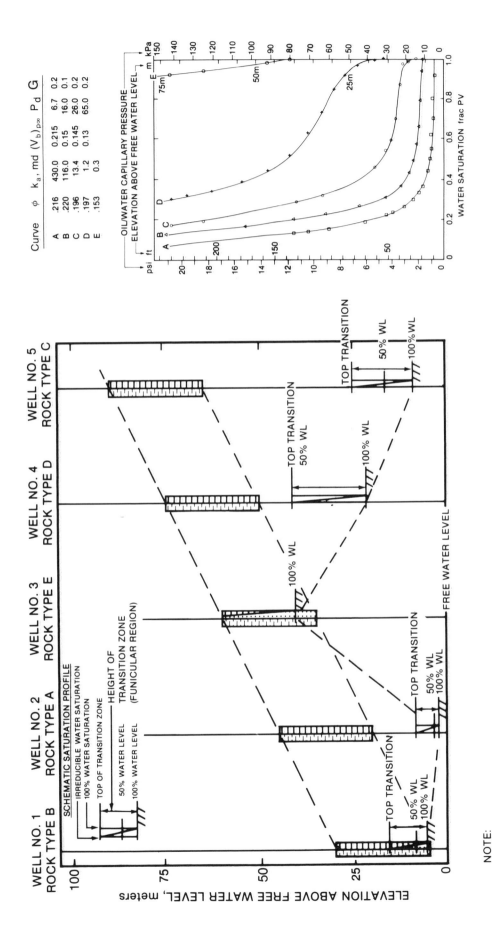

NOTE:

Conversion factors used to convert (1) from laboratory Hg/A capillary pressure to subsurface O/W capillary pressure and (2) then to subsurface elevation above free water level are for illustrative purposes only, and are not necessarily correct.

Fig. 2.19—Schematic example of static fluid distribution.

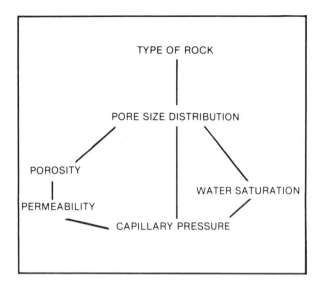

Fig. 2.20—Relationships of fundamental reservoir properties (after Archie[1]).

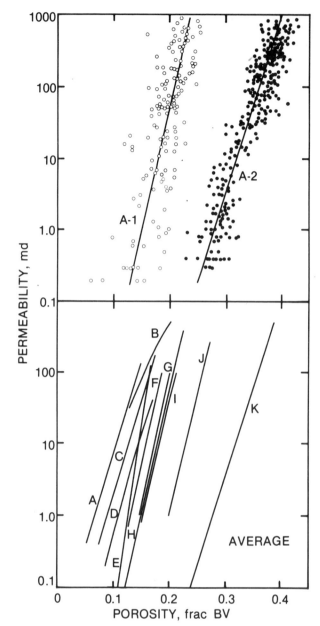

each pair of three fundamental petrophysical/reservoir properties: porosity, permeability, and water saturation for a particular rock type.

2.4.1 Porosity/Permeability Relationships

Figs. 2.21 through 2.23 show examples of porosity/permeability relationships from the literature.[1,13,34] Correlations between porosity and permeability are commonly expressed as either

$$k = A'_1 \, A_2'^{\phi}; \quad \log k = A_1 + A_2 \phi , \quad \ldots \ldots \ldots (2.10)$$

or

$$k = A'_3 \phi^{A'_4}; \quad \log k = A_3 + A_4 \log \phi , \quad \ldots \ldots (2.11)$$

where A's are constants. Most of the theoretical models relating porosity and permeability suggest the form of Eq. 2.11. However, these models are so simplified and often unrepresentative of real rocks that either Eq. 2.10 or 2.11 can be used properly. In practice, porosity/permeability plots are plotted more often in the semi-log format (i.e., Eq. 2.10).

No specific values or limits have been put on the constants in Eqs. 2.10 and 2.11 for any specific rock type or formation. The nearly constant slope of the porosity/permeability plots of Fig. 2.21 for several rock types suggests that constant A_2 of Eq. 2.10 may have a single value. Generalized porosity/permeability relationships for many formations are found in the literature.

Neasham[13] demonstrates a wide variation in permeability for a given porosity because of different occurrences of pore-filling clay (i.e., different pore-space properties). As said earlier, any rock can be unique in its pore-size-distribution (porosity, permeability, and fluid-distribution) characteristics.

2.4.2 Porosity/Water Saturation Relationships

Figs. 2.24 through 2.26 show literature examples of porosity/water-saturation relationships.[39,40] Buckles[39]

A-1. UPPER WILCOX (MERCY)
A-2. NACATOCH (BELLEVUE) FINE GRAINED

A. OOLITIC SMACKOVER (MAGNOLIA) COARSE GRAINED
B. PALUXY (QUITMAN)
C. GLOYD (JEFFERSON)
D. SAN ANDRES (WASSON)
E. LOWER WILCOX (SHERIDAN)
F. BARTLESVILLE (AVANT)
G. BARTLESVILLLE (TALALA)
H. UPPER WILCOX (MERCY)
I. UPPER WILCOX (SHERIDAN)
J. LOOSELY CONSOLIDATED (GULF COAST)
K. NACATOCH (BELLEVUE) FINE GRAINED

Fig. 2.21—Example of porosity/permeability relationships (after Archie[1]).

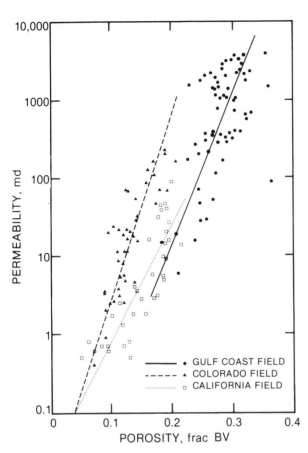

Fig. 2.22—Example of porosity/permeability relationships (after Timur[34]).

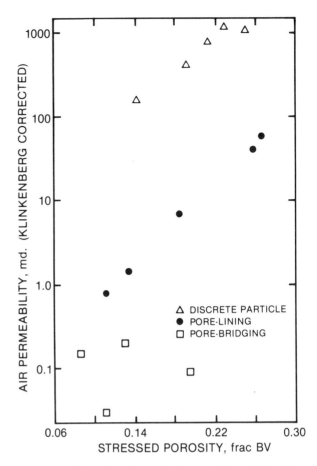

Fig. 2.23—Example of porosity/permeability relationships (after Neasham[13]).

shows that, for a given rock type, an equilateral-hyperbola equation of the form

$$\phi S_w = C , \dots\dots\dots\dots\dots\dots\dots\dots(2.12)$$

where

ϕ = porosity,

S_w = water saturation, and

C = correlation factor,

often fits porosity/irreducible-water-saturation data reasonably well. Fig. 2.25[40] shows that transition zones (with water saturation greater than irreducible) fail to form coherent hyperbolic patterns in a porosity/saturation crossplot. Such lack of coherence also can be caused by variations in rock type. In Fig. 2.26,[40] the data appear incoherent and typical of a transition zone until distinguished by rock type; then a typical hyperbolic relationship for each rock type is apparent.

Buckles demonstrates that a correct average saturation (i.e., the same as a volumetrically weighted average reservoir-water saturation) can be obtained by using an average reservoir porosity and a relationship of the form of Eq. 2.12.

Buckles[39] shows that a particular formation in a particular field has a definite value of C (the correlation factor in Eq. 2.12). Although no catalog of C values has been found in the literature, Hilchie[41] presents a

porosity/water-saturation crossplot (Fig. 2.27) that shows a correlation between C value and formation type. The source of these data is not explicitly stated.

2.4.3 Permeability/Water Saturation Relationships

Figs. 2.28[42] and 2.29[34] show literature examples of permeability/water-saturation relationships.

2.5 Compositions of Formation Waters

The subsurface formation-water properties of most interest to the formation-evaluation specialist are resistivity, dielectric constant, acoustic velocity, density, hydrogen index, thermal neutron capure cross section, and thermal conductivity. Also of interest is how these properties vary with dissolved solids concentration, temperature, and pressure.

Three major difficulties occur when formation-water properties are used in formation evaluation: (1) confusion concerning the proper and consistent nomenclature and units to express the concentration of dissolved solids in formation waters; (2) failure to use the water properties appropriate to the particular conditions of dissolved solids concentration, temperature, and pressure, because their functional dependence is not well known; and (3) a lack of knowledge about the water compositions appropriate for certain geologic formations in particular geographic areas.

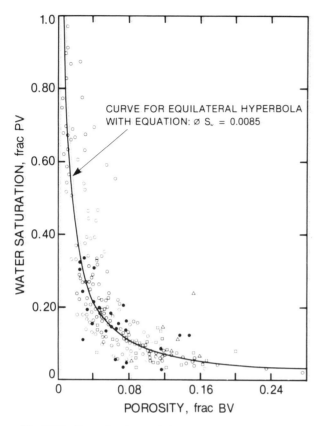

Fig. 2.24—Example of porosity/water-saturation relationship (after Buckles[39]).

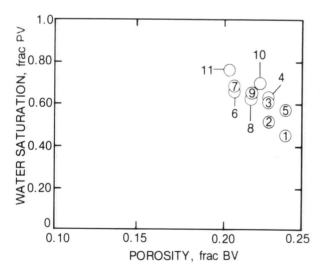

Fig. 2.25—Example of porosity/water-saturation relationship (modified after Morris and Biggs[40]).

This book of the well logging monograph presents a nomenclature and units for concentration. Other books, particularly Books II and III, will provide specific relationships on how certain properties vary with composition, temperature, and pressure.

This monograph set will not provide a catalog of produced water compositions. Ref. 43 provides a significant

bibliography up to 1942 of compositions of oilfield waters in specific geologic formations/provinces. The reference sections in Chaps. 5, 7 through 11, and 13 of Ref. 44 also list (in scattered format) papers on water composition. Several commercial and university- or government-sponsored computer data bases contain water-composition data.

Table 2.17 summarizes the nomenclature and units for expressing the concentration, C, of dissolved solids in formation waters. Also given are the appropriate equations for converting among various expressions. Most commercial oilfield concentration data are reported in either parts per million (ppm) or milligrams per liter (mg/L). The relationship between the two is

$$C_{ppm} = C_{mg/L}/\rho , \quad \dots\dots\dots\dots\dots\dots (2.13)$$

where ρ is density in g/mL.

Following the API recommendation,[45] this monograph set uses mg/L as the standard unit of concentration.

2.6 Summary Comments

Unfortunately, formation evaluation is often perceived as synonymous with wireline log analysis. In reality, all the major tools and techniques of formation evaluation (mud logging, wireline logging, etc.) should be viewed only as means to understand and evaluate the rocks in the subsurface. Effective formation evaluation requires the integrated use of every piece of available data.

Formation evaluation specialists can use the well logging tools and evaluation methods described in following chapters of this monograph set most effectively if they clearly understand the physical and chemical properties of rocks and their fluid content. This chapter attempts to clarify and systematize that understanding by reviewing the fundamental properties needed to evaluate a hydrocarbon reservoir. Perhaps the most important characteristic of a rock is its pore-size distribution, which strongly influences porosity, permeability, and fluid distribution. The petrophysical models used to relate porosity, etc., to borehole-measured parameters should be internally consistent; for example, a model used to evaluate porosity should be consistent and compatible with a permeability model for that same rock. Such models will be consistent if they are based on knowledge and a model of pore-size distribution.

The publications cited in this chapter offer some outstanding insights about the properties of reservoir rock. The textbooks by Grim,[6] Pettijohn,[2] and Van Olphen are highly recommended summaries dealing with the various properties of rock solids. Archie's paper[1] on the petrophysics of reservoir rocks and Leverett's work[37] on capillary phenomena and fluid distributions are early classics that still provide lucid insights 30 to 40 years later. Thomeer's method[10] of quantifying the capillary-pressure curve is suggested as a systematic way to understand rock pore systems. The work of Beard and Weyl[26] is useful in understanding the petrophysical/ reservoir properties of clastic rocks. The carbonate rock classification schemes presented by Archie,[28] Dunham,[9] and Lucia[30] are recommended for practical field use.

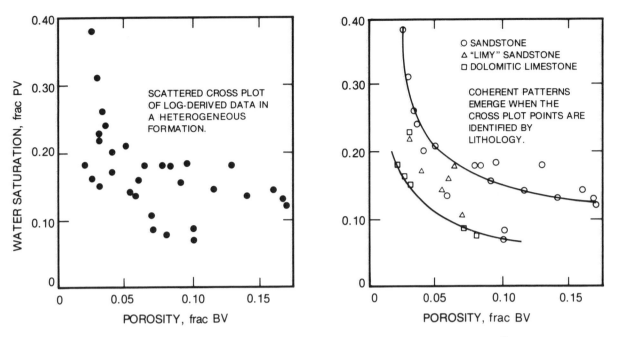

Fig. 2.26—Example of porosity/water-saturation relationships (modified after Morris and Biggs[40]).

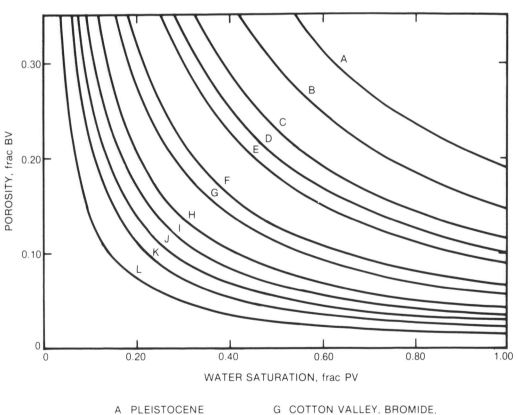

A   PLEISTOCENE
B   MIOCENE
C   FRIO OLMOS
D   WILCOX
E   RED CAVE
F   STRAWN, TUBB

G   COTTON VALLEY, BROMIDE,
    ATOKA, WOODBINE
H   MORROW, AUSTIN CHALK
I   SPIRO
J   SMACKOVER, BROWN DOLOMITE
K   ARBUCKLE
L   HUNTON, ELLENBURGER

Fig. 2.27—Porosity/water-saturation relationships for various formations (after Hilchie[41]).

TABLE 2.17—SUMMARY OF NOMENCLATURE AND UNITS FOR CONCENTRATION OF DISSOLVED SOLIDS IN FORMATION WATERS

Term	Definition	Equations
Molality	$\dfrac{\text{g-mol solute}}{1{,}000\text{ g solvent}}$	$C_m = \dfrac{W_{su}(\text{g-mol})}{W_{sv}(\text{g})} \times 1{,}000.$
Molarity	$\dfrac{\text{g-mol solute}}{1{,}000\text{ mL solution}}$	$C_M = \dfrac{W_{su}(\text{g-mol})}{V_{sl}(\text{mL})} \times 1{,}000.$
Normality	$\dfrac{\text{g-eq solute}}{1{,}000\text{ mL solution}}$	$C_N = \dfrac{W_{su}(\text{g-eq})}{V_{sl}(\text{mL})} \times 1{,}000.$
Weight percent	$\dfrac{\text{g solute}}{100\text{ g solution}}$	$C_W = \dfrac{W_{su}(\text{g})}{W_{sl}(\text{g})} \times 100.$
Parts per million	$\dfrac{\text{mg solute}}{10^6\text{ mg solution}}$	$C_{ppm} = \dfrac{W_{su}(\text{g})}{W_{sl}(\text{g})} \times 10^6 = C_W \times 10^4.$
Milligrams/liter	$\dfrac{\text{mg solute}}{\text{L solution}}$	$C_{mg/L} = \dfrac{W_{su}(\text{mg})}{V_{sl}(\text{mL})} \times 1{,}000 = \rho C_{ppm} = \rho C_W \times 10^4.$
Grains/gallon	$\dfrac{\text{grains solute}}{\text{gal solution}}$	$C_{g/gal} = \dfrac{W_{su}(\text{grains})}{V_{sl}(\text{gal})} = 17.1\,C_{mg/L} = 17.1\,\rho C_{ppm}.$

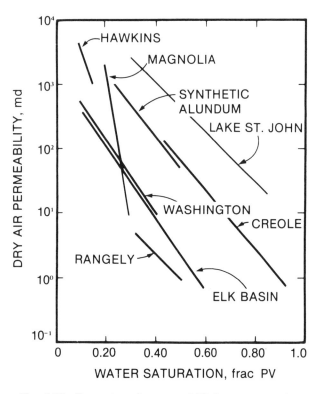

Fig. 2.28—Example of permeability/water-saturation relationships (after Bruce and Welge[42]).

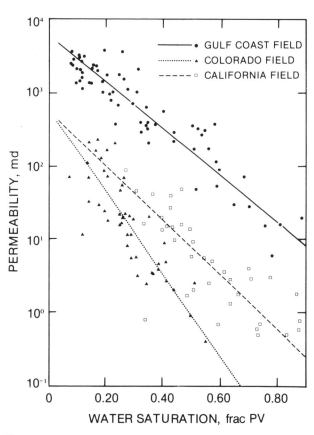

Fig. 2.29—Example of permeability/water-saturation relationships (after Timur[34]).

References

1. Archie, G.E.: "Introduction to Petrophysics of Reservoir Rocks," *Bull.*, AAPG (1950) **34**, 943-61.
2. Pettijohn, F.J.: *Sedimentary Rocks*, third edition, Harper & Row Publishers Inc., New York City (1975).
3. *Physical Properties of Rocks and Minerals*, Y.S. Touloukian and C.Y. Ho (eds.), McGraw-Hill/CINDAS Data Series on Material Properties, Volume II-2, McGraw-Hill Book Co. Inc., New York City (1981).
4. *Handbook of Physical Constants*, S.P. Clarke Jr. (ed.), Memoir 97, GSA, Boulder, CO (1966) 459-82.
5. Wells, L.E., Sanyal, S.K., and Mathews, M.A.: "Matrix and Response Characteristics for Sonic, Density, and Neutron," *Trans.*, SPWLA Annual Symposium (1979) paper Z.
6. Grim, R.E.: *Clay Mineralogy*, second edition, McGraw-Hill Book Co. Inc., New York City (1968) 32.
7. Rittenhouse, G.: "A Visual Method of Estimating Two-Dimensional Sphericity," *J. Sed. Petrol.* (1943) **13**, 79.
8. Powers, M.C.: "A New Roundness Scale for Sedimentary Particles," *J. Sed. Petrol.* (1953) **23**, 117.
9. Dunham, R.J.: "Classification of Carbonate Rocks According to Depositional Texture," *Classification of Carbonate Rocks*, Memoir 1, AAPG, Tulsa (1962) 108-21.
10. Thomeer, J.H.M.: "Introduction of a Pore Geometrical Factor Defined by the Capillary Pressure Curve," *Trans.*, AIME (1960) **219**, 354-58.
11. Choquette, P.W. and Pray, L.C.: "Geologic Nomenclature and Classification of Porosity in Sedimentary Carbonates," *Bull.*, AAPG (1970) **54**, 207-50.
12. Pittman, E.D.: "Porosity, Diagenesis and Productive Capability of Sandstone Reservoirs," *Aspects of Diagenesis*, Special Publication 26, Soc. of Economic Paleontologists and Mineralogists, Tulsa (1979) 159-74.
13. Neasham, J.W.: "The Morphology of Dispersed Clay in Sandstone Reservoirs and Its Effect on Sandstone Shaliness, Pore Space, and Fluid Flow Properties," paper SPE 6858 presented at the 1977 SPE Annual Technical Conference and Exhibition, Denver, Oct. 9-12.
14. Carmen, P.C.: "Fluid Flow Through Granular Beds," *Trans.*, Instn. of Chem. Eng. (1937) **15**, 150-66.
15. Purcell, W.R.: "Capillary Pressures—Their Measurement Using Mercury and the Calculation of Permeability Therefrom," *Trans.*, AIME (1949) **186**, 39-48.
16. Burdine, N.T., Gournay, L.S., and Reichertz, P.P.: "Pore Size Distribution of Petroleum Reservoir Rocks," *Trans.*, AIME (1950) **189**, 195-204.
17. Fatt, I. and Dykstra, H.: "Relative Permeability Studies," *Trans.*, AIME (1951) **192**, 249-55.
18. Gates, J.I. and Tempelaar-Leitz, W.: "Relative Permeabilities of California Cores by the Capillary Pressure Method," *Drill. and Prod. Prac.*, API (1950) 285-302.
19. Wyllie, M.R.J. and Spangler, M.B.: "Application of Electrical Resistivity Measurements to Problems of Fluid Flow in Porous Media," *Bull.*, AAPG (1952) **36**, 359-403.
20. Berg, R.R.: "Method for Determining Permeability from Reservoir Rock Properties," *Trans.*, Gulf Coast Assn. of Geologic Soc. (1970) **20**, 303-17.
21. Wyllie, M.R.J. and Gregory, A.R.: "Formation Factors of Unconsolidated Porous Media: Influence of Particle Shape and Effect of Cementation," *Trans.*, AIME (1953) **198**, 103-09.
22. Fatt, I.: "The Network Model of Porous Media, I—Capillary Pressure Characteristics," *Trans.*, AIME (1956) **207**, 144-59.
23. Rose, W.: "Studies of Waterflood Performance, III—Use of Network Models," Circular 237, Illinois State Geological Survey, Urbana, IL (1957) 1-31.
24. Simon, R. and Kelsey, F.J.: "The Use of Capillary Tube Networks in Reservoir Performance Studies: I. Equal-Viscosity Miscible Displacements," *Soc. Pet. Eng. J.* (June 1971) 99-112.
25. Simon, R. and Kelsey, F.J.: "The Use of Capillary Tube Networks in Reservoir Performance Studies: II. Effect of Heterogeneity and Mobility on Miscible Displacement Efficiency," *Soc. Pet. Eng. J.* (Aug. 1972) 345-51.
26. Beard, D.C. and Weyl, P.K.: "Influence of Texture on Porosity and Permeability of Unconsolidated Sand," *Bull.*, AAPG (1973) **57**, 349-69.
27. Enos, P. and Sawatsky, L.H.: "Pore Networks in Holocene Carbonate Sediments," *J. Sed. Pet.* (1981) **51**, 961-85.
28. Archie, G.E.: "Classification of Carbonate Reservoir Rocks and Petrophysical Considerations," *Bull.*, AAPG (1952) **36**, 278-98.
29. Jodry, R.L.: "Pore Geometry of Carbonate Rocks," in *Oil and Gas Production from Carbonate Rocks*, American Elsevier Publishing Co. Inc., New York City (1972) 35-82.
30. Lucia, F.J.: "Petrophysical Parameters Estimated From Visual Descriptions of Carbonate Rocks: A Field Classification of Carbonate Pore Space," *J. Pet. Tech.* (March 1983) 629-37.
31. Hubbert, M.K.: "Darcy's Law and the Field Equations of the Flow of Underground Fluids," *Trans.*, AIME (1956) **207**, 222-39.
32. Seevers, D.O.: "A Nuclear Magnetic Method for Determining the Permeability of Sandstone," *Trans.*, SPWLA Symposium (1966) paper L.
33. Krumbein, W.C. and Monk, G.D.: "Permeability as a Function of the Size Parameters of Unconsolidated Sand," *Trans.*, AIME (1943) **151**, 153-63.
34. Timur, A.: "An Investigation of Permeability, Porosity, and Residual Water Saturation Relationships," *Trans.*, SPWLA Symposium (1968) paper J.
35. Thomeer, J.H.: "Air Permeability as a Function of Three Pore Network Parameters," *J. Pet. Tech.* (April 1983) 809-14.
36. Rose, W.D. and Bruce, W.A.: "Evaluation of Capillary Character in Petroleum Reservoir Rock," *Trans.*, AIME (1949) **186**, 127-42.
37. Leverett, M.C.: "Capillary Behavior in Porous Solids," *Trans.*, AIME (1941) **142**, 152-68.
38. Brown, H.W.: "Capillary Pressure Investigations," *Trans.*, AIME (1951) **192**, 67-74.
39. Buckles, R.S.: "Correlating and Averaging Connate Water Saturation Data," *J. Cdn. Pet. Tech.* (Jan.-March 1965) 42-52.
40. Morris, R.L. and Biggs, W.P.: "Using Log-Derived Values of Water Saturation and Porosity," *Trans.*, SPWLA Symposium (1967) paper X.
41. Hilchie, D.W.: *Well Log Interpretation (Basic)*, D.W. Hilchie, Golden, CO (1977) ESI2.
42. Bruce, W.A. and Welge, H.J.: "The Restored State Method for Determination of Oil in Place and Connate Water," *Drill. and Prod. Prac.*, API (1947) 166-74.
43. Case, L.C. *et al.*: "Selected Annotated Bibliography on Oil-Field Waters," *Bull.*, AAPG (1942) **26**, 865.
44. Collins, A.G.: *Geochemistry of Oilfield Waters*, Elsevier Scientific Publishing Co., Amsterdam (1975).
45. "Analysis of Oil-Field Waters," *Recommended Practice 45*, second edition, API, Dallas (1968).

Chapter 3
Borehole Logging Environment

The numerous caliper logs already taken in wells over an extensive area show that the difference between bit sizes and actual hole sizes is much greater than expected...

from C.P. Parsons' 1943 paper,[1] shortly after the commercial introduction of electromechanical tools considered the forerunner of modern caliper logging systems.

3.0 Introduction. Wireline log data answer questions about subsurface formations and the fluids they contain. The reliability of such answers often depends on the environment in which the measurements were made. Unfortunately, drilling practices and procedures that optimize drilling efficiency do not always provide the ideal environment for formation evaluation. Therefore, many logging tools are designed to minimize adverse borehole conditions. In other situations, expert knowledge is required to recognize such conditions and to deal with the effects of less-than-optimal environments. These conditions and some ways to deal with them are discussed in this chapter.

3.1 Borehole Geometry

Rotary drilling creates a cavity, or *borehole*, wherein drilling mud replaces formation material and the virgin formation is exposed to a drilling-induced environment (Fig. 3.1). Dealing with this environment requires knowing the borehole shape, size, and inclination, and how these change with time.

Applying corrections based on ideal borehole models to nonideal conditions can result in erroneous interpretation of well logs. Ideally, the hole is modeled as a vertical cylinder of a uniform diameter penetrating horizontally bedded formations. However, ideal conditions are not common in real wells. Typical boreholes can deviate from the vertical, penetrate dipping beds, and have hole dimensions that are larger or smaller than the bit size. Holes often have noncircular cross sections and rugose walls. Fortunately, correction for nonidealities is often possible, but for some borehole conditions the only alternative is to identify intervals with uncorrectable conditions and label those intervals "not interpretable."

3.1.1 Size and Shape

Borehole size, or *gauge*, has been measured with *caliper* devices for many years. Beckstrom[2] wrote "Open Hole Diameter Changes Located and Measured by Recording Calipers" in 1935, and commercial services have been available, at least on a limited basis, since 1938. Early services were stimulated by a need for more accurate calculation of the amount of cement used for setting casing. Parsons[1] in 1943 and Guyod[3-6] in 1945 discussed this and other uses. Calipering is now a routine component of wireline logging and provides data essential for accurate log analysis.

The caliper devices used on different tools respond differently in the same noncylindrical hole. Fig. 3.2 shows four standard configurations: (a) "one arm" that also serves as an eccentering device; (b) "two arms" extending equidistant from a centralized tool body; (c) "three arms," which center the tool body; and (d) "four arms" consisting of two calipers at right angles to each other.

One-arm devices tend to seek the longest dimension of the borehole cross section—especially if the long axis is in a vertical plane. They are used with some density and neutron tools. Such tools (with eccentering devices) are also likely to take a position that puts their body or skid in contact with the low side of the hole during logging. The low side of the hole can have a different mudcake thickness and character than the side or top, because of greater exposure to scraping by the bit and wearing by the drillstring.

Two-arm calipers tend to record the long axis of out-of-round holes. They are used with microresistivity tools. The one- and two-arm calipers could be considered different versions of the same calipering configuration. Both tend to measure the long axis of the hole but contact the borehole wall and sense irregularities differently.

Three-arm devices maintain their arms equidistant from the body of the tool and therefore measure only one diameter—something between the minimum and maximum of a noncircular hole section (Fig. 3.3).[7] This design is used in three-arm dipmeters and some acoustic tools. There is an independent three-arm caliper module that can be used with almost any combination of tools.

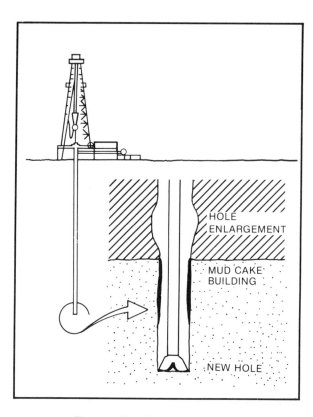

Fig. 3.1—Simplified borehole model.

Four-arm calipers typically use two pairs of arms that extend independently of the other. One pair seeks the long dimension of an out-of-round hole; the other measures the dimension at right angles. Some dipmeters and special caliper tools use this configuration. Fig. 3.4 compares calipers recorded in a noncylindrical hole.

In addition to the number of arms, the nature of the tool contacts also affects the caliper response when a hole is not cylindrical or contains mudcake. The contact area, shape, and pressure varies among the different tools pictured in Fig. 3.5.

Devices that use "finger-type" arms (Fig. 3.5a) have small contact areas and can sense small-scale borehole irregularities. Contact pressure is usually high enough to cut through any mudcake. Tools for high-resolution calipering or borehole geometry investigation typically have small contact areas. Pad-type devices (Fig. 3.5b) have somewhat larger contact areas than finger-type contacts and, when operated at lower contact pressures, override mudcake. Microresistivity, dipmeter, and some density and sidewall acoustic tools use pads. Tools that use an eccentering arm and skid (Fig. 3.5c) with different contact areas may or may not cut through the mudcake, depending on contact pressure and mudcake properties. Often the skid overrides and the eccentering arm cuts through. Some density and neutron tools use an eccentering arm. Some tools use a "bowspring" (Fig. 3.5d) for centering the tool body and/or calipering the hole. The spring can be wide, as for the acoustic tools; or narrow, as for some special calipering devices. The contact pressure varies with the length and width of the bow, the size of the hole, the strength of the spring, and the

hole inclination. In highly deviated holes, the weight of the tool can collapse the caliper.

Borehole cross sections are often described as circles and ellipses because only these shapes can be defined from the one or two dimensions usually available from one logging run. When the entire borehole section is defined, more complex shapes are revealed. Fig. 3.6 shows examples of irregular hole shapes obtained with a modified Borehole Televiewer.[8] The dotted circle is concentric with the tool and represents an 8.5-in. diameter. Borehole walls are shown by the inner edge of the long traces. Studies[8] of four-arm dipmeter calipers indicate that borehole elongation is preferentially in one direction while the section at right angles tends to stay in gauge. Moreover, the borehole tends to be more wrinkled, or *rugose*, in the direction of maximum elongation. This helps explain the improved accuracy of density-log measurements when special positioning devices keep the skid in contact with the formation face at a right angle to the elongation.

Rapid changes in hole shape may not be sensed, depending on how the tool contacts the borehole wall. Fig. 3.7 shows a situation where the lower enlarged segment (d) will be correctly sensed by the backup pad and skid, while the upper enlarged segment (b) will not, because only the backup arm will enter it. The rugose section (c) will be calipered as bit size because both tool contacts override the enlargements. The in-gauge segment (a) will be calipered as bit size less some fraction of the mudcake thickness.

Most calipering tools are designed to operate in 5- to 20-in. holes, but specialized devices can measure up to a 40-in. diameter. Larger holes or caverns can be investigated with sonar-type calipers.[9]

3.1.2 Inclination and Direction

Borehole deviation affects the accuracy of logging data and the reliability of wellsite operations. Ideally, the hole is vertical, permitting rapid and safe descent and retrieval of tools. Vertical holes and horizontally bedded formations provide radial symmetry that makes interpretation easier.

Specialized tools are available for logging borehole geometry. Fig. 3.8 shows a tool designed for this purpose. It has small contact pads (for high vertical resolution), arms with optional extensions, an inclinometer for measuring the tool's position with respect to the Earth's magnetic and gravitational fields, and an integrator (at the surface) to compute hole volume. Data recorded with such a tool (Fig. 3.9) are sufficient to compute a three-dimensional course for the well. Projections of the well course into vertical and horizontal planes (Fig. 3.10) reveal places where the hole doubles back on its direction, causing "keyseats" created by the drillpipe and centralizers wearing and cutting on the low side of the hole. In those intervals one caliper records greater than bit size, and the other records bit size or smaller (Fig. 3.11). Campbell[8] considers this a typical response when a key seat is encountered.

3.1.3 Degradation With Time

Borehole conditions often degrade as drilling continues. Fig. 3.12 shows an example of significant hole deterioration between two logging runs.[8] Hole condi-

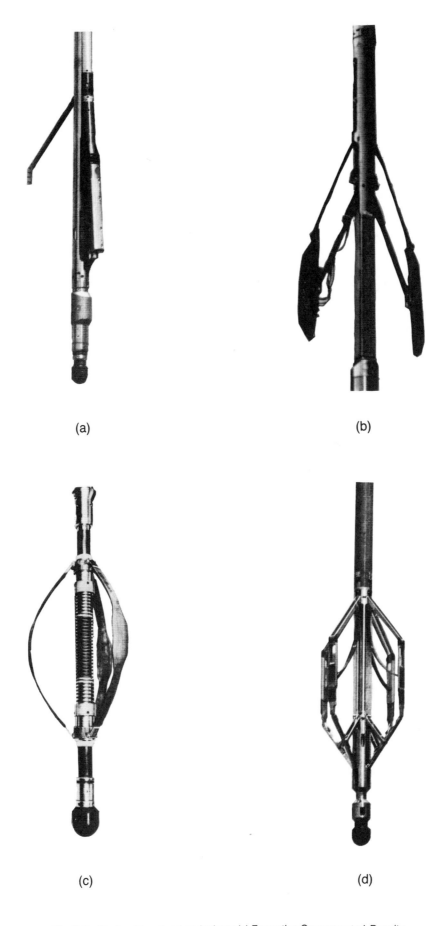

(a)

(b)

(c)

(d)

Fig. 3.2—Tools with calipering devices: (a) Formation Compensated Density,
(b) Microlaterolog, (c) Sonic Caliper, and (d) High Resolution
Dipmeter (courtesy Schlumberger Well Services).

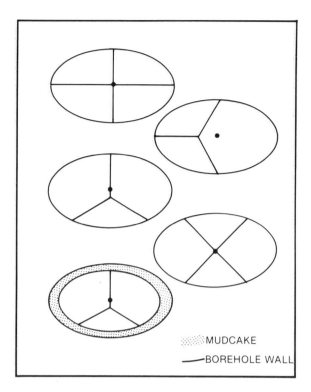

MUDCAKE

BOREHOLE WALL

Fig. 3.3—Position of caliper arms in an elliptical hole (after Hilchie[7]).

tions sometimes deteriorate enough that logging measurements cannot be sufficiently corrected to permit accurate interpretation. Then the alternatives are to use other (and often more expensive) evaluation methods or accept the risk of evaluating a prospective interval inadequately. It is better to use drilling procedures and muds that slow the deterioration or to log often enough that the hole condition is within the range necessary for making valid environmental corrections.

3.1.4 Comments

In summary, caliper data may not completely describe borehole geometry, which can be much more complex than a vertical, right, and smooth-sided cylinder with a diameter that is the same as bit size.

3.2 Invasion

Drilling fluids composed to overbalance formation pore-fluid pressures tend to invade permeable formations, replacing the native fluid in the region adjacent to the borehole. Many logging methods derive their response from the near-borehole region; therefore, evaluating the consequences of drilling-fluid invasion is critical to interpreting well logging data correctly.

3.2.1 Impregnation

Laboratory experiments and core studies have revealed the potential for drilling mud to *impregnate* a freshly cut formation. This is driven by the pressure differential between the drilling mud and formation fluid.

Solids Mobility

The experimental results of Donaldson and Baker[10] on solids mobility in sandstones demonstrate that quartz particles readily migrate through sandstone samples with

mean pore-throat sizes not much larger than the average size of the mobile particles.

Clay-particle migration is another matter. Such particles penetrate only a limited distance before bridging at pore constrictions or earlier bridges, or plating onto a surface (Fig. 3.13).[11] Glenn *et al.*[12,13] simulated drilling conditions with Alundum[TM] samples in contact with flowing mud. During one part of the experiment, the samples were continuously scraped by a bit as is done when a well is drilled. Downhole pressure differentials were also simulated, but not size-scale nor temperature. Under these conditions, clay penetration was about 3 cm.

Core studies provide more evidence of solids migration through the pores of some rocks. For example, Webb and Haskin[14] evaluated the effects of coring techniques on the integrity of the recovered cores. Those from pressure and rubber-sleeve coring tools were characterized by a series of concave-downward, poorly sorted, but generally very fine-grained bands (Fig. 3.14).[14] Scanning-electron-microscope examination and X-ray diffraction analysis indicate that the fine-grained bands are native formation material mixed with drilling debris and whole mud. The mud and drilling debris appear to have impregnated the underlying rocks before they were cut by the core bit. Cores cut with large-diameter barrels having different bottomhole hydrokinetics did not display this phenomenon.

Solid-particle invasion has also been defined by analysis of the barite content of full cores. For example, in Fig. 3.15 barium and sulfur are present throughout the outer 1 in. of the core. Their co-presence indicates that barite, an uncommon mineral in rocks, was put there by drilling-mud impregnation.

Solids movement during the surge phase is resisted by internal buildup of particles within the pores from gravity settling, bridging or plugging at pore constrictions, and attracting of particles to pore surfaces. Eventually a surface cake (Fig. 3.16) forms and restricts further movement of solids into the formation. No predictive model incorporates all these factors, but factors that control solids migration before the forming of an external mudcake are reasonably well understood.

Controlling Factors

Impregnation is most likely in higher-permeability rocks with pore throats larger than the mud solids. This was investigated by Glenn *et al.*[12] and Beeson and Wright,[15] who measured the flow rates of bentonite/water slurries and drilling muds into various porous and permeable media under differential pressure. They observed an initially rapid flow rate (or *surge*) while the medium was being bridged by clay solids. The rate declined to a more constant-value flow after mudcake formed. Accordingly, the total fluid loss can be considered in two parts: a surge (or spurt) loss and a filtrate loss (Fig. 3.17).[15] The surge loss is interpreted as the volume indicated by the point where the line defining the flow rate after mudcake formation crosses the zero time axis. Table 3.1 lists surge losses for a range of permeabilities and, presumably, pore sizes.[15] Impregnation occurs only during the surge period before mudcake buildup stops mud solids from moving into the formation.

The surge loss varies with mud type and characteristics, including the particle-size distribution.[13,16]

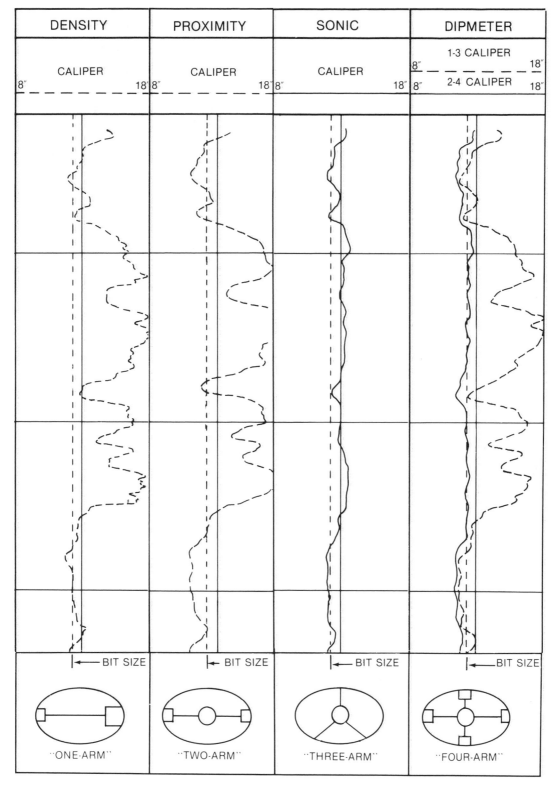

Fig. 3.4—Caliper surveys from different tool types in the same noncylindrical hole.

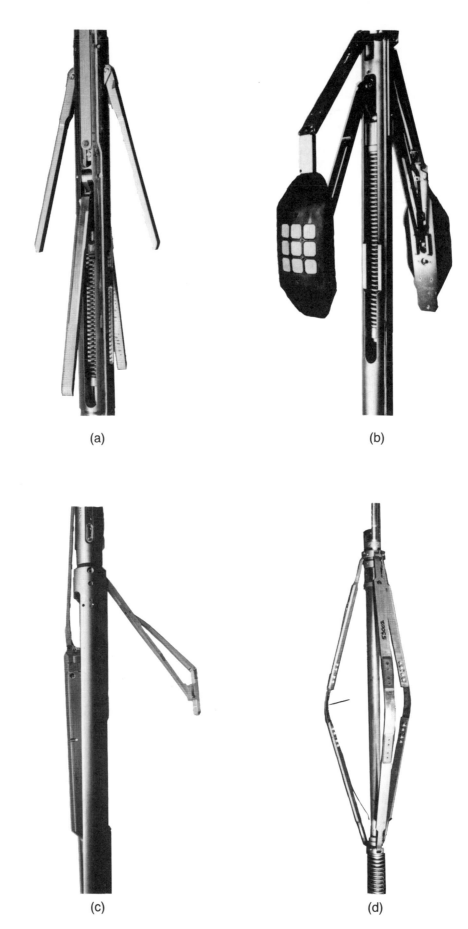

(a)

(b)

(c)

(d)

Fig. 3.5—Tools with calipering devices: (a) Four-Arm Power Caliper, (b) Microlaterolog, (c) Compensated Densilog, and (d) Bow Spring Caliper Module (courtesy Dresser-Atlas).

Laboratory measurements by Glenn and Slusser[13] demonstrated that a 3.2 wt% bentonite/water slurry could flow through porous samples unless particles larger than the makeup clay (1 μm) were added (Fig. 3.18).[13] Some artificial muds used for laboratory experiments and low-solids muds used in the field are deficient in larger particles, encouraging impregnation. Desilters also encourage impregnation by removing certain sizes of solids. Discontinuing desilting should be considered when drilling or coring highly permeable reservoirs.

Solids movement into a rock's pores increases with differential pressure (Fig. 3.19[12] and Table 3.2[15]). This occurs when partly depleted reservoirs are drilled with regular muds or when weighted muds are used in normally pressured intervals. Balanced pressure differentials between the pore fluid and mud column help control impregnation and reduce its adverse effects.

Impregnation is resisted by surface forces between the

TABLE 3.1—EFFECT OF PERMEABILITY ON SPURT LOSSES IN A CONSOLIDATED SAMPLE (after Beeson and Wright[15])

Permeability		Mud Spurt
Air (md)	Water (md)	Loss (mL)
31	7	2.3
60	42	2.5
77	43	6.5
243	254	7.1
390	171	6.9
520	303	5.6
650	469	7.0

migrating solids and pore walls. Because clays have higher surface activity than quartz, mud solids move more freely in a clean rock than in a shaly one. Impregnation does not occur when pore sizes are smaller than the suspended mud solids, such as in shales.

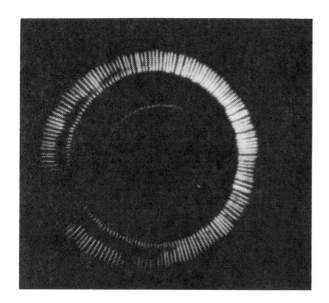
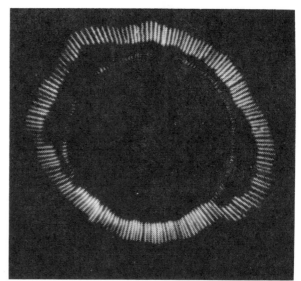
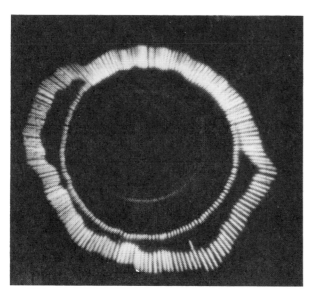
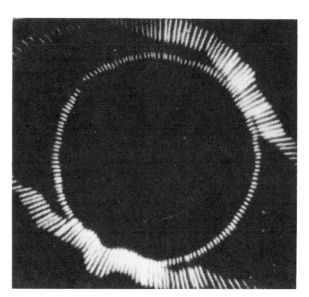

Fig. 3.6—Examples of irregular hole shapes (after Campbell[8]).

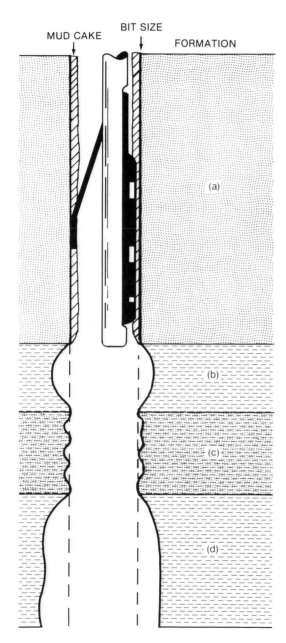

Fig. 3.7—Effect of tool design on caliper response.

TABLE 3.2—EFFECT OF PRESSURE DIFFERENTIAL AND PERMEABILITY ON SPURT LOSSES (after Beeson and Wright[15])

Water Permeability (md)	Mud Spurt Loss (mL)	Pressure (psi)
133	5.0	100
157	3.5	100
279	6.0	100
60	14.6	500
98	18.8	500
82	20.0	1,000
83	22.0	1,000
89	22.0	1,500
39	21.6	1,500

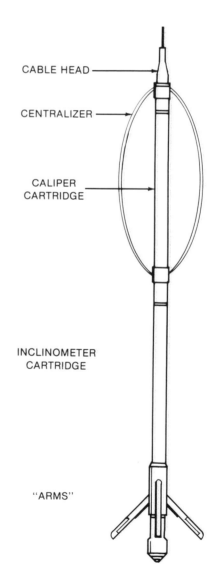

Fig. 3.8—Tool for logging borehole geometry (after Campbell[8]).

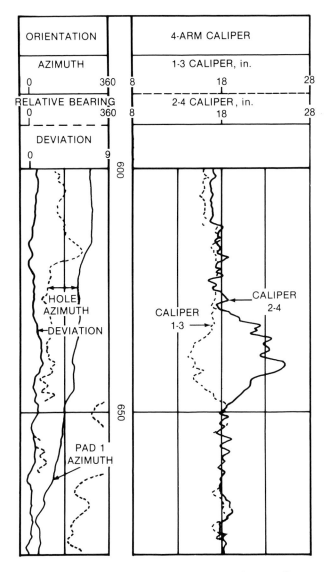

Fig. 3.9—Log of borehole geometry (after Campbell[8]).

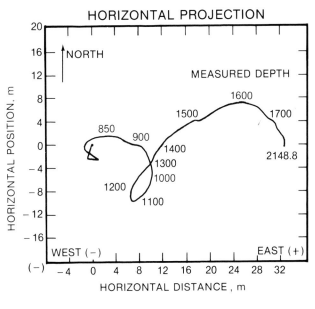

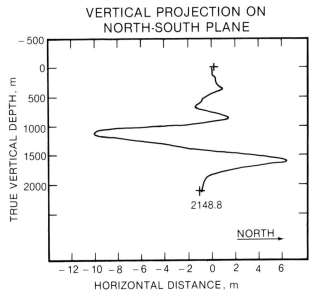

Fig. 3.10—Well profile projections (modified after Campbell[8]).

Effect on Formation Evaluation

Drilling muds contain not only the initial mud materials (makeup clays, high-density weighting additives, complex polymers, surfactants, etc.), but also previously drilled formation solids and fluids. Such materials, even in small amounts, can affect the responses of electrical, acoustical, radiation, and nuclear magnetism surveys. For example, barite impregnation can cause underestimation of porosity from interpretation of bulk density (Fig. 3.20).[17] Montmorillonite impregnation can affect resistivity (Fig. 3.21),[17] and therefore also affect estimates of porosity, permeability, and hydrocarbon saturation from shallow-sensing resistivity logs.

Impregnation can also reduce the reliability of analysis methods based on flushing near the borehole. Fertl and Hammack[18] report anomalously low "movable oil" (calculated from logs) in sandstones with permeabilities greater than 1 darcy. They attribute this to mud-solids penetration into the pores.

Exposing core samples to laboratory conditions that simulate impregnation impairs their permeabilities. The Alundum samples exposed to circulating mud in the

drilling simulations performed by Glenn and Slusser[13] were segmented and analyzed. In segments where clay was found (Fig. 3.22), the permeability after exposure was a fraction of the original.[13] The original Alundum sample did not contain clay, so all the clay found was from the mud. Even backflushing (reverse flow) did not restore the initial permeabilities. If conditions during drilling favor impregnation, formation damage can be expected.[19]

Some investigators consider impregnation insignificant; however, convincing evidence indicates that mud solids do migrate into some reservoir rocks during coring and drilling. Thus, one should remain aware that impregnation can cause formation damage and affect log responses.

Drilling fluid can also leave the hole through fractures or vugs. This can result in loss of circulation and recovery of returns needed for mud logging analysis.

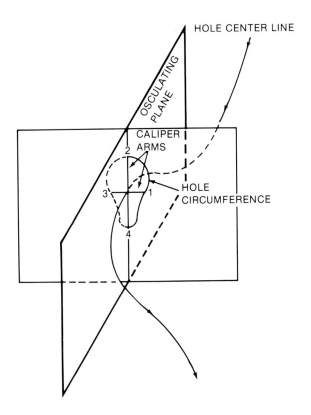

Fig. 3.11—Typical "key seat" pattern (after Campbell[8]).

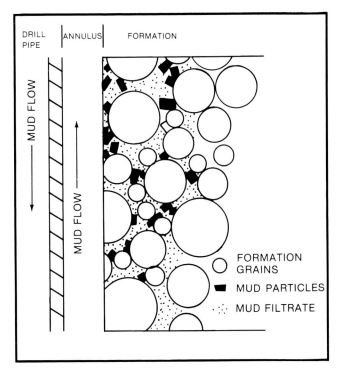

Fig. 3.13—Conceptualization of mud solids migrating into formation before mudcake develops (modified after Dresser-Magcobar[11]).

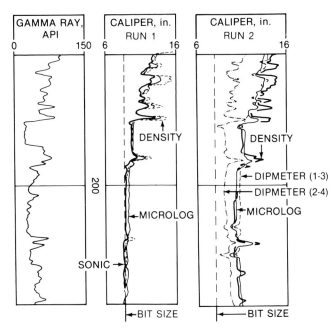

Fig. 3.12—Caliper logs obtained at different times in the same hole (after Campbell[8]).

3.2.2 Infiltration

The mud surge is stopped by *mudcake*, the buildup of mud solids on the borehole face. This limits invasion to what and how much can filter through the ultrafine pores of a highly porous but barely permeable mud-solids deposit. After mudcake forms, infiltration is limited to a fluid phase called *mud filtrate*, which replaces formation fluids and develops an *infiltered* region. The combined impregnated and infiltered regions are called the *invaded zone*. The depth of invasion is usually described by its diameter, d_i, which is referenced from the hole axis (Fig. 3.23).[20]

Filtration

The filtration of suspended solids from a slurry can be considered[21] in terms of mudcake volume, V_{mc}, being deposited as a filtrate volume, V_{mf}, is produced. No mudcake forms after filtrate production ceases.

The filtrate production rate is typically determined by a low-temperature filtration test, according to API Recommended Practice 13 B. A sample of mud is placed in the reservoir, where a 7.1-sq in. paper filter covers the outlet end. A 100-psi pressure is applied to the mud reservoir, and the filtrate is collected in a graduated receptacle. The amount collected (V_{mf}) in 30 minutes is usually reported as the fluid loss in cubic centimeters. The mudcake thickness, h_{mc}, on the filter paper is reported to the nearest $\frac{1}{32}$ in.

Low-pressure mud filtrate production is, for the first few hours, almost a linear function of the square root of time, t.

$$V_{mf} = c\sqrt{t}, \quad \ldots\ldots\ldots\ldots\ldots\ldots\ldots\ldots\ldots\ldots (3.1)$$

NATURAL   U.V.

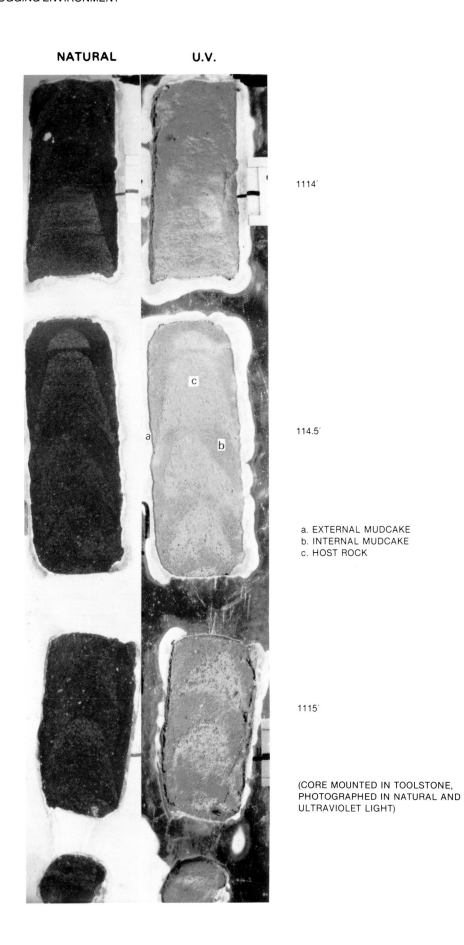

1114'

114.5'

a. EXTERNAL MUDCAKE
b. INTERNAL MUDCAKE
c. HOST ROCK

1115'

(CORE MOUNTED IN TOOLSTONE,
PHOTOGRAPHED IN NATURAL AND
ULTRAVIOLET LIGHT)

Fig. 3.14—Photograph of slabbed core showing features attributed to impregnation (after Webb and Haskin[14]).

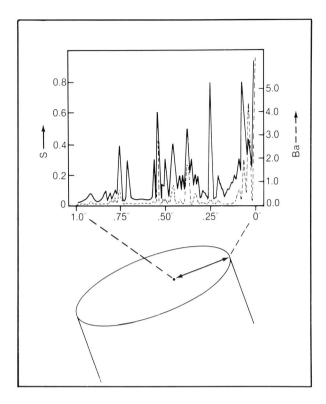

Fig. 3.15—Barium and sulfur response from electron micro-
probe scan across core.

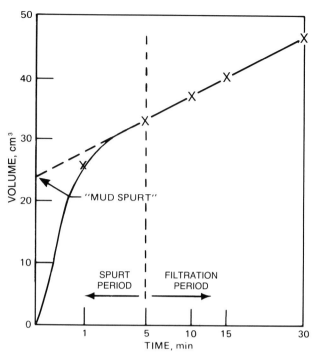

Fig. 3.17—Fluid loss vs. cumulative time showing surge and
filtration flow periods (modified after Beeson and
Wright[15]).

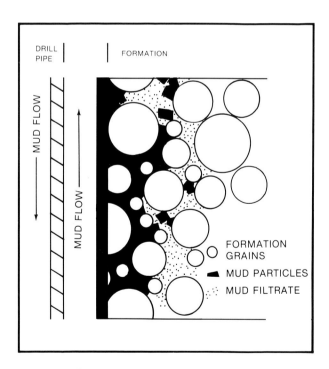

Fig. 3.16—Conceptualization of impregnated region after mudcake forms (modified after Dresser-Magcobar[11]).

where c is a constant that depends on mud type, pressure, and temperature. A gradual loss of linearity with time is attributed to mudcake compressibility[21] and increasing heterogeneity.[22]

Filtrate losses through a mudcake are higher when the mud is moving than when it is still.[23] This is caused partly by diagenesis of the mudcake, which tends to form during trips and to erode during drilling. As operations alternate between drilling (circulation) and tripping (no circulation), the mudcake is perceived as forming in stratified layers, each with its own filtration characteristics. When the bit knocks off old cake, new patches form with different filtration characteristics. This perception casts doubt on the significance of a filtration test involving a uniform, uncompacted layer.

Laboratory tests indicate that filtration rates through a mudcake depend on the annular mud velocity (Fig. 3.24).[23] Thus, several investigators[23-26] consider static fluid-loss tests inadequate for predicting actual downhole filtration—especially during drilling. Moreover, some muds with low static filtration rates have high dynamic losses.[23]

The preceding considerations pose the following questions.

1. How is filtration affected by formation permeability?

2. When and how fast does mudcake form?

3. How do temperature and pressure affect filtration?

4. What are typical invasion depths?

5. Can invasion depths be predicted?

To help answer these questions, it is instructive to consider filtrate flow through a series of concentric cylinders representing the mudcake, the impregnated zone, and the

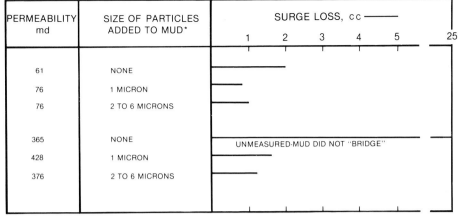

PERMEABILITY md	SIZE OF PARTICLES ADDED TO MUD*	SURGE LOSS, cc ————
61	NONE	
76	1 MICRON	
76	2 TO 6 MICRONS	
365	NONE	UNMEASURED-MUD DID NOT "BRIDGE"
428	1 MICRON	
376	2 TO 6 MICRONS	

*ALL ADDITIONS ONE LB/BBL

Fig. 3.18—Effect of particle-size distribution on surge loss in high-permeability rock samples (modified after Glenn and Slusser[13]).

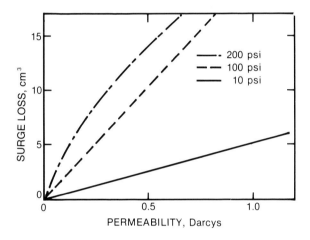

Fig. 3.19—Effect of permeability and pressure differential on surge loss in porous media (after Glenn et al.[12]).

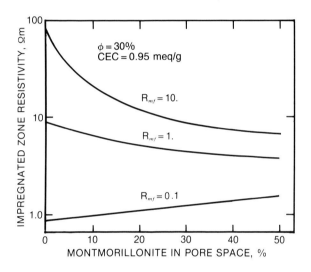

Fig. 3.21—Effect of montmorillonite impregnation on resistivity (after Campbell[17]).

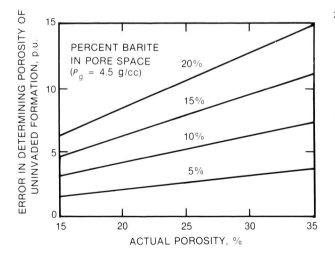

Fig. 3.20—Effect of barite concentration on porosity calculated from bulk density; grain density is assumed (after Campbell[17]).

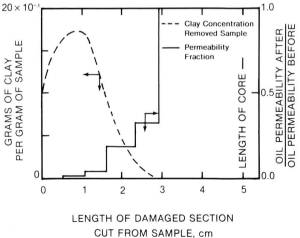

LENGTH OF DAMAGED SECTION CUT FROM SAMPLE, cm

Fig. 3.22—Clay concentration and permeability damage in inert porous sample exposed to simulated drilling conditions (modified after Glenn and Slusser[13]).

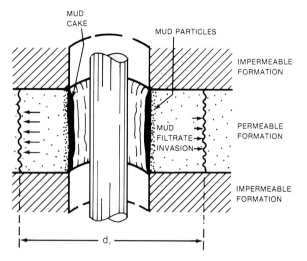

Fig. 3.23—Schematic of borehole region (after Breitenbach[20]).

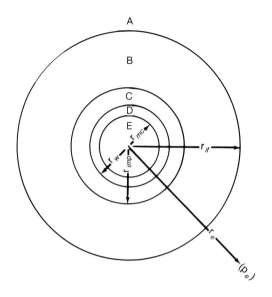

LEGEND

A UNDISTURBED FORMATION (k_f, μ_f, p_e)
B INFILTERED ZONE (k_{if}, μ_{if})
C IMPREGNATED ZONE (k_{imp}, μ_{imp})
D MUD CAKE (k_{mc}, μ_{mf})
E BOREHOLE (p_w)

Fig. 3.25—Invasion-filtration model, with nomenclature for equations (modified after von Engelhardt[21]).

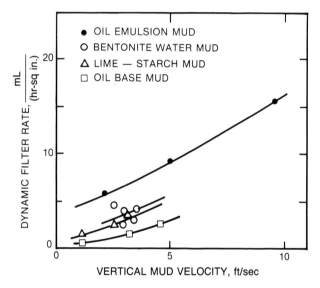

Fig. 3.24—Effect of vertical mud velocity on filtration rates (modified after Ferguson and Klotz[23]).

darcy, centimeter, centimeter, and centipoise, respectively. This equation is useful for considering how formation permeability, fluid viscosity, and impregnation depth affect filtration rates and subsequent mudcake buildup.

Formation Permeability

Substituting typical permeability and viscosity values into Eq. 3.2 generates four cases of special interest.

1. When formation permeability is smaller than mudcake permeability (e.g., shale intervals), filtrate production and subsequent mudcake development are very small. This explains why mudcake is not usually observed in shale and other low-permeability sections.

2. When formation permeability is significantly larger than mudcake permeability, the filtration rate will be almost the same regardless of whether the formation permeability is 0.1 md or 1 darcy—ignoring the possibility of impregnation. Accordingly, assuming that the formation permeability is greater than 0.1 md, no conclusions about rock permeability can be drawn from the thickness of the filter cake.

3. When the formation oil is more viscous than the filtrate, filtration is reduced and thinner mudcakes are produced.

4. When the impregnated zone permeability is lower than mudcake permeability, filtration can be reduced (to the point that no external mudcake is produced).

infiltered zone. These cylinders have radii r, permeabilities k, pressures p (as shown in Fig. 3.25), and a height h_f.[21] The filtration rate, dV_{mf}/dt, of mud filtrate with viscosity μ, in accordance with Darcy's law, modified after von Engelhardt[21] is

$$\frac{dV_{mf}}{dt} = \frac{2\pi h_f(p_w - p_e)}{\dfrac{\mu_{mf}}{k_{mc}}\ln\dfrac{r_w}{r_{mc}} + \dfrac{\mu_{imp}}{k_{imp}}\ln\dfrac{r_{imp}}{r_w} + \dfrac{\mu_{if}}{k_{if}}\ln\dfrac{r_{if}}{r_{imp}} + \dfrac{\mu_f}{k_f}\ln\dfrac{r_e}{r_{if}}} .$$

$$\dots\dots\dots\dots\dots\dots\dots\dots\dots (3.2)$$

The filtration rate is in cubic centimeters divided by seconds if the units for p, k, h, r, and μ are atmosphere,

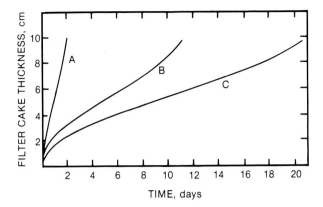

Fig. 3.26—Effect of time and mud type on mudcake thickness. A is a "normal" mud with NaCl added. B is "normal" mud. C is "normal" mud with NaCl and cellulose added (after von Engelhardt[21]).

Time

Mudcake forms rapidly. Its rate of formation can be evaluated by simplifying the model used in deriving Eq. 3.2 to assume full water saturation, no impregnation, and a formation permeability greater than 1 md. The necessary relationships are derived in Ref. 21. Filtercake thicknesses as a function of time are presented in Fig. 3.26 for three mud types.[21]

Temperature

Temperature affects the filtrate viscosity and sometimes the structure and permeability of the mudcake. Fig. 3.27 shows filter loss behavior of some clay/water muds at temperatures above 150°F.[27] Schremp and Johnson[27] report that low-temperature tests will not predict filter losses at high temperature—especially for some emulsion and oil-base fluids. The combined effects of temperature tend to increase the amount of invasion (Fig. 3.28).[20]

Pressure

The effect of pressure on filter loss is unpredictable as temperature increases (Fig. 3.29). Above 150°F and 200°F there is a tendency for filter loss to increase with increasing pressure, but at 250°F both increases and decreases can be observed with increasing pressure. The amount of pressure differential is important in considering impregnation during the mud surge before mudcake forms.

Invasion Depth

Infiltration depth for a given time, formation thickness, and porosity can be calculated from Eq. 3.2. However, this equation does not include the effects of mudcake compressibility, mud velocity, and two-phase fluid saturations. Thus, infiltration depth is better evaluated through laboratory simulation and log studies.

Ferguson and Klotz[23] investigated drilling-fluid behavior around a bit in a model consisting of a sandstone sample suspended in a pressure vessel where full-scale tools could be operated. Field well geometry and pressure differences were duplicated, but temperature was not. With this model, they evaluated filtration losses from several types of drilling fluids. Their data can be used to estimate the depth of filtrate penetration into a

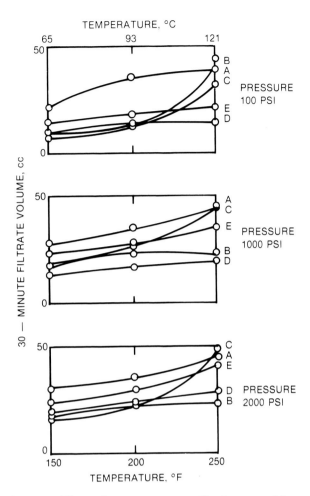

Fig. 3.27—Effect of temperature on filtration rate (after Schremp and Johnson[27]).

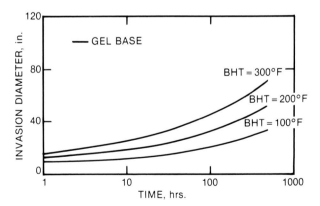

Fig. 3.28—Invasion depth as a function of bottomhole temperature (modified after Breitenbach[20]).

permeable interval after a given sequence of operations. For example, with the typical operations schedule shown in Table 3.3, the invasion diameter of a sandstone assumed to be at 7,000 ft is estimated to reach 43.4 in. during drilling to 7,500 ft.[23] In this example, invasion

TABLE 3.3—DRILLING SCHEDULE AND FILTRATE INVASION
(modified after Ferguson and Klotz[23])

Operation	Time (hours)	Filtrate Volume (mL/sq in.)	Invasion Diameter (in.)
1. Drill through zone at 5 ft/hr			14.6
2. Drill below zone at 5 ft/hr	50	120	36.8
3. Round trip to replace bit	8	3.5	37.2
4. Drill below zone at 5 ft/hr	50	61.5	42.2
5. Pull pipe, log well, run pipe	12	2.9	42.6
6. Condition hole to run casing			
a. Circulate drilling mud	2	2.9	43.0
b. Pull drillpipe	4		
7. Run casing	12	2.9	43.4
8. Cement casing, end of filtration	—	—	—
Total mud filtration	138	192	43.4

TABLE 3.4—INVASION DIAMETER (in.),
WILLISTON BASIN
(after McVicar et al.[29])

d_i	Porosity (%)
20	15 to 18
40	12 to 15
80	9 to 12

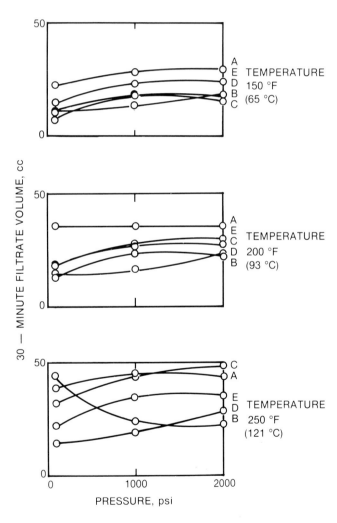

Fig. 3.29—Effect of pressure on filtration rate (after Schremp and Johnson[27]).

reached 85% of its maximum depth after the first drilling period. Ferguson and Klotz concluded that filtrate invasion from beneath the bit could be as much as one hole diameter before filter cake controls filtration. However, resistivity measurements while drilling often indicate lower initial rates of invasion.

Studies by Miesch and Albright[28] of resistivity log data from 676 zones in 26 midcontinent area wells indicated that invasion diameters of 60 in. could be estimated when no other information was available. In the Williston basin, McVicar et al.[29] reported invasion diameters of 20 to 80 in., depending on the porosity (Table 3.4),[29] which determines the volume available to store the invading fluid (Fig. 3.30). A high filtration rate plus low porosity causes "deep" invasion; a low filtration rate plus high porosity causes "shallow" invasion.

An approximate invasion depth can be estimated from the mud type, filter loss, and annular velocity, bottomhole temperature, pressure, porosity, hole diameter, and circulating/noncirculating times. The necessary relationships for gel-base, oil-emulsion, and oil-base muds were developed by Breitenbach[20] from experimentally derived data in the literature. In the previously cited midcontinent studies,[28] these relationships predicted invasion diameters with an average deviation of 53.2% from log calculations assuming "average" values for the pressure, surface temperature, and mud velocity terms in Breitenbach's relationship.

Satisfactory evaluation of water saturation from deep resistivity measurements requires that invasion diameters be no more than 80 to 100 in. for optimal conditions; less for typical hole and formation conditions. Limiting depths can be reached in a few days when the water loss is high and porosity is low. Fig. 3.31 shows the effect of invasion on the short normal after only 6 days.

Analysis of logging runs repeated over a given interval at different times is helpful for estimating invasion rates. It is good practice always to overlap the bottom segment of a previous logging run to check on hole degradation and invasion.

Invasion depth increases with time, but the rate slows as the mudcake compresses, and larger volumes of filtrate are required for each incremental advance of the invasion front.

3.2.3 Invasion Patterns

Mud filtrate moving into formation pores displaces formation fluids. This displacement can be visualized as pistonlike. However, laboratory experiments and field observations show that invasion patterns are not simply pistonlike. Flow paths are irregular and changing; resident fluid can be bypassed; and the invading-fluid boundary is neither sharp nor simple. A more realistic view can be achieved after these questions are answered:

   1. Does filtrate displace oil and water at the same rate?

   2. Is all the connate water displaced or will some remain?

   3. Does gravity modify the filtrate distribution?

Flushed Zone

Infiltration during drilling can replace the pore fluid near the wellbore several times. One or two pore volumes will displace nearly all the connate water from a homogeneous medium. A few pore volumes of filtrate will displace most of the movable hydrocarbon, providing their mobilities are similar. The near-wellbore region in which most of the original pore fluid has been replaced is called the *flushed zone*, designated by the subscript *xo*. The resistivity of the flushed zone will be higher than the undisturbed formation if the invading filtrate is fresher than the connate water (Fig. 3.32).

Formation Water Annulus

Injection of water into a water-wet petroleum-bearing reservoir displaces the connate water.[31] Similarly, filtrate invasion into a petroleum-bearing reservoir can displace connate water creating an *annulus* of high water saturation between the flushed zone and the undisturbed formation. When the filtrate is fresher than the formation water, the resistivity is lower in the annulus than in the flushed zone (Fig. 3.33).[30] The presence of a low-

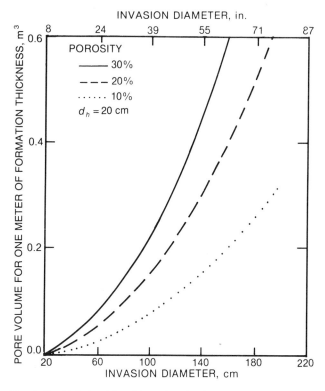

Fig. 3.30—Relationship of invasion depth and porosity, with other factors constant (after Campbell[17]).

resistivity region around a borehole can be detected by a resistivity survey that uses a multiple-electrode array to investigate different depths from the hole. The low-resistivity zone in the electrical survey, using electrodes spaced from 6 to 52 in. (Fig. 3.34), is evidence of an annulus and the presence of hydrocarbons.[32]

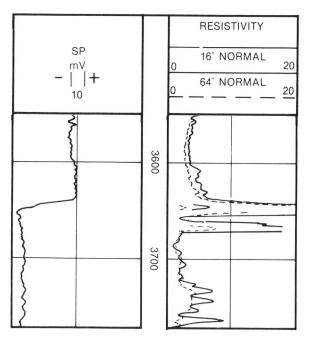

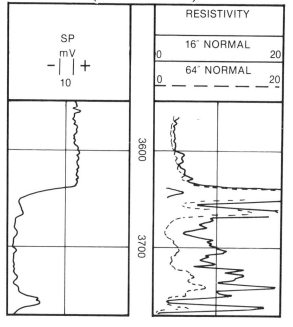

Fig. 3.31—Example of invasion between two logging runs.

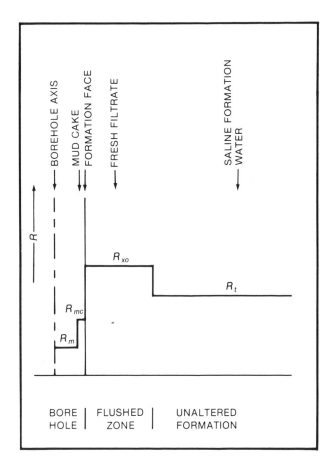

Fig. 3.32—Resistivity profile for an invasion pattern from piston-like displacement of connate water by fresher mud filtrate in a water-saturated medium.

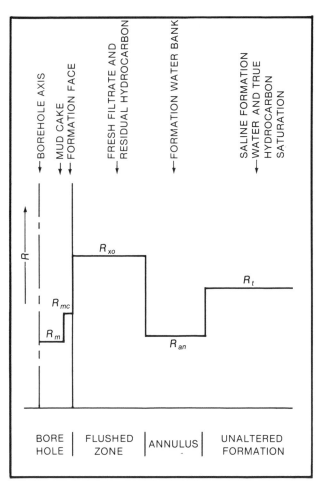

Fig. 3.33—Resistivity profile for an invasion pattern with an annulus of formation water (modified after Gondouin and Heim[30]).

The absence of an annulus does not prove that hydrocarbons are absent. Laboratory studies[30] have proved that banks of filtrate, formation water, and hydrocarbons move with different velocities, creating complex, transient, and often ambiguous profiles. These are demonstrated in Fig. 3.35, which shows the results of displacing kerosene and brine (in a permeable sample) with fresh water.[30] The displacement and consequent saturation changes were monitored by electrical measurements along the length of the sample. The second-day profile clearly defines a low-resistivity region, interpreted as a bank of "connate" water. In later profiles this bank is not clearly defined. Field evidence has also shown that an annulus can form and disappear.

Some analysts disavow annulus-detection methods as too pessimistic. However, this should not preclude their use provided they are not taken as final proof of the absence or presence of petroleum.

Transition Zone
The shape, regularity, and extent of the boundary between the flushed zone and undisturbed formation influence electric log responses.

In an ideal medium, the invasion boundary should be steplike, but coreflood experiments show more gradual transitions between invading and resident fluids (Fig. 3.36).[30] Molecular diffusion is among possible explanations, but the calculated diffusion distances are smaller than those observed.[33] Pore microheterogeneity could cause an irregular frontal advance—fingering[34,35]—hence, a region of mixed invading and native fluids with resistivities that are intermediate between the two. Thus, when expressed in electrical equivalents, an exact definition of the diameter of the invaded zone is ambiguous. In a water-saturated interval it can be defined as a diameter midway between the flushed zone and unflushed zone. This is not entirely satisfactory for asymmetrical transitions, which generate different calculated invasion diameters from focusing-electrode logs than from focusing-coil logging devices. The paths of currents for these devices are different, giving them different sensitivities to the distribution of resistivities in the transition zone. A study of 500 intervals[30] recognized this difference in almost all cases, confirming the existence of asymmetric transitions.

Evaluation of water saturation from electrical measurements requires accurate determination of the uninvaded formation's resistivity or conductivity. An ideal deep-sensing resistivity or conductivity measurement would not be affected by the mud or mudcake nor by the impregnated, flushed, or transition zones (Fig.

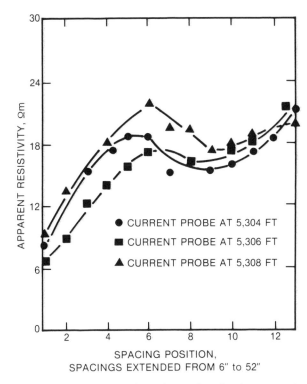

Fig. 3.34—Resistivity vs. electrode spacings for three current-probe depths (modified after Campbell and Martin[32]).

3.37).[36] In the absence of ideality they are affected; therefore, the effects of invasion need to be considered. Otherwise, the hydrocarbon saturation will be underestimated when R_{xo} is less than R_t or overestimated when greater. The hydrocarbon saturation can also be underestimated if a deep resistivity measurement is significantly affected by a low-resistivity annulus.

Gravity Effects

Filtrate entering a formation moves as the resultant of two forces: one is the result of the pressure gradient between the mud and the formation and the other is the result of the density difference between fresh filtrate and saline formation fluid or the less common reverse case. The ascending filtrate spreads out under impermeable barriers (Fig. 3.38).[37] This increases the depth of invasion. Simultaneously, the invasion depth at the bottom of the interval is reduced.

A gravity separation pattern is most easily recognized in thick, rather uniform rocks and when a microresistivity log is available to help define impermeable intervals.

3.2.4 Comments

Invasion begins as a surge of whole mud into the formation's pores. This can be most severe when the best reservoirs of older fields are being cored with low-solids mud. This situation combines factors that favor impregnation—large pores, partly depleted reservoirs, slow penetration, and muds with dispersed, uniform-size particles.

A rapidly formed mudcake, behaving like a compressible filter, limits drilling-fluid movement to only

the fluid phases. After mudcake forms, the filtration rate varies with mud type, circulation conditions, and temperature. Filtrate production is highest during drilling and circulating.

The depth of invasion is influenced by the amount of mud filtrate moving into the formation, and by the formation porosity, but not by formation permeabilities greater than about 0.1 md. The filtrate flow patterns may not completely displace formation fluids nor move within as regular cylindrical boundaries, further complicating the prediction and analysis of invasion.

Invasion continues with time, but at progressively slower rates. Good muds and drilling practices can slow but not stop it. Accordingly, the time between logging runs should be coordinated with expected invasion rates so that the invasion depth does not extend beyond the investigating limits of deep-resistivity tools.

3.3 Temperature Disturbance

Drilling fluids pumped into boreholes are usually warmer than the shallow formations and colder than the deeper ones. As a result, radial temperature gradients form in the near-borehole formation during drilling and dissipate during trips or logging. These disturbances can extend several feet into the formation (Fig. 3.39).[38]

A drilling-induced temperature disturbance can affect the region sensed by log surveys. For example, the temperature of the near-borehole region investigated by a microresistivity device can be higher or lower than that sensed by a macroresistivity tool (Fig. 3.40). The temperature used to adjust a surface-measured water resistivity to formation conditions is properly that of the formation volume — not that of the borehole region. Calculations of water saturation from surface-measured formation-water resistivities adjusted to borehole temperature, rather than formation temperature, can lead to underestimating oil or gas content—sometimes by 10% or more.

The borehole temperature changes with time. For example, at a depth of 9,184 ft in Fig. 3.39, the borehole temperature changed almost 15°F in the first 14 hours after circulation was stopped. Therefore the bottomhole temperature should be measured before each logging run.

The temperature differences between flushed, invaded, and uninvaded regions begin to decrease when circulation stops. Therefore, the temperature difference between shallow and deep regions is minimized if the deep-resistivity survey is run early in the logging sequence and the shallow-resistivity survey is run last.

Temperature logging and analysis are discussed in Chap. 5.

3.4 Stress Disturbance

Boreholes encounter stress conditions that influence the well logging environment.

3.4.1 Earth Stresses

The earth's stress field can be represented by three mutually orthogonal stresses (Fig. 3.41). Here these are assumed to be oriented almost vertically and horizontally, allowing the vertical stress, σ_v, to be equated to the overburden load, σ_{zo}, which can be estimated from

$$\sigma_v \simeq \bar{\rho}_b hg = \sigma_{zo} , \qquad \dots \dots \dots \dots \dots (3.3)$$

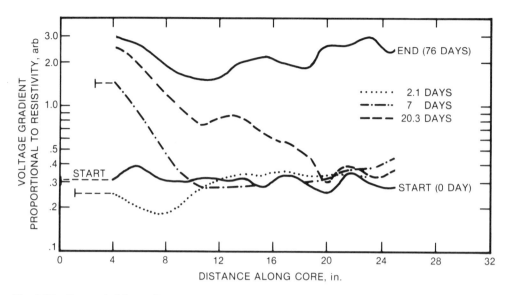

Fig. 3.35—Core resistivity profiles during flooding—immiscible case (modified after Gondouin and Heim[30]).

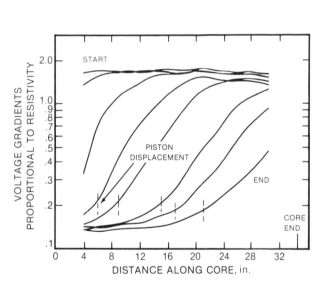

Fig. 3.36—Core resistivity profiles during flooding—miscible case (modified after Gondouin and Heim[30]).

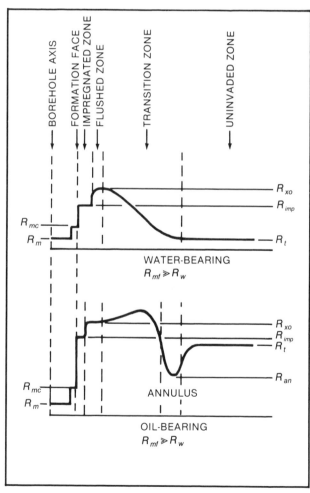

Fig. 3.37—Resistivity profiles for a composite invasion pattern for oil- and water-bearing formations (modified from Schlumberger Well Services[36]).

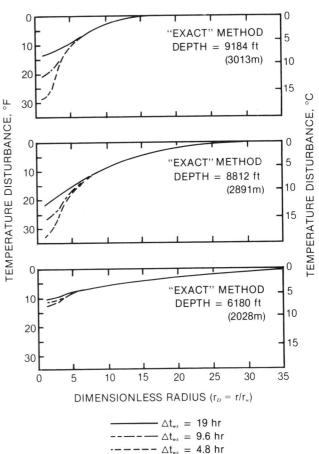

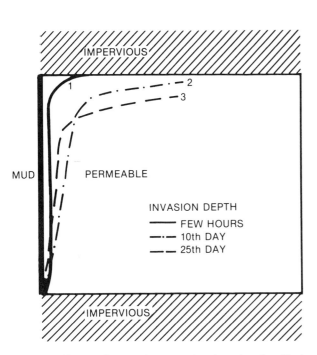

Fig. 3.38—Pattern for gravity-separation invasion (modified after Doll[37]).

Fig. 3.39—Example of radial temperature disturbances at various depths (after Edwardson *et al.*[38]).

where $\bar{\rho}_b$ is bulk density, h is true vertical depth, and g is the acceleration of gravity. The stress or overburden load is given in dynes/cm^2 when $\bar{\rho}_b$ is in g/cm^3, h is in cm, and g is in cm/sec^2. Assuming a typical value of gravity near the earth's surface, the overburden load can be expressed in g/cm^2 or psi or as a gradient (g/cm^2/m or psi/ft). The average overburden pressure gradient near the earth's surface is often assumed to be about 231 g/cm^2/m or 1.0 psi/ft, which corresponds to a force exerted by a rock column with an average bulk density of 2.31 g/cm^3. However, the overburden stress gradient varies from area to area. For example, Fig. 3.42 shows the gradients from three different areas as a function of depth.[39] The overburden stress includes the weight of the overlying pore fluids above a given depth (here designated as the pore-fluid pressure, p_f) given by

$$p_f = \rho_f hg, \quad\ldots\ldots\ldots\ldots\ldots\ldots\ldots\ldots (3.4)$$

where ρ_f is the fluid density. p_f is given in dynes/cm^2 when ρ_f is in g/cm^3, h is in cm, and g is in cm/sec^2. Pore-fluid pressures are normally equal to a hydrostatic head of water, but can be higher (supernormal) or lower (subnormal) as shown in Fig. 3.43.[39]

The horizontal earth stresses are generally of unknown orientation and magnitude unless inferred from the geologic setting or determined from special investigations.[40] Their relative magnitudes depend on geologic

conditions, which vary from area to area. In geologically stable areas, the maximum principal stress is vertical; the intermediate and least principal stresses are horizontal and about equal in magnitude. In areas characterized by normal faulting, the maximum principal stress acts vertically; the intermediate and least principal stresses are horizontal, unequal, and less than the overburden. Where thrust faulting dominates the structural style, the minimum stress is vertical; the maximum stress is horizontal and greater than the overburden.

When rock behavior is considered, it is sometimes necessary to evaluate the effective stress, σ_e, which represents the grain-to-grain (or rock-frame) stress as follows.

$$\sigma_e = \sigma_t - p_f, \quad\ldots\ldots\ldots\ldots\ldots\ldots\ldots\ldots (3.5)$$

where σ_t is the bulk or total stress and p_f is the pore-fluid pressure, expressed in the same units as σ_e and σ.

3.4.2 Borehole Stresses

The stresses acting on the borehole face are derived from the outlying earth stresses and the wellbore fluid pressure. The resultant stress condition can be represented by three stresses oriented axially, tangentially, and radially to the hole (Fig. 3.44).[41] These are assumed to be principal stresses. For a model consisting of a horizontal layer (which is porous, homogeneous, and elastic) penetrated by a vertical borehole with no

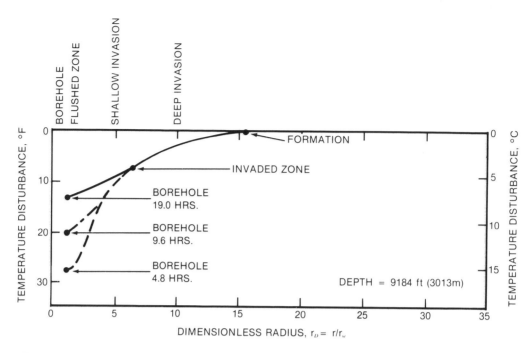

Fig. 3.40—Relationship between region of temperature disturbance and depths of investigation of various logging devices (modified after Edwardson et al.[38]).

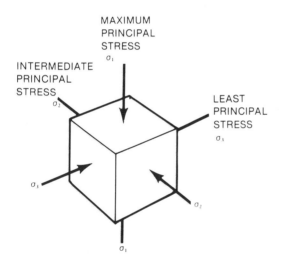

Fig. 3.41—Representation of earth stress conditions.

fluid flow, the stresses at the borehole face are

$$\sigma_{zi} = \sigma_{zo} \, , \quad \dots\dots\dots\dots\dots\dots\dots\dots\dots\dots\dots (3.6)$$

$$\sigma_{\theta i} = \frac{2\nu}{1-\nu}\sigma_{zo} - \frac{\nu}{1-\nu}\beta p_f \, , \quad \dots\dots\dots\dots (3.7)$$

and

$$\sigma_{ri} = p_w = p_f \, , \quad \dots\dots\dots\dots\dots\dots\dots\dots (3.8)$$

where ν is Poisson's ratio, p_w is the borehole fluid pressure in the same units as used for the stresses, and β is the difference between unity and the ratio of the bulk compressibility to the rock matrix compressibility. θ is

the angular position around the borehole wall. Fig. 3.45 shows how these stresses vary from the borehole face to the undisturbed formation.[41] The greatest disturbance is at the borehole wall. The borehole-induced distortion of the earth's stress field can extend far enough into the formation to affect some electric- and acoustic-log responses.

Borehole stress can change some rocks from an elastic to a plastic state. This is most likely to happen in poorly consolidated rocks with low inherent shear strength, τ_r. Risnes et al.[41] investigated borehole-induced stress around a vertical borehole. They assumed the region to be elastic and homogeneous and located in an outlying stress field where the maximum stress is vertical and the two horizontal stresses are equal. Fig. 3.46 shows the stress distribution in a very poorly consolidated rock ($\tau_r = 14.7$ psi) for a given set of subsurface conditions.[41] The plastic zone is predicted to extend about 0.9 m from the center of the wellbore. An example is shown in Fig. 3.47 for the same formation conditions except for a somewhat better-consolidated rock ($\tau_r = 147$ psi), where the extent of plastic characteristics is 0.3 m.[41] Because many well logs respond to a region shallower than 1 m, the properties determined from their response may be from the disturbed region. Acoustic and electric logs are especially sensitive to properties affected by the elastic-to-plastic transformation.

3.4.3 Borehole Stability

The borehole wall must support the loads resulting from the outlying earth stresses and the pressure of the wellbore fluid. Failure can enlarge, reduce, or collapse the hole, or fracture the formation (Fig. 3.48), depending on the rock strength, stress on the borehole wall, drilling-fluid pressure, and formation-pore pressure.[42]

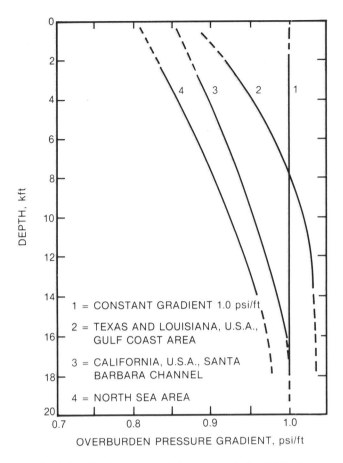

Fig. 3.42—Overburden load for compacted siliciclastic sequences (after Fertl[39]).

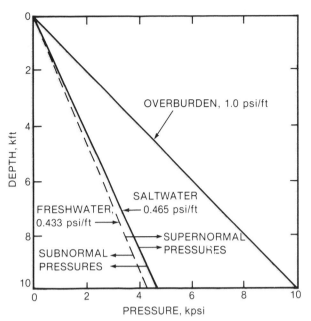

Fig. 3.43—Subsurface pressure definitions (after Fertl[39]).

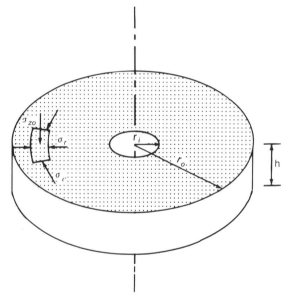

Fig. 3.44—Borehole model showing principal stresses (after Risnes *et al.*[41]).

Fracturing can occur when the mud weight exceeds the effective tangential stress, $\sigma_\theta - p_f$, by an amount sufficient to overcome the rock's tensile strength.[40] The rock's pore pressure, p_f, is assumed to be close to the borehole fluid pressure. This type of failure is prevented by reducing the effective mud weight.

Some rocks fail in a brittle manner when the borehole stress exceeds the rock's compressive strength. Because borehole stress can vary circumferentially, such failure can result in an out-of-round hole and very rugose hole walls. This type of failure is controlled by increasing the mud weight.

Some rocks fail by plastic flow when their compressive strength is exceeded. Flow failure is most likely in salts, shales, and unconsolidated sands, and is recognized by hole sizes that are smaller than the bit-size-minus-mudcake thickness. Obviously, a partly collapsed hole is a hostile environment for logging. This instability is controlled by increasing the mud weight.

The borehole's angle and direction can affect its stability, depending on the natural stress field and mud weight. Bradley[42] found that in areas where the principal horizontal stresses are equal, hole direction does not affect stability; inclination from the vertical does. An example from this study (Fig. 3.49) shows that increasing the borehole angle from 0 to 60° requires reducing the mud weight from 15.3 to 12.5 lbm/gal to prevent fracturing the formation; but the same change requires increasing the mud weight from 9.5 to 12.0 lbm/gal to prevent

collapse.[42] The shaded region represents the combinations of mud weights and hole angles at which the hole will be stable for the conditions in this example.

In areas where principal stresses are not equal, Bradley states that borehole stability depends on the relative orientations of the hole and the regional stress field. Fig. 3.50 shows the stability/instability fields for two borehole orientations.[42]

3.5 Chemical Alteration

Drilling-fluid interaction with rocks around the wellbore can change the logging environment from ideal to hostile. Solution of minerals can create large cavities in

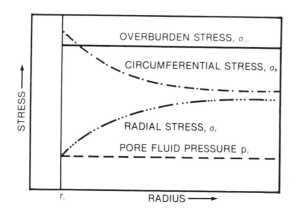

Fig. 3.45—Stress distribution around a borehole—elastic case (after Risnes *et al.*[41]).

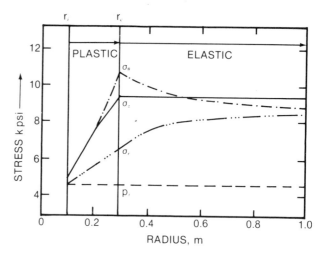

Fig. 3.47—Stresses around a borehole—poorly consolidated case (after Risnes *et al.*[41]).

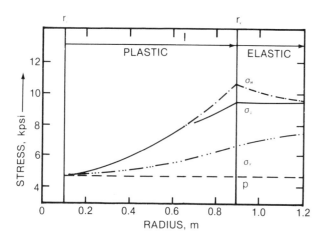

Fig. 3.46—Stresses around a borehole—slightly consolidated case (after Risnes *et al.*[41]).

some intervals and false porosity in others. Ion exchange and hydration between the mud and formations can alter formation properties measured by wireline logging. Although a detailed review of the controlling processes and remedial actions is beyond the scope of this chapter, some examples are included to stimulate an awareness of potential problems.

3.5.1 Solution Effects

Salt beds dissolve when contacted by water-base drilling fluids undersaturated with chloride. Fig. 3.51 shows examples of a salt section drilled with different muds. The hole enlargement at 8,560 to 8,575 ft and 8,660 to 8,698 ft in Run 2 is greater than the depth of investigation of most logging methods; as a result, the drilling fluid's properties are logged rather than the formation's. This problem can be minimized by using salt-saturated drilling fluids. However, it is not always possible to maintain a fully salt-saturated condition at bottomhole temperature. Oil-base drilling fluids are better for maintaining hole gauge in evaporite sections. Fig. 3.52 compares logs in nearby wells penetrating an evaporite section. The quality of the logging data was improved by drilling Well 2 with oil-base mud.

The solution and removal of intergranular salt cements around the borehole creates a fluid-filled pore volume not present in the unaltered formation. This near-borehole alteration is usually shallow and affects the microresistivity, neutron, and density devices more than the deep resistivity surveys. In the example shown in Fig. 3.53, conventional interpretation did not reveal the solution-induced porosity and predicted hydrocarbon saturation. This interval was tested in many wells in the area (without any fluid recovery) before the correct interpretation relating the high Laterolog® resistivity to low porosity was made.

Recognizing salt solution is made easier by examining cores or cuttings. Solution is indicated by cubic casts and, sometimes, remnant patches of salt cement. Mud logging indicators of this condition are the absence of staining in the cuttings and increased chloride content and lack of gas in the mud.

The apparent porosities and permeabilities of cores can be increased by salt solution during coring or preparing shaped samples for analysis. When this happens, the core-analysis results do not represent formation properties.

3.5.2 Clay-Alteration Effects

Drilling fluid can also alter formation clays affecting density and acoustic measurements. Figs. 3.54 and 3.55 show examples of significant alteration of shale properties near the borehole.[43,44]

Sandstones cemented with certain clays may not be stable in the presence of some drilling muds. Fig. 3.56 shows an example where hole gauge was improved by drilling with mud containing potassium chloride. Well C in this example can be more accurately evaluated by wireline logging than Wells A or B.

3.6 Tool Performance in Nonideal Logging Environments

Departure from an ideal borehole environment degrades the accuracy of well logging measurements. Fortunately, some tools are less affected than others in a given en-

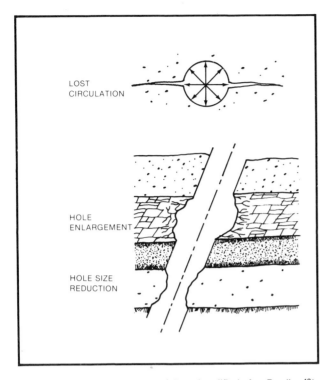

Fig. 3.48—Types of borehole failure (modified after Bradley[42]).

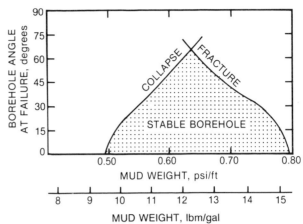

Fig. 3.49—Effect of borehole angle on hole stability (after Bradley[42]).

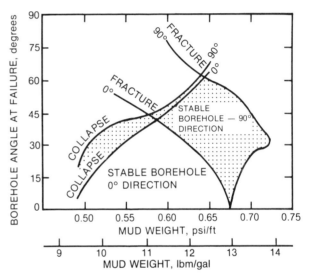

Fig. 3.50—Effect of borehole direction on hole stability (after Bradley[42]).

vironment. Specifying an optimal logging program requires knowledge and awareness of well logging tool sensitivities to problems with the borehole fluid, mudcake, hole geometry, invaded zone, or an altered region.

3.6.1 Spontaneous Potential (SP)

SP measurements must be made in water-base borehole fluids. Holes that are empty or filled with oil-base mud are not suitable. Ideally, the borehole fluid contains NaCl. If $CaCl_2$ or $MgCl_2$ is significant, the interpretation should account for the relative activities of the sodium, calcium, and magnesium ion concentrations.[45] Fig. 3.57 compares the SP from a well drilled with NaCl-type mud and the SP from a nearby well drilled with a mud that contained significant amounts of $CaCl_2$. The SP's are different here, although the mud resistivities in the two wells were about the same. Changes caused by calcium or magnesium ion concentration can be misinterpreted as a change in shaliness or sandstone thickness.

The effects of borehole size and depth of invasion on the SP are discussed in Chap. 6.

3.6.2 Deep Resistivity

Tools with macrospaced focusing electrodes are designed to evaluate deep, unaltered resistivity—especially when formation resistivity is high and the mud resistivity is low (salt muds). Such tools are often optimized for an 8-in. hole, so some correction is necessary for larger boreholes. Focused currents that pass through the mud, mudcake, and invaded zone to reach the undisturbed formation tend to be most responsive where the formation resistivity is the highest. These tools perform best when

the flushed zone resistivity, R_{xo}, is lower than the formation resistivity, R_t.

Tools with focusing coils (such as deep induction logs) are designed to investigate formation resistivities lower than their invaded-zone resistivities. This happens when the porosity is high, the formation water is saline, and the mud is fresh. Induction tools are also typically optimized for an 8-in. borehole filled with fresh mud, oil-base mud, or air. Such tools are usually designed to be run with a 1½-in. standoff from the hole wall, so some correction may be needed when the borehole size varies or different standoffs are used. Such tools tend to be most responsive to conductive (low-resistivity) zones and perform best when the invaded-zone resistivity is not lower than that of the formation.

Selection of the appropriate deep-investigation device depends on mud salinity, hole size, invasion character, and formation resistivity.

Deep resistivity measurements are discussed in Chap. 6.

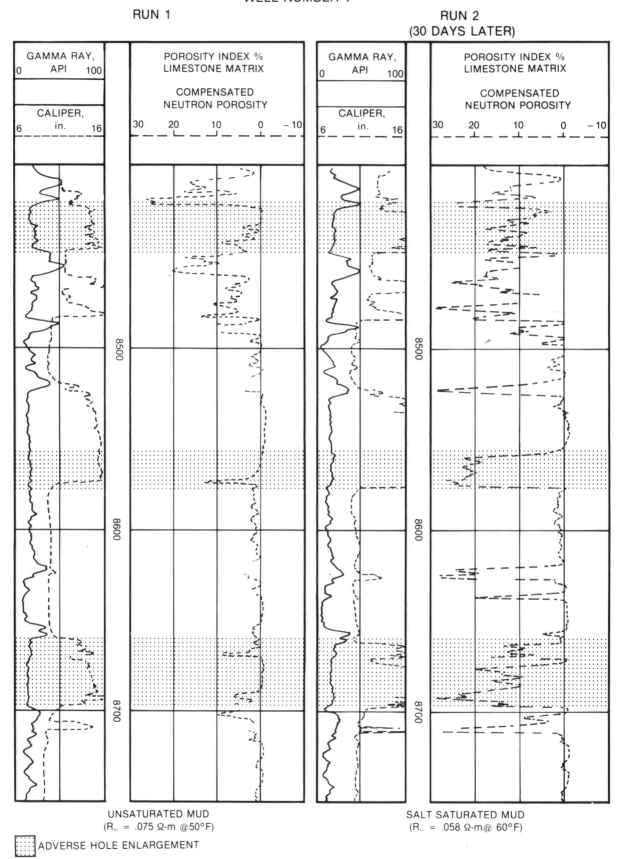

Fig. 3.51—Examples of hole conditions and log responses in salt sections drilled with different muds.

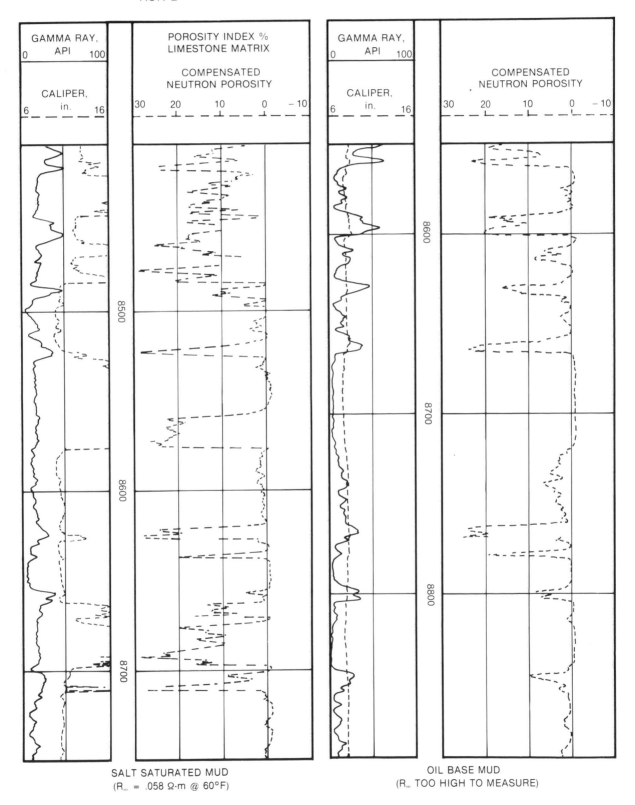

Fig. 3.52—Comparison of logs obtained from nearby holes drilled with different muds.

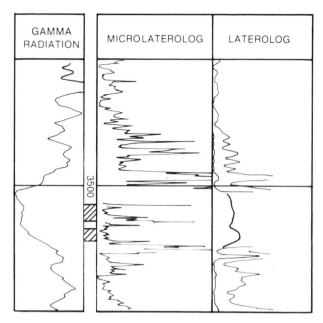

Fig. 3.53—Log response in section where intergranular cement has been removed. The affected interval is marked with crosshatching where the microlaterolog indicates porosity variations not shown by the Laterolog.

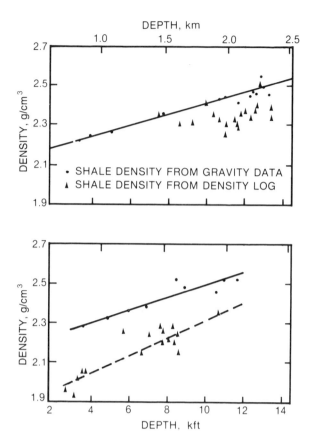

Fig. 3.54—Comparison of bulk densities measured with shallow and deep investigating devices (after Pritchett[43]).

3.6.3 Shallow Resistivity

Tools with microspaced conventional or focusing-electrode devices have shallow investigation ranges designed to evaluate the invaded zone. Borehole effects are minimized by mounting the electrodes in an insulated pad that is forced against the side of the hole. This configuration eliminates current paths in the mud, but the pad overrides the mudcake, requiring mudcake-thickness corrections. Effects of borehole size and shape are small unless severe rugosity lets mud between the pad and the hole face, reducing the measured resistivity. Positioning the tool along the short diameter of the hole may result in better pad contact and more reliable measurements.

The selection of shallow-investigating resistivity tools is based on expected mudcake thickness and invasion depth.

Shallow-resistivity measurements and analyses are discussed in Chap. 6.

3.6.4 Acoustic Travel Time

Acoustic measuring devices require a fluid-filled hole. Modern tools automatically compensate for borehole size and tool tilt. Fig. 3.58 demonstrates that the interval transit time is not affected by the change in hole diameter that occurred during the few days between logging runs.[46] Spurious effects from borehole rugosity may be partly compensated.

When changes in rock properties around the borehole have modified the formation velocity, long-spaced acoustic tools should be considered. Fig. 3.59 shows an example where 8- to 10-ft and 10- to 12-ft spacings are providing data more representative of formation properties than are 3- to 5-ft spacings.[46]

Acoustic logging is discussed in Chap. 7.

3.6.5 Compensated Gamma-Gamma Attenuation (Density)

Density-measuring devices can be operated in any borehole fluid. To minimize fluid effects, the source and detector are mounted on a skid that is forced against the borehole wall by an eccentering arm. Dual detectors are used to compensate for mudcake. Fig. 3.60 shows that borehole changes between Logging Runs 1 and 2, except for a few thin intervals where "spikes" are observed, were adequately handled by the compensation features.[46] Thin mudcakes from normal clay-base muds require less compensation than thick cakes or those containing weighting materials.

Inadequate compensation for mud between the skid and the hole wall (caused by rugosity) can produce unreliable results (Fig. 3.61).[47] The skid and arm tend to align naturally in the direction of maximum hole enlargement where rugosity is often the greatest. Density measurements can be improved by positioning the tool to locate the face or skid containing the source and detector on the minimum borehole diameter, where the surface is likely to be less rugose (Fig. 3.62).[46]

Density measurements are discussed in Chap. 8.

3.6.6 Natural Gamma Ray

Gamma ray measurements can be made in any borehole fluid. However, most openhole tools are calibrated in conditions representing an 8-in. hole filled with

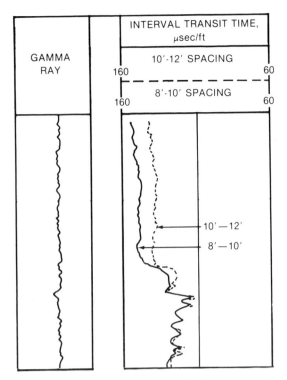

Fig. 3.55—Comparison of interval transit time measured with long-spaced acoustic surveys. The different velocities measured by the 8- to 10-ft and 10- to 12-ft surveys indicate a shallow altered zone (after Timur[44]).

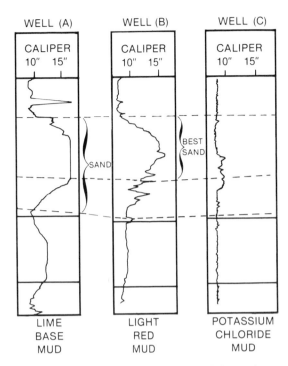

Fig. 3.56—Examples of hole conditions in shaly sandstones drilled with different muds. Dashed lines connect depth of equivalent stratigraphic position. Solid lines are 50-ft depth marks.

10-lbm/gal mud. Fig. 3.63 shows the results of gamma ray and neutron surveys traversing an air/fluid contact. In both, the sensitivity is greater in the air than in the fluid-filled interval.

Because potassium in the borehole fluid contributes gamma ray activity, KCl muds hinder quantitative interpretation of the formation response (Fig. 3.64).[46] Interpretation of gamma ray measurements should include the possibility of radioactive filtrate invading the formation.

Tool position in the borehole affects log response. Some gamma ray surveys are run centered and some are run eccentered, depending on what is needed for the other tools combined for the logging run. This often explains why two gamma ray surveys in the same hole did not repeat.

Variations in borehole diameter affect the observed gamma ray intensity, particularly in heavy muds. Uncorrected measurements may not distinguish washed-out shales from in-gauge sandstones.

Natural gamma ray logging is discussed in Chap. 8.

3.6.7 Compensated Neutron

Neutron logs are usually calibrated in conditions representing a 7⅞- or 8-in. hole filled with fresh water at 75°F and atmospheric pressure. Calibration conditions assume a specific tool position in the hole. Departures from calibration conditions require that the log readings be corrected for hole diameter, mudcake thickness, borehole fluid salinity, mud weight, standoff distance, pressure, and temperature. Some corrections can be made automatically during logging. For example, the neutron-porosity logs in Fig. 3.65 were automatically corrected for hole size.[46] Note the good repeat, even though the hole diameter changed 2 to 3 in. between

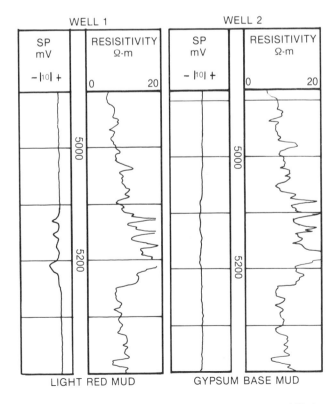

Fig. 3.57—Log responses in sandstone-shale sequence drilled with different muds.

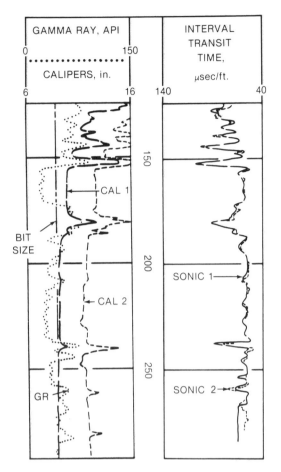

Fig. 3.58—Comparison of caliper and interval transit time measurements from two logging runs (after Campbell[46]).

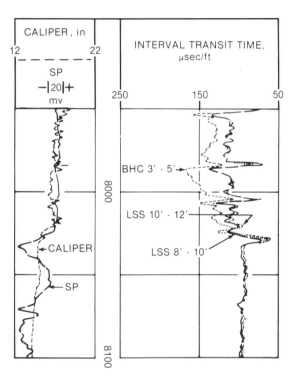

Fig. 3.59—Comparison of interval transit times measured by tools with different transmitter-receiver spacings (after Campbell[46]).

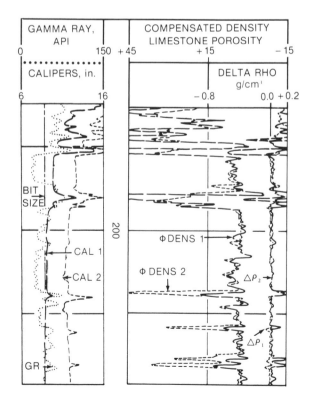

Fig. 3.60—Comparison of caliper and density-porosity from two logging runs (after Campbell[46]).

runs. However, some hole conditions are not overcome by automatic compensation. Severe rugosity or caves put mud between the tool and the formation. This mud will be sensed and combined with the formation-fluid response, indicating a falsely high porosity.

Neutron logging is discussed in Chap. 8.

3.6.8 Comments

An ideal borehole fluid for some logging methods can be a hostile one for others.

The effects of mudcake and/or weighting materials are minimized by compensation features of certain tools.

Most openhole logging tools are designed for optimal performance in a 7⅞- to 8-in. cylindrical hole. Correction for departures from cylindrical shape are not commonly available for most tools. Rugose hole walls can degrade the performance of pad- and skid-type tools, but better logging conditions are usually present in the short dimension of the hole. Special positioning devices can be used to take advantage of this.

An invaded zone affects most logs—especially electrical devices. Deep invasion increases the risk in formation evaluation.

Drilling-induced changes around the borehole affect the responses from short-spaced acoustic and density logs. Other methods, such as long-spaced acoustic or borehole gravity, are available for reaching the undisturbed regions.

Finally, different tools actually "see" different parts

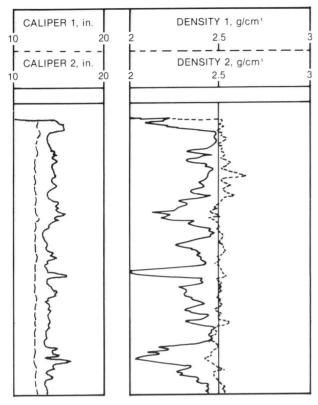

Fig. 3.61—Comparison of caliper and bulk density measurements from logging runs 6 days apart (after Misk *et al.*[47]).

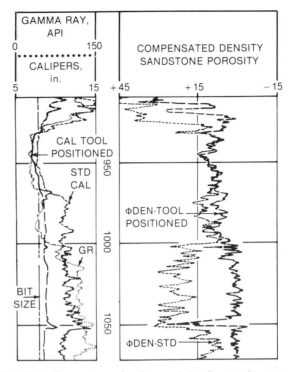

Fig. 3.62—Comparison of caliper and density-porosity measurements with and without positioning device (after Campbell[46]).

of the borehole and formation. For example, the compensated density sees directly in front of the skid position, but the induction log is omnidirectional and investigates more vertical length.

3.7 Recommended Practices

The risk of abandoning a potentially economic well can be minimized by reducing uncertainties caused by the borehole environment.

3.7.1 Drilling Programs

One way to reduce uncertainties is a drilling program that produces in-gauge holes. Logging tool performance degrades above an optimal size, typically about 8 in. and the effects of rugosity are often not correctable. This should be a significant consideration in specifying hole size.

Rate-of-penetration logs are more useful when obtained with relatively constant torque and weight on bit. Alternatively, normalizing these factors by use of drilling models is good practice.

The importance of drilling-fluid selection and maintenance on lowering the risk in formation evaluation cannot be overemphasized. Critical uncertainties caused by deep invasion are avoided by minimizing fluid loss, including exposure time before logging. Low-solids mud lacking in larger particles can encourage impregnation. Turning off the desilter should be considered when drilling highly permeable reservoirs. The use of oil-base or nonsaline water-base muds requires that special consideration be given to selecting and interpreting wireline logs. Balanced mud-formation fluid pressures help maintain good hole conditions.

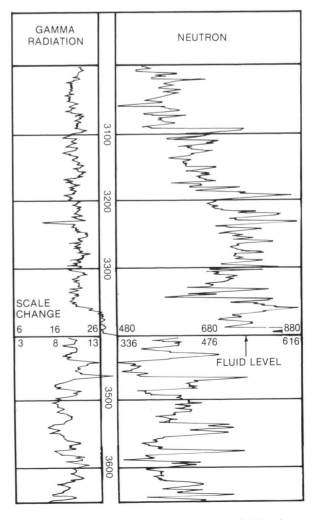

Fig. 3.63—Gamma ray-neutron survey across fluid level.

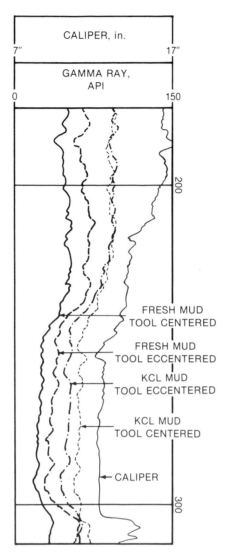

Fig. 3.64—Effect of KCl mud on gamma ray response (after Campbell[46]).

Some combinations of drilling parameters and fluids produce better borehole quality than do others. In-gauge holes are efficient to drill and good hole conditions reduce completion risks. Thus, some interests of well drilling, formation evaluation, and completion are served by good holes, so should be closely coordinated.

3.7.2 Borehole-Compensated Tools

Tools that automatically compensate for departures from ideal conditions help to minimize borehole effects on interpretation. Compensation techniques are used in modern acoustic, density, and neutron logging tools. Focused resistivity and electromagnetic devices help minimize effects from the hole and invaded zone. Such tools have greatly improved the quality of measurements needed for evaluating formation properties.

3.7.3 Deep-Investigation Tools

Drilling-induced changes around the borehole cannot always be avoided. When altered regions are developed, use of the borehole gravimeter and long-spaced acoustic logging is recommended. Macrospaced focusing-electrode or coil devices are recommended for shallow-to-moderately deep invasion. Very deep invasion may not be resolved with present technology.

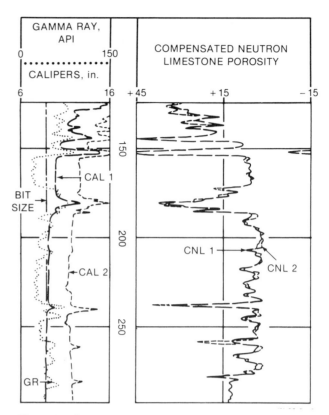

Fig. 3.65—Comparison of caliper and neutron-porosity measurements from two logging runs (after Campbell[46]).

3.7.4 Documentation

Inadequate documentation leads to ambiguous and unnecessarily risky evaluations. Good log interpretation for a well requires a complete history of drilling-fluid properties and drilling conditions.

A completed log heading is not adequate for some interpretation problems; an incomplete heading is asking for trouble.

3.7.5 Comments

Minimizing borehole-induced interpretation problems starts (and sometimes ends) with selecting appropriate drilling fluids and procedures. Further uncertainties can be avoided by the use of tools that compensate for nonidealities. The remaining uncertainties are further reduced by appropriate combinations of mud logging, coring, testing, and wireline logging. This overcomes the limitations inherent to each.

3.8 Summary Comments

The usefulness of wireline logging measurements often depends on the borehole environment, which can cause observed responses to depart from the true formation properties.

To minimize formation evaluation risks:
1. Drill a straight and in-gauge hole.
2. Minimize fluid loss and pressure-overbalance.
3. Maintain good particle-size distribution in mud.
4. Keep mudcakes thin.
5. Log soon after drilling.
6. Overlap prior runs.
7. Document drilling and logging history.
8. Specify and monitor log quality.
9. Use borehole-compensated tools.
10. Integrate log combinations into the interpretation.

References

1. Parsons, C.P.: "Caliper Logging," *Trans.*, AIME (1943) **151**, 35–47.
2. Beckstrom, R.C.: "Open Hole Diameter Changes Located and Measured by Recording Calipers," *Oil Weekly* (May 1935) 77.
3. Guyod, H.: "Caliper Logging—Part I," *Oil Weekly* (Aug. 27, 1945).
4. Guyod, H.: "Caliper Logging—Part II," *Oil Weekly* (Sept. 3, 1945).
5. Guyod, H.: "Caliper Logging—Part III," *Oil Weekly* (Sept. 10, 1945).
6. Guyod, H.: "Caliper Logging—Part IV," *Oil Weekly* (Sept. 17, 1945).
7. Hilchie, D.W.: "Caliper Logging—Theory and Practice," *The Log Analyst* (Jan. 1968) 3–11.
8. Campbell, R.L.: "Borehole Geometry," *Notes*, American Assn. of Petroleum Geologists Short Course on the Borehole Environment, San Francisco, CA (May 1981).
9. Dawson-Grove, G.E.: "Sonar Applications in Western Canada," *Trans.*, SWPLA Annual Symposium (May 1969) paper E.
10. Donaldson, E.C. and Baker, B.A.: "Particle Transport in Sandstones," paper SPE 6905 presented at the 1977 SPE Annual Technical Conference and Exhibition, Denver, Oct. 9–12.
11. *Mud Engineering*, Dresser-Magcobar, Div. of Dresser Industries Inc., Houston (1968).
12. Glenn, E.E., Slusser, M.L., and Huitt, J.L.: "Factors Affecting Well Productivity—I. Drilling Fluid Filtration," *J. Pet. Tech.* (May 1957) 126–31; *Trans.*, AIME, **210**.
13. Glenn, E.E. and Slusser, M.L.: "Factors Affecting Well Productivity—II. Drilling Fluid Particle Invasion into Porous Media," *J. Pet. Tech.* (May 1957) 132–39; *Trans.*, AIME, **210**.
14. Webb, M.G. and Haskin, C.A.: "Pressure Coring Used in Midway-Sunset's Unconsolidated Sands," *Oil and Gas J.* (April 10, 1978) 51–55.
15. Beeson, C.M. and Wright, C.C.: "Loss of Mud Solids to Formation Pores," *Pet. Eng.* (Aug. 1952) 40–52.
16. Gatlin, C. and Nemir, C.E.: "Some Effects of Size Distribution on Particle Bridging in Lost Circulation and Filtration Tests," *J. Pet. Tech.* (June 1961) 575–78; *Trans.*, AIME, **222**.
17. Campbell, F.L.: "Invasion," *Notes*, American Assoc. of Petroleum Geologists Short Course on the Borehole Environment, San Francisco, CA (May 1981).
18. Fertl, W.H. and Hammack, G.W.: "Solids Particle Penetration Into Porous Reservoir Rocks and Its Effect on Well Log Analysis," *Trans.*, SPWLA Annual Symposium (1976) paper F.
19. Darley, H.C.H.: "Prevention of Productivity Impairment by Mud Solids," *Pet. Eng.* (Sept. 1975) 102–10.
20. Breitenbach, E.A.: "A New Technique for Approximating Drilling Fluid Filtration," *Trans.*, SPWLA Annual Symposium (1965) paper I.
21. von Engelhardt, W.: "Filter Cake Formation and Water Losses in Deep Drilling Muds," Illinois State Geological Survey Circular 191 (1954) 1–24.
22. Outmans, H.D.: "Mechanics of Static and Dynamic Filtration in the Borehole," *Soc. Pet. Eng. J.* (Sept. 1963) 236–44; *Trans.*, AIME, **228**.
23. Ferguson, C.K. and Klotz, J.A.: "Filtration From Mud During Drilling," *J. Pet. Tech.* (Feb. 1954) 30–43; *Trans.*, AIME, **201**, 29–42.
24. Prokop, C.L.: "Radial Filtration of Drilling Mud," *Trans.*, AIME (1952) **195**, 5–10.
25. Horner, V. *et al.*: "Microbit Dynamic Filtration Studies," *J. Pet. Tech.* (June 1957) 183–89; *Trans.*, AIME, **210**.
26. Krueger, R.F.: "Evaluation of Drilling-Fluid Filter-Loss Additives Under Dynamic Conditions," *J. Pet. Tech.* (Jan. 1963) 90–98; *Trans.*, AIME, **228**.
27. Schremp, F.W. and Johnson, V.L.: "Drilling Fluid Filter Loss at High Temperatures and Pressures," *Trans.*, AIME (1952) **195**, 157–62.
28. Miesch, E.P. and Albright, J.C.: "A Study of Invasion Diameter," *Trans.*, SPWLA Annual Symposium (1967) paper O.
29. McVicar, B.M., Heath, J.L., and Alger, R.P.: "New Logging Approaches for Evaluations of Carbonate Reservoirs," *Proc.*, Williston Basin Symposium, Bismarck, ND (1956).
30. Gondouin, M. and Heim, A.: "Experimentally Determined Resistivity Profiles in Invaded Water and Oil Sands for Linear Flows," *J. Pet. Tech.* (March 1964) 337–48; *Trans.*, AIME, **231**.
31. Brown, W.O.: "Mobility of Connate Water During a Waterflood," *J. Pet. Tech.* (July 1957) 190–95; *Trans.*, AIME, **210**.
32. Campbell, W.M. and Martin, J.L.: "Displacement Logging—A New Exploratory Tool," *J. Pet. Tech.* (Dec. 1955) 233–39; *Trans.*, AIME, **204**.
33. Wyllie, M.R.J.: "Theoretical Considerations Involved in the Determination of Petroleum Reservoir Parameters from Electric Log Data," *Proc.*, Third World Pet. Cong., Leiden, The Netherlands (1951) Sec. 2.
34. Craig, F.A. Jr.: *The Reservoir Engineering Aspects of Waterflooding*, Monograph Series, SPE, Dallas (1971) 35.
35. van Meurs, P.: "The Use of Transparent Three-Dimensional Models for Studying the Mechanism of Flow Processes in Oil Reservoirs," *J. Pet. Tech.* (Oct. 1957) 295–300; *Trans.*, AIME, **203**.
36. *Schlumberger Log Interpretation, Vol. I—Principles*, Schlumberger Ltd., New York City (1972).
37. Doll, H.G.: "Filtrate Invasion in Highly Permeable Sands," *Pet. Eng.* (Jan. 1955) 53–66.
38. Edwardson, M.J. *et al.*: "Calculation of Formation Temperature Disturbances Caused by Mud Circulation," *J. Pet. Tech.* (April 1962) 416–26; *Trans.*, AIME, **225**.
39. Fertl, W.H.: *Abnormal Formation Pressures*, Elsevier Scientific Publishing Co., Amsterdam/New York City (1976).
40. Hottman, C.E., Smith, J.H., and Purcell, W.R.: "Relationship Among Earth Stresses, Pore Pressure, and Drilling Problems Offshore Gulf of Alaska," *J. Pet. Tech.* (Nov. 1979) 1477–84; *Trans.*, AIME, **267**.
41. Risnes, R., Bratli, R.K., and Horsrud, P.: "Sand Stresses Around a Wellbore," *Soc. Pet. Eng. J.* (Dec. 1982) 883–98.
42. Bradley, W.B.: "Failure of Inclined Boreholes," *Trans.*, ASME (1979) **101**, 232–39.
43. Pritchett, W.C.: "Physical Properties of Shales and Possible Origin of High Pressures," *Soc. Pet. Eng. J.* (Oct. 1980) 341–48.
44. Timur, A.: "Examples," *Notes*, American Assn. of Petroleum Geologists Short Course on the Borehole Environment, San Francisco, CA (May 1981).
45. Gondouin, M., Tixier, M.P., and Simard, G.L.: "An Experimental Study on the Influence of the Chemical Composition of Electrolytes on the SP Curve," *J. Pet. Tech.* (Feb. 1957) 58–70; *Trans.*, AIME, **210**; *Well Logging*, Reprint Series, SPE, Dallas (1971) **1**, 65–79.
46. Campbell, R.L.: "Tool Performance," *Notes*, American Assn. of Petroleum Geologists Short Course on the Borehole Environment, San Francisco, CA (May 1981).
47. Misk, A. *et al.*: "Effects of Hole Conditions on Log Measurements and Formation Evaluation," SAID, Annual Symposium (June 1976) paper 22.

Chapter 4
Mud Logging

. . . and it is for the fluid contents, rather than for the rock itself, that wells are drilled.

from J.T. Hayward,[1] whose innovations
helped establish oil and gas monitoring
applications, which have become known as
mud or hydrocarbon logging.

4.0 Introduction. As new borehole is excavated, formation rock and fluid contents are mixed into the drilling fluid and carried to the surface, where they are available for
  1. gas-in-mud analysis,*
  2. oil-in-mud analysis,
  3. gas-in-cuttings analysis,
  4. oil-in-cuttings analysis,
  5. cuttings description,
and sometimes
  6. nonhydrocarbon gases identification,
  7. cuttings density determination, and
  8. drilling-fluid properties measurement.
Observations and data collected from hydrocarbon analyses, combined with drilling rate and cuttings descriptions, are organized and recorded as a function of well depth and called a *mud log*.

Hydrocarbons in drilling returns can be compelling evidence that prospective oil- or gas-bearing formations have been encountered. This evidence is provided by sensors that respond directly to hydrocarbon presence, in contrast with indirect evidence derived from most wireline logging measurements. Mud logging data are available early in the formation-evaluation cycle, and these provide timely guidance for follow-up evaluation procedures such as coring, testing, and wireline logging.

Some mud logging services provide monitoring capabilities that assist the drilling operation. Sensors on the surface are available to monitor:
  1. mud weight, flow, and temperature in and out,
  2. mud salinity and resistivity in and out,
  3. pit level and volume,
  4. standpipe pressure,
  5. hook load (weight on bit),
  6. rotary torque and revolution rate (speed),
  7. pump stroke rate and pressure,
  8. total bit revolutions,
  9. penetration (depth increment),
  10. rate of penetration,
and, sometimes, sensors on the drillstring near the bit monitor:
  11. direction and inclination of the hole,
  12. resistivity of formation,
  13. natural gamma radiation,
  14. mud temperature and resistivity,
  15. weight on bit,
  16. torque on bit, and
  17. mud column pressure.
Data from these monitors are organized and presented as reports and logs with contents and formats useful for achieving drilling objectives.

Safe and cost-effective drilling operations are supported by availability of comprehensive data on the drilling performance and mud conditions. For example, continuous monitoring of the drilling-fluid properties and volumes provides early warning of potentially hazardous conditions associated with unusual mud loss, abnormal formation-fluid flows, hydrogen sulfide presence, and salt-section penetration. Continuous feedback from the mud logging personnel to the company representatives and drilling crew helps obtain optimal drilling performance and reduces the risk of encountering catastrophic problems. The already impressive value of mud logging for formation evaluation is extended by the benefits provided to drilling operations.

The formation evaluation, drilling optimization, and rig-site safety roles of modern mud logging services are sometimes inseparable. For example, weight-on-bit and rotary-torque relationships are useful not only for optimizing bit performance but also for evaluating formation properties such as fractures. Monitoring gas

---

*In the discussions that follow, *gas* refers to vaporized hydrocarbons. After extraction of ''gas'' samples from the mud, it would be more accurate to refer to gas in air liberated from the mud stream.

from the mud not only helps identify prospective reservoirs but also helps evaluate pore pressure needed to specify mud weight for safe drilling. The presence of hydrogen sulfide affects both safety and formation-evaluation considerations. The rate of penetration is important to both formation evaluation and drilling interests. So the drilling, mud, and hydrocarbon monitoring systems of modern mud logging provide data for both the formation-evaluation interests emphasized in this chapter and the drilling optimization and safety interests, which are outside the scope of this monograph.

4.1 The Mud Logging Environment

Mud logging operations are performed primarily at the wellsite, a hostile environment for complex and delicate analytical procedures. The instruments are subjected to vibration and power-supply variation. Ambient temperature and humidity conditions may be less than ideal. Maintenance at remote locations requires special efforts.

4.1.1 Mud Logging Unit

Personnel, analytical instruments, and supporting facilities for mud logging operations are sheltered in portable housing, or logging units, located near the sample collection area. The interrelationship between a modern mud logging unit and a drilling rig is shown in Chart 4.1.

There are mud logging units and mud logging units. The mud logging service can consist of a house trailer with a portable gas detector, or a mud logging service can have complete hydrocarbon, drilling, and mud monitoring facilities. Quality mud logging services are backed up with maintenance, training, and research and development facilities. Service options are discussed in Sec. 4.6.

4.1.2. Drilling-Fluid Circulation

The principal components of a drilling-fluid circulation system are depicted in Fig. 4.1 and briefly discussed in this section. This section is limited to an overview. Interpretation considerations are discussed in more detail in Secs. 4.2 through 4.5.

Drilling Fluid

Drilling fluid, called *mud*, influences hydrocarbon monitoring in many ways as are discussed later and is a source of contaminants that interfere with analysis. However, the pressure from the mud column warrants special consideration.

Drilling mud is formulated to control formation-fluid pressure. Because mud pressure usually exceeds formation pressure, mud filtrate invades newly drilled permeable formation and flushes hydrocarbon ahead of the drill bit. Flushing tendencies are increased as the pressure overbalance is increased. The present desire to drill wells in an environmentally safe way has increased the frequency of drilling with mud pressures that significantly exceed formation pressures. This may explain why some people believe mud logging is not as effective a formation evaluation tool as was perceived in the past.

For mud logging purposes, an optimal drilling fluid provides in-gauge holes, minimum overbalance, effec-

tive cuttings-carrying capacity, and no hydrocarbon contaminants.

Drillstring

The drilling fluid is pumped to the bottom of the hole through the drillpipe and collars and arrives there after a time depending in part on the drillstring volume. The drillstring is also a source of contaminants. Stain and fluorescence from particles of joint lubricant (*pipe dope*) can be a nuisance in cuttings examination. Reactions between the drillstring and some muds can produce hydrogen gas. Hydrogen gas causes some detectors to respond as if hydrocarbon gases were present.

Drill Bit

Drill-bit design can affect sample quality and hydrocarbon monitoring. Fluid flow ports, which increase drilling-fluid pressure and velocity at the formation/bit interface, influence how formations are disaggregated during drilling. Increased pressure tends to flush formation fluid ahead of the drill-bit/formation interface. The shape and size of the bit teeth affect cuttings size.

Annulus

The annular space between the borehole face and drillpipe is the conduit for circulating drilling fluid and its entrained formation contents to the surface. The circulation exposes the drilling fluid to previously drilled formations where cavings or produced fluids can enter the returns. The quality of mud logging data is improved by drilling practices that result in a stable and in-gauge hole.

Mud Return Flowline

Drilling returns are moved from the wellhead to surface processing equipment through a *return flowline* or *ditch*. This relatively short part of the circulation system is an important variable in gas content evaluation. Gas in the drilling fluid can escape from a return line before sampling. Gas losses from a flowline are reduced by keeping it filled, eliminating slope or direction changes that create turbulence, avoiding use of sections that are open to the atmosphere, and reducing the elevation of the fluid drop entering the shale shaker.

Shale Shaker

One or more shale shakers are used to separate cuttings from drilling mud. A shale shaker has a vibrating screen whose purpose is to separate the coarse drilling solids from the drilling fluid. In addition to the screen, a shale shaker consists of (1) a feed tank or *possum belly* or *shaker box* to receive the drilling fluid and control its flow onto the screens, (2) a vibrating unit, (3) a catch basin to confine the flow passing over the screen, and (4) supporting structures. Hoberock[2-7] reviews the current knowledge and practice on the application of shale shakers. Sampling techniques and recommended practices are discussed in Sec. 4.3.2.

Sand Trap, Desander, and Desilter

The mud slurry passing through and, if any, bypassing the shale shaker screen flows into a compartment or tank that traps coarser solids by gravity settling. Subsequently, hydrocyclone desanders and desilters can be used to

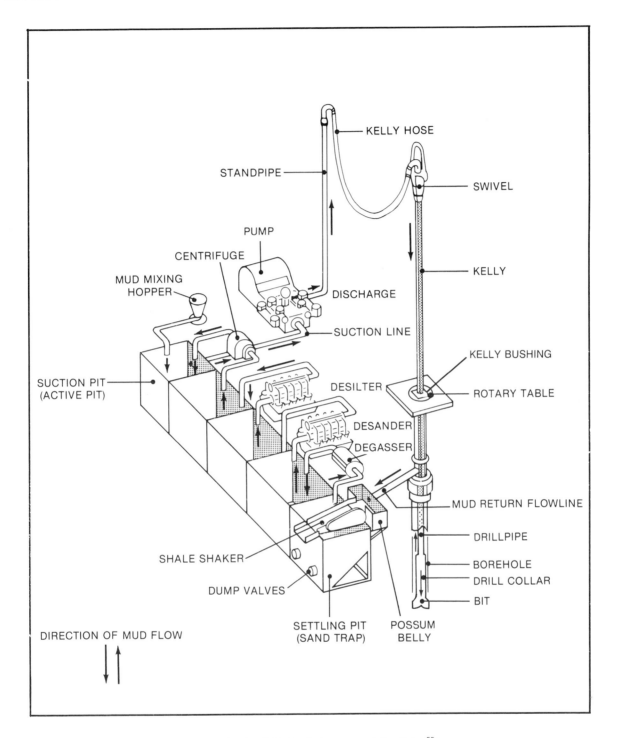

Fig. 4.1—Drilling-fluid circulation system (after Exlog[55]).

separate solids from the drilling returns. Separation and removal of coarser solids from the active mud system reduces the recirculation of previously drilled formation materials that could be confused with returns from newly drilled intervals. A comprehensive discussion of solids control is given by Ormsby.[8]

Mud Tanks

Drilling returns are circulated through a series of tanks or pits before they are pumped back into the borehole. These tanks are used for mixing and conditioning mud. Formation solids are separated by gravity settling in the tanks. Gas content is reduced while the mud is in the

tank. Reducing solids and gas content from the circulating mud is assisted by large mud tank capacity.

Degassers

The gas content of drilling returns should be minimized before recirculation. This avoids contending with recycled gas background in the next circulation cycle and is especially desirable when prospective formations are characterized by relatively small gas-in-mud increases.

Although circulation across a shale shaker and through the mud tanks removes most entrained hydrocarbon gases, special degassing equipment can be used for more complete removal. This is discussed by Liljestrand.[9,10]

Mud Pumps

The mud pump capacity and rate are important and affect the time it takes samples to travel from the bottom of the hole to the surface. Many mud logging operations monitor pump displacement with instrumentation that provides continuous data on the displacement rate of mud being pumped into the borehole. Use of the pumping rate data to determine accurate sample depth assignments is discussed next.

4.1.3 Circulation Rate and Sample Depth Determination

Circulating drilling mud carries cuttings and liberated formation fluids from the bottom of the hole to the surface where they can be sampled. Because this takes a while, there is a *lag* between the time of drilling an interval and sampling returns from it. Because of lag, the current driller's depth when the sample is collected will be deeper than where it originated if drilling has continued during part or all of the lag period. Thus, to determine a sample's true depth of origin, one must know how much the well has been deepened between a potential sample's departure from the bottom of the hole and its arrival at the surface. To do this, lag is systematically monitored and used to assign a "true" depth to each sample.

Lag varies with circulation rate, drillstring and hole size, depth, and the relative velocities of the mud and the cuttings or gases. Other factors being constant, lag increases with hole size and depth. As both change slowly, "lag vs. depth" can be plotted and extrapolated for predicting changes in lag between actual determinations.

Lag can be evaluated by timing the circulation of a tracer, assuming the pumping rate is constant, which it rarely is. Preferably, lag can be determined by counting the pump strokes required to circulate a tracer from the bottom of the hole:

$$n_\ell = n_1 - n_2, \dots\dots\dots\dots\dots\dots\dots (4.1)$$

where n_ℓ is the number of pump strokes required to circulate from the bottom to the surface, n_1 is the pump-stroke count when the sample arrived at the surface, and n_2 is the pump-stroke count when the sample was drilled. After n_ℓ is determined, this equation and a record of drilling depths with their associated pump-stroke counts can be used to assign the depth associated with n_2 to the sample collected at n_1. Such depth assignments are called *lagged* depths.

It is more convenient to put the tracer in at the surface. Then the strokes required to displace the mud in the drillstring are subtracted from the stroke count between insertion and reappearance of the tracer. The drillstring volume can be estimated from Chart 4.2.

Tracer material can be any easily identifiable substance that does not interfere with sample examination or gas-in-mud determination. The most common tracer is calcium carbide, which reacts with water to produce acetylene gas, detectable by the gas-in-mud analyzer. Visible material is also used, such as shredded cellophane, oats, or crushed brick.

Buoyancy can cause gas to "creep" ahead of cuttings during circulation to the surface, especially in low-gel-strength muds. It is good practice to determine lags with both solid and gas tracers.

A hole in the drillstring can cause the tracer, especially acetylene gas, to arrive at the surface before returns from the bottom. The appearance of two tracer arrivals, with the second one at a pump-stroke count consistent with normal lag, is strong evidence that the first arrival was from a hole in the pipe. The approximate depth of the "leak" can be estimated from "lag vs. depth" plots, assuming the hole has remained in gauge since drilling.

Lag should be evaluated after every trip, at the start of each 8- to 12-hour shift (tour), and when mud pumps have been added, exchanged, or modified. Cuttings taken during a distinctive change in lithology, accompanied by a drilling break, can be used to check the lag. The observed lag can also be checked with an estimate of the "ideal" lag by the calculation of an annular volume (assuming the hole is in gauge) and its displacement when given pump volume and stroke rate. These practices improve the quality of depth determinations. Good depth determinations are needed to relate lithology and hydrocarbon logs with drilling time and, later, wireline logs (Fig. 4.2). Consistent depth relationships among these logs lower the risk in formation evaluation.

4.2 Logging Drilling Time

The drilling depth and time data are collected to determine the drilling rate. This is recorded as the rate-of-penetration log.

4.2.1. Measurement and Recording

Penetration rate is recorded by a measurement of the distance and rate the kelly moves down through the kelly bushing. The instrumentation required varies among service companies, who are the best sources for more information.

Drilling rates are presented as either the time required to penetrate a fixed interval (minutes per foot or minutes per meter); or as the depth penetrated in a fixed time (feet per hour or meters per hour). Presentation and scales are chosen to emphasize changes—especially the onset of faster penetration, called a *drilling break* (Fig. 4.3). If plotted on linear scales, interval-per-fixed-time presentation is preferred when drilling is fast; time-per-fixed-interval presentation is better when drilling is slow. Chart 4.3 shows some alternative formats and scales for recording rate of penetration.

4.2.2. Factors Influencing Rate of Penetration

The drillbit penetrates as mechanical and hydraulic forces overcome a rock's resistance to being crushed, disaggregated, or dissolved. This resistance is controlled by properties affecting the rock's strength and density. The forces applied to overcome a rock's resistance are determined by drilling conditions. Penetration is also resisted by drilling debris, which must be removed, or "cleaned," by hydraulic action of the mud. The effectiveness of bottomhole cleaning is determined by drilling-fluid circulation and flow properties.

Drilling Conditions

The penetration rate depends partly on the nature, amount, and application rate of forces at the bit. These are determined by rotary speed, torque and weight on the bit (here considered synonymous with force on the bit),

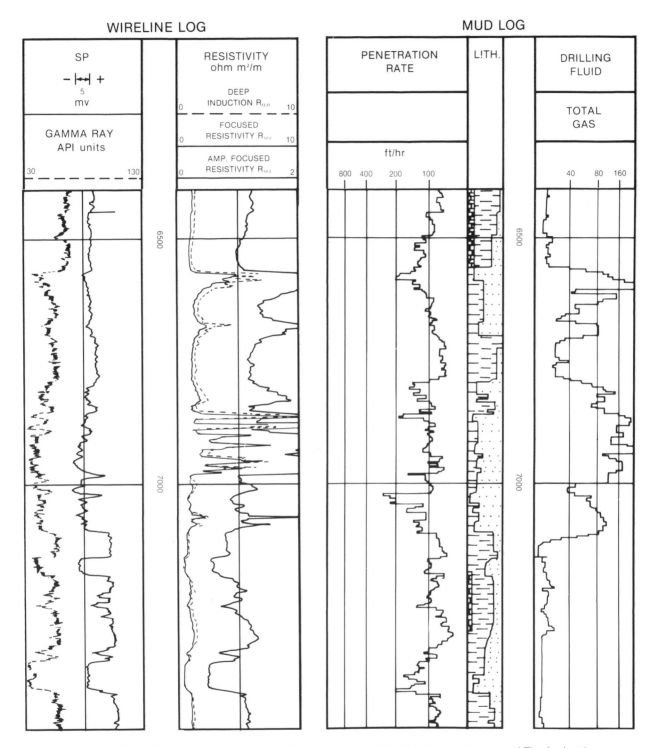

Fig. 4.2—Comparison of wireline log and mud log illustrating good depth coherency (courtesy of The Analysts).

bit size, type, and wear, pump pressure, and hydraulic jetting characteristics. Other conditions being the same, the penetration rate varies inversely with bit diameter. Bit wear or failure slows drilling. The mud log should document the bit's size, type, and condition, plus weight on the bit, torque, and rotary speed (Table 4.1).

Penetration can be assisted by hydraulic jetting through the bit. Jetting effectiveness depends on the bit type, pump pressure, and circulation rate, which should be recorded for use in interpreting the drilling rate.

TABLE 4.1—BIT DESCRIPTION AND HISTORY RECORD

Bit number
Feet drilled
Weight
Pump pressure
Wear code
Bit types
Time on bottom
Rotary speed
Mud circulation rate
Other

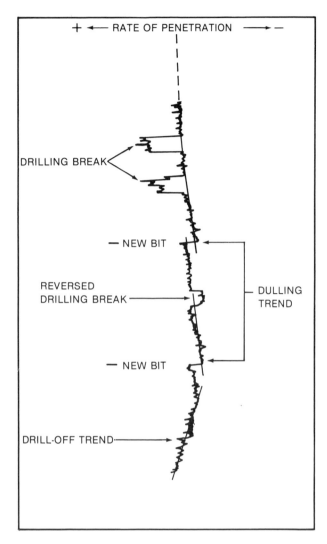

Fig. 4.3—Schematic drilling rate log (courtesy of The Analysts).

Rock Properties

Drillability is determined in part by a rock's resistance to being crushed, disaggregated, or dissolved. This resistance depends mostly on the amount and nature of cementation and/or grain interpenetration. Resistance to drilling also depends on porosity. Other factors being constant, a high-porosity rock can be drilled faster than one with lower porosity. Porosity, and therefore penetration rates, typically decreases with depth.

Some rock-forming minerals are dissolved by untreated natural (fresh water) muds, thereby increasing penetration rates. Salt beds should be suspected when the mud salinity and drilling rate increase rapidly.

Mud Properties

Optimal drilling performance requires effective mud circulation patterns around the bit and adequate cuttings-carrying capacity. The mud's carrying capacity depends on its circulation rate and rheology—especially density, viscosity, and gel strength.

The differential pressure (overbalance or underbalance) between the circulating mud column and formation also affects the drilling rate. Overbalanced muds tend to hold the cuttings down, which interferes with the efficient application of drilling forces and reduces the rate of penetration. Hydraulic jetting tends to correct this problem.

Drilling Models

The factors influencing the drilling rate can be incorporated into formulations useful for predicting or evaluating drilling performance. Bingham[11] proposed a relationship incorporating rate of penetration, R, weight on bit, W, rotary speed, f, and bit diameter, d_b:

$$\frac{R}{f} = a\left(\frac{W}{d_b}\right)^d , \quad \dots\dots\dots\dots\dots\dots\dots\dots\dots(4.2)$$

where a is a constant that depends on rock strength, and d is the formation drillability exponent, called the *d-exponent*. Differential pressure affects rock strength.[12] Fig. 4.4 shows the relative influence of differential pressure on rock strength and "chip hold-down" as they affect rate of penetration. These data indicate that "chip hold-down" affects rate of penetration more than does rock strengthening because of pressure differential. Rehm and McClendon[13] describe an empirically formulated "correction" to account for the pressure differential between the mud and formation as

$$d_{cs} = d\left(\frac{\rho_{m1}}{\rho_{m2}}\right), \quad \dots\dots\dots\dots\dots\dots\dots\dots(4.3)$$

where d_{cs} (sometimes called d_{xc}) is the *corrected d-exponent*, ρ_{m2} is the equivalent circulating density, and ρ_{m1} is the normal mud weight for the area. In a given rock type and constant pressure differential, d and d_{cs} increase gradually with depth.

A normalized rate of penetration can be derived from a d-exponent model. Ideally this rate should respond only to formation properties. Actually the relationships among drilling and formation factors influencing penetration rates are more complex than implied by d-exponent formulations. Drilling hydraulics, drill-bit design, and formation stress are not considered in Eqs. 4.2 and 4.3. The more complex formulations now in use[14-16] are beyond the scope of this review.

4.2.3 Use of Drilling-Rate Data

Rate-of-penetration data are used to (1) identify changes in rock types or porosity indicating prospective reservoir intervals, (2) make well-to-well correlations, and (3) detect abnormal pressure conditions.

Lithology and Porosity

A drilling break is the first indication of porosity in a prospective lithology. When a drilling break occurs, drilling can be stopped until returns are circulated to the surface for analysis before a decision is made to core, test, log, complete, or resume drilling.

Rate-of-penetration data are expected to correlate with

SP, gamma ray, density, or acoustic velocity logs, considering the effects of porosity and lithology on each. Fig. 4.2 shows a good correlation between drilling rate and an SP log. Correlation can be improved with normalized penetration rates that minimize changes caused by drilling conditions. The use of drilling rates for porosity interpretation is discussed by Zoeller[14] and Bourgoyne and Young.[16]

Well-to-Well Correlation

A penetration-rate log is useful for making stratigraphic or structural correlations before wireline logs are available, and is especially important should a hole be lost before wireline logs could be run. Shepherd and Atwater[17] discuss the use of drilling-rate data for well-to-well correlation.

Abnormal Pressure Detection

Jorden and Shirley[18] proposed using drillability to detect the onset of abnormal formation pressures. They made Eq. 4.2 lithology-specific and introduced units consistent with oilfield usage as:

$$d = \frac{\log\left(\dfrac{R}{60f}\right)}{\log\left(\dfrac{12W}{10^6 d_b}\right)}, \quad \ldots\ldots\ldots\ldots\ldots (4.4)$$

where R is in feet per hour, f is in revolutions per minute, d_b is in inches, and W is in pounds. Jorden and Shirley related the d-exponent to subsurface pressure conditions and found that when an abnormal pressure zone is first penetrated, the expected regular increase with depth is reversed (Fig. 4.5). Plots using the corrected d-exponent show a similar reversal. Hole size, lithology, and mud circulating conditions also affect the d-exponent, regardless of formation pressure.

Evaluation of formation pressure is complex and should be interpreted from more than d-exponent data. Abnormal pressure can also be indicated by mud gas after connections or trips, shale density profiles, cuttings size and shape, and mud temperature and salinity. Interpretation of pressure indication is discussed in Sec. 4.5.4 and Chap. 17.

4.2.4 Comments

Drilling-rate data are useful for recognizing prospective zones, correlating with nearby wells before wireline logs are run, and detecting abnormal pressures. Normalized rate-of-penetration logs derived from drilling models compensate for changes in drilling weight, bit size, rotary speed, circulating mud weight, bit tooth characteristics, mud hydraulics, drillstring configurations, and torque. Ideally a normalized rate of penetration will respond only to lithology, porosity, and pressure. Drilling models are not perfect, so compensation does not always remove effects from all the drilling operations. Therefore, recommended interpretation strategies combine the rate of penetration, description of cuttings, and mud gas behavior.

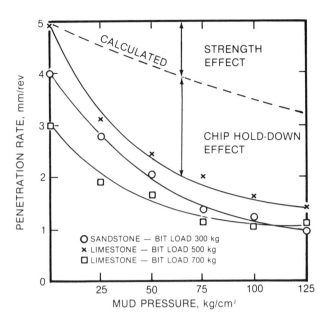

Fig. 4.4—Penetration rate as a function of mud pressure at atmospheric pore pressure (after Garnier and van Lingen[12]).

4.3 Logging Hydrocarbons in Drilling Returns

Hydrocarbon sensing is a critical component of the mud logging operation. Logging of drilling time and cuttings lithology is important for reducing potential ambiguities in identifying the origins of entrained oil and gas. However, the ultimate success or failure of a mud logging operation depends on the sensitivity and reliability of its hydrocarbon monitors.

4.3.1. Origins of Oil and Gas in Drilling Returns

Identifying the sources of oil and gas in drilling returns is a prerequisite to successful formation evaluation. Oil and gas enter the drilling fluid not only as a result of current drilling of a hydrocarbon-saturated interval but also as production from a previously drilled interval, contamination, or possibly thermocatalytic generation during drilling. Mercer[19] provides an excellent basis for considering hydrocarbon origination; his definitions are used in this discussion.

Liberated and Expelled Oil and Gas

As new hole is drilled, a cylindrical volume of formation contents is broken up and mixed into the circulating drilling fluid. This process releases (*liberates*) some formation oil or gas from saturated formations into the drilling fluid.

Cuttings from a newly drilled interval can retain part of their formation fluids in the chips after drilling. The cuttings and retained fluid enter the mud column under bottomhole (mud column) pressure. As the cuttings travel to the surface, reduced pressure causes some of that fluid to expand and to be produced (or *expelled*) into the drilling returns. Some formation fluid may be retained in the cuttings. The expelled formation fluid and the liberated component appear at the surface at approximately the same time, so there is no practical way to dif-

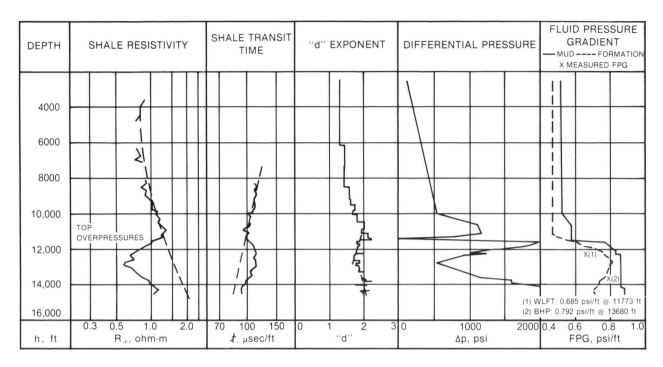

Fig. 4.5—Correlation of normalized penetration rate with other indications of abnormal pressure (after Jorden and Shirley [18]).

ferentiate them. The combined liberated, expelled, and retained hydrocarbons constitute a *show* and indicate the presence of a prospective oil and/or gas accumulation.

Produced Oil and Gas

While drilling proceeds with underbalanced pressures or while the hole is swabbed during trips, oil and gas can be produced into a borehole from previously drilled intervals.

Recycled Oil or Gas

Some formation contents may be recirculated as drilling continues. *Recycled* oil and gas are defined as that hydrocarbon not removed before the mud is pumped back down the hole and which appears again at the surface. Although good drilling practice requires the removal of oil, gas, and cuttings before the mud is recirculated, some can persist through more than one cycle. Recycled oil and gas can obscure a new show or be detected as a false show, so special elimination procedures are justified.

Contamination

Contamination gas (or oil) is defined as hydrocarbons artificially introduced into the drilling fluid from a source other than formations penetrated in the well. A common contaminant is diesel fuel. Diesel generally has small amounts of volatile components at ambient conditions and therefore usually contributes relatively small amounts of new gases. Alternatively diesel can act as a scavenger and can deplete the mud of formation gas. Consequences of diesel contamination vary from a nuisance (small background gas-in-mud levels of gas and slightly fluorescent coatings on cuttings) to a serious problem. Use of Grades 1 or 2 diesel fuel, delivered and stored in clean tanks, is least likely to cause significant

contamination; the use of other grades of diesel, bunker fuel, or crude oil is more risky.

Hydrocarbon gases in a mud can originate from the breakdown of organic additives, which also can decompose to generate hydrogen sulfide or carbon dioxide. Both can come from degradation of lignosulfonates at temperatures above 200°C and can interfere with some gas-in-mud measurements.

Thermocatalytic Generation

The conversion of organic content of rocks to hydrocarbons by thermal processes associated with drilling action has been postulated but not convincingly proved. Thermocatalytic generation should be greatest during slow drilling of organic-rich shales.

4.3.2 Collection and Preparation of Samples

Samples of gas, mud, and cuttings are separated (*caught*) from drilling returns by various methods. The shale shaker (Fig. 4.6) is usually used for sample collection, but sampling devices can also be located on a flow diversion line. Which method is preferable depends on the mud properties, weather conditions, and drilling rig configuration. Sample-collection systems are sources of problems and require close attention by mud logging personnel. If representative samples are not obtained, the potential value of mud logging is seriously compromised.

Requirements for sampling gas, cuttings, and mud are different and so will be considered separately.

Gas Sampling

A sampling device called a *trap* is used to remove gas samples from drilling returns. Ideally, a trap should be capable of extracting the gas from drilling fluid,

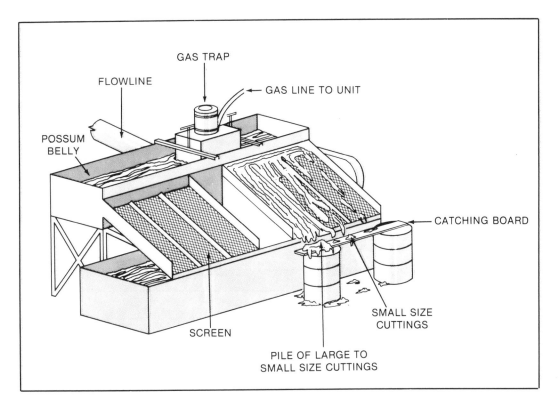

Fig. 4.6—Gas and cuttings collection sites at shale shaker (after Exlog[20]).

regardless of its density, viscosity, and gel strength. Sampling must be consistent and reliable regardless of the flow rate in the main mud circulation system. No gas trap of currently available design performs all these functions, but among presently used types, mechanical agitation is preferred.

A mechanical-agitation device (Fig. 4.7) consists of a means to regulate flow so as to sample a constant mud volume per unit of time, an electric-powered impeller to agitate the mud, and an outlet for delivering the gas sample from the atmosphere above the sample to the detector. The efficiency and reliability of mechanical agitators depend on impeller design, rotational speed, vacuum level used to withdraw gases, and mud properties. Although not much information on such trap performance has been published, estimates that only 25 to 75% of the gas is extracted under typical conditions seem realistic.

The gas trap is located either in the possum belly of a shale shaker or in a sluice box on a flow diversion line. The trap must be kept clean of cuttings accumulations, lost-circulation material, and congealed mud, all of which can modify the desired flow rate. Automatic warning devices that signal malfunctions are very desirable. The magnitude of carbide tracer responses are good checks on trap and vacuum line performance. A sudden change in background gas level should be viewed as either a show or a delivery malfunction.

The gas-in-air from the trap flows through a carrier system to reach the detector (Fig. 4.8). The amount of flow is regulated at a level that is compatible with the detector's reactivity. This desired flow level can be reduced or blocked by water condensation and freezing so that filters can be used to control the buildup of fluids

in the flow line. After moving through the detector cell, any unaltered gas sample, reaction product, or carrier is exhausted to the atmosphere. The flow through the detector is continuous, thereby providing an uninterrupted monitor of the flow stream.

Continuous sampling is sometimes supplemented with batch collection and analysis. One such system uses distillation analysis, which yields a more complete extraction, especially of heavier hydrocarbons, than mechanical agitators. Gas composition of a sample obtained from a conventional trap is compared with the results of a distillation extraction in Fig. 4.9.

The results from continuous gas monitoring are reported by various authors or contractors as "continuous ditch gas," "mud analysis," "drilling fluid gas," "gas detector response drilling fluid," and "fluid logging units."

Mud Sampling

Mud samples are usually caught at the same time as cuttings samples. Attention should be given to consistency of procedures, cleanliness of containers, and potential evaporation of gases or fluids. Mud with oil should be stored in glass or metal containers; mud without oil may be stored in plastic containers.

Cuttings Sampling

Cuttings are used in identifying intervals of oil and gas saturation and in estimating reservoir characteristics. Data derived from cuttings clarify interpretation of gas-in-mud logs. The importance of collecting good cuttings samples cannot be overemphasized.[20,21] Cuttings collection is discussed in Sec. 4.4.1.

Special samples should be taken whenever gas-in-mud

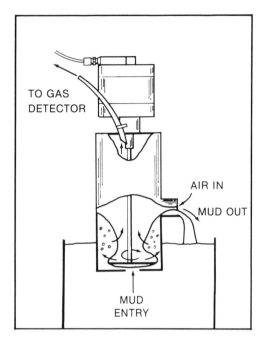

Fig. 4.7—Schematic gas trap—mechanical agitator type (modified from Choate[21]).

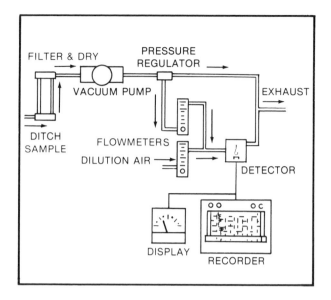

Fig. 4.8—Flowpath of the gas analysis system (after Exlog[20]).

levels increase or one lag time after drilling breaks. Samples for gas and oil analyses are processed as soon as possible and with a minimum of handling.

Samples from wells drilled with oil-base or oil-emulsion muds can have surface coatings that can be removed by "washing" with either a detergent solution or a nonfluorescent solvent such as naphtha. Such washing can risk removing indigenous oil staining so should be avoided if possible.

4.3.3 Detection and Analysis of Hydrocarbon in Drilling Returns

After removal of the gas from the drilling fluid and cuttings, the gas samples are processed with instruments designed to *detect* hydrocarbons and to *analyze* their physical or chemical characteristics. These processes are applied in an orderly sequence that yields gas-in-mud, oil-in-mud, gas-in-cuttings, and oil-in-cuttings content data. These data, presented as a continuous record organized by well depth, constitute a *hydrocarbon log*, which is an integral part of a mud log.

Gas in Mud

Different types of sensing elements have been used to analyze air/hydrocarbon mixtures, with objectives of
   1. detecting hydrocarbons,
   2. determining their relative abundances, and
   3. providing data on their molecular compositions.
Some analyses are done in a continuous mode, but others are better suited for batch-processing.

Catalytic Combustion Detector. Since the earliest days of mud logging, the standard instrument for monitoring gas-in-mud content has been the *hot-wire detector* (or analyzer), which is based on thermal catalytic combustion principles and thus is more descriptively called a catalytic combustion detector.

A catalytic combustion detector responds to the reaction of gases around a platinum or platinum-coated wire heated to a high temperature by an electrical current. The steady-state temperature around the wire depends on the balance between the rates of heat generated in the wire and dissipated through the surrounding material.

A typical catalytic combustion detector uses a Wheatstone bridge circuit (Fig. 4.10) in which two of the usual resistors are replaced by a pair of electrically matched platinum filaments. The temperature of the filaments can be varied by changing the bridge voltage (Fig. 4.11). When conditions for heat generation and loss are identical for both, a balance control resistor can be adjusted so that the bridge meter senses no potential difference, and the recorder senses no current flow. At this state, the bridge is said to be balanced. Heating or cooling one filament with respect to the other unbalances the bridge and results in a meter reading proportional to the amount of unbalance.

The filaments are operated within a chamber or cell (Fig. 4.12). One filament functions as a sensor and the other functions as a reference depending on their relationship with the sample stream. The sensor filament is exposed to the sample flowing through the cell; however, the reference filament is excluded from the sample by an enclosure or coating depending on the type of filament. One type of catalytic combustion detector excludes the sample by an impermeable or slightly permeable case that encloses the reference filament. Another type of catalytic combustion detector uses a reference filament that is coated to reduce its catalytic reactivity so that the reference filament has the same contact with the sample stream as the sensor filament has. This is an advantage when nonhydrocarbon gases are in the sample.

The bridge is balanced by air flowing through the cell. After balancing, the bridge signal by convention is positive when the sensor is heated, compared with the reference, assuming the bridge response has the conventional polarity.

Catalytic combustion filaments are operated at high-

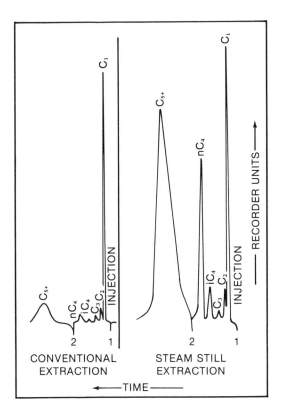

Fig. 4.9—Gas compositions of samples extracted by steam distillation and mechanical agitation (after Choate[21]).

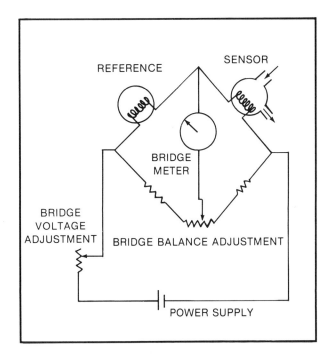

Fig. 4.10—Wheatstone bridge circuit used for catalytic combustion detector (courtesy of The Analysts).

enough voltages (hence temperatures) to oxidize (with catalysis) a hydrocarbon-gas/air mixture rapidly. The oxidation/combustion generates heat at the sensor (but not at the reference), producing a positive bridge signal. Fig. 4.13 shows the response for lean mixtures (less than stoichiometric, which is the ideal mixture for complete combustion) of methane and air for one type of sensor. Depending on the methane concentration, 1.55 to 2.40 V are needed to produce the maximum signal for this type of sensor. Other types may respond differently.

The voltage required to ignite lean mixtures of hydrocarbons and air decreases with molecular weight (Fig. 4.14). Thus, when operated at "high" voltage (more than needed to ignite methane) the catalytic combustion detector becomes a total gas analyzer; operated at "low" voltage (less than needed to ignite C_1 but more than needed to ignite C_{2+}) the catalytic combustion detector becomes a heavier-than-methane analyzer. The catalytic combustion detector recorder reading for the high-voltage operation is preferably called "total gas," but also "high-voltage gas," or "x voltage gas" (where x is the operating voltage). The lower voltage operation is called either "low-voltage gas," "wet gas," "petroleum vapors," "heavies," or "y voltage gas" (where y is the operating voltage), which can be reported as either the bridge or filament measurement (typically the filament voltage is about half the bridge voltage).

Ideally, the difference between the high- and low-voltage readings would represent the methane concentration. In practice, however, the heat of combustion from heavier-molecular-weight gases can raise the cell temperature sufficiently to ignite methane, even at "low" voltage. When this happens, the difference no longer represents methane abundance. Alternatively, the methane can be measured without interference if the sample is passed through a filter that removes the heavier compounds. Such measurements are reported as either "methane direct," "methane only," "methane," or "C_1."

For lean hydrocarbon/air mixtures the bridge signal increases up to a certain concentration, then decreases (Fig. 4.15). Theoretically the peak position corresponds to the maximum concentration of hydrocarbon at which complete combustion in air is possible (the stoichiometric composition), which is 9.5% for methane/air, 5.6% for ethane/air, 4.01% for propane/air, and 3.11% for butane/air. Actual sensor response may vary depending on cell design, sample flow, filament vibration, filament reactivity, contaminants such as water vapor, and deviations from simple oxidation/combustion effects including thermal cracking, branch reactions, and conduction effects from unburned hydrocarbons and combustion products. The decrease of bridge signal with increasing concentration is a serious limitation. After the peak signal is reached, the sample can be diluted with known volumes of air to operate the detector within the "linear" response region. However, exact dilution and quantitative calibration become increasingly difficult to achieve with increasing concentration. The meter reading is scaled to compensate for the amount of dilution.

The meter or recorder can be calibrated to be read in "gas units" or equivalent methane in air. Sensor calibration is best performed with three concentrations of methane: zero, at a point below the lower explosive limit, and well above that limit. These requirements are satisfied with air for the zero concentration, 2% methane

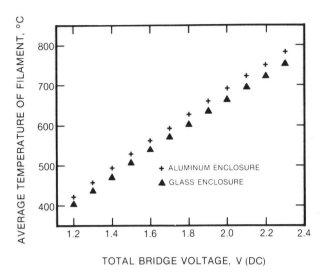

Fig. 4.11—Average temperature of a typical catalytic filament operated at different voltages (courtesy Delphian Corp.).

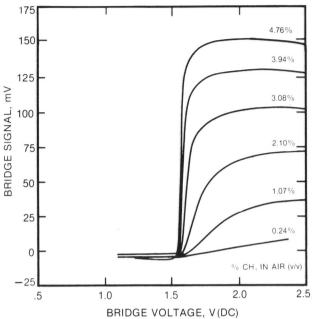

Fig. 4.13—Catalytic combustion detector response as a function of bridge voltages for different methane concentrations (courtesy of Delphian Corp).

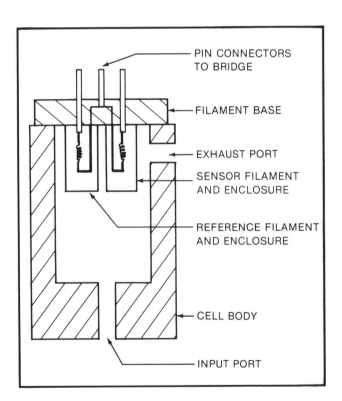

Fig. 4.12—Catalytic combustion detector cell (modified from Exlog[55]).

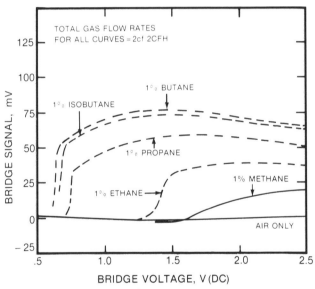

Fig. 4.14—Catalytic combustion detector response as a function of bridge voltage for different gasses (courtesy of Delphian Corp.).

in nitrogen or air for the point below the explosive limit, and 20% methane in nitrogen or air for the high concentration. The gas response is reported as the volume-to-volume (hydrocarbon/air) ratio. A catalytic combustion system should detect 200 ppm hydrocarbon in air.[22]

Nonhydrocarbon gases affect performance of the catalytic combustion detector. Hydrogen, acetylene, and hydrogen sulfide react within the same voltage range as heavier hydrocarbon gases. Carbon dioxide response

should be evaluated for each sensor. Water vapor affects the responses of some types of catalytic combustion detectors more than others. It is a good practice to filter out as much water vapor as possible.

The platinum filament of a hot-wire detector can have its catalytic reactivity "poisoned" by sulfur and silicone compounds. At lower voltages, the filament surface can become coated with incompletely burned hydrocarbons, which reduce the reactivity and hence sensitivity.

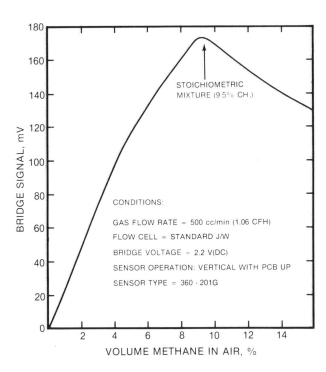

Fig. 4.15—Catalytic combustion response as a function of methane concentration (courtesy of Delphian Corp.).

TABLE 4.2—THERMAL CONDUCTIVITIES OF SOME COMMON GASES AT 212°F (after Lynch[22])

Gas	Thermal Conductivity Btu/(hr-sq ft-°F/ft)
Helium	0.101
Hydrogen	0.129
Air	0.0183
Methane	0.0235
Ethane	0.0175
Propane	0.0151
Butane	0.0135
Carbon dioxide	0.0126
Water vapor	0.0160

Therefore, a hot-wire detector should be checked regularly. Warnings of degrading filament performance are provided by variations in background gas, carbide lag response, or instrument calibrations. Filament performance is sensitive to alignment and distance to the enclosure. Therefore, the filament should be mounted vertically to minimize sag of the hot element. Vibration should be minimized.

A hot-wire detector provides a record of gas concentration by continuously analyzing samples collected from a trap. Although a logger or interpreter must deal with serious limitations, this is a useful technique for detecting hydrocarbons, especially when supplemented by other analytical procedures such as gas chromatography.

Thermal Conductivity Detectors. One of the oldest forms of gas detection is based on thermal conductivity. This property describes the ability of substances to transfer heat across a temperature gradient. Table 4.2 lists the thermal conductivities of some common gases.

A thermal conductivity detector consists of a flow cell, a means for maintaining a temperature gradient across the sample, and a sensor responsive to a temperature change within the cell. One embodiment employs two or four electrically heated filaments located in cavities within a metal block (Fig. 4.16). By regulating the electrical current passing through the filaments, the temperature can be adjusted to produce the required gradient across the gas flowing through the cavity. Another embodiment employs a conventional catalytic combustion detector with two filaments operated in a single flow cell (Fig. 4.12). In either type of device, the filaments are operated below the combustion temperature of any hydrocarbons in the sample.

Differential measurements of thermal conductivity are more practical than absolute measurements. One way to make differential measurements employs two flow cavities and corresponding heated filaments, which are incorporated into a Wheatstone bridge circuit (Fig. 4.17). The bridge can be balanced to zero output signal when the same gas flows past both filaments. When a gas with a thermal conductivity different from that used to balance the bridge enters one of the cells, heat transfer is modified there, thus changing the temperature of the filament in the sensor cell relative to the reference cell. This changes the sensor filament resistance relative to the reference filament resistance, imbalances the circuit, and creates an output signal. If a conventional catalytic combustion detector is used, both filaments are typically in one flow cell, but only one element is directly exposed to the sample and the other is sealed in an enclosure containing air, which becomes the reference environment. As with the other embodiment, changes in the resistance of the sensor filament imbalance a bridge circuit and produce an output signal.

Thermal conductivity detectors are the least-sensitive gas detection devices used in mud logging. The sensitivity depends partly on the reference gas. Air must be used for the reference environment when total gas is monitored from the mud, even though its thermal conductivity is not much different from those of light hydrocarbons. Better sensitivity is achieved with helium as the reference gas, as is possible when chromatograph systems using helium carriers are employed. The sensitivity can be improved by use of four heated filaments in the bridge (Fig. 4.17).[24]

The thermal conductivities of mixtures of heavier gases can be relatively independent of individual volume fractions. When heavy reference or carrier gases such as air or nitrogen are used, the detector filament is sometimes cooled even though the lower thermal conductivity of the sample component would seem to indicate less heat transfer and increased filament temperature. Such occurrences are consistent with predictions from relationships that account for the molecular weights and diameters of the components, as well as their proportions and thermal conductivities.[24]

The response does not saturate at high methane concentrations (Fig. 4.18), unlike what happens with the most widely used gas detectors. As a result, thermal conductivity detection is an alternative to diluting the sample and using catalytic combustion or flame ionization detection when the hydrocarbon concentrations are above the saturation level of those detectors.

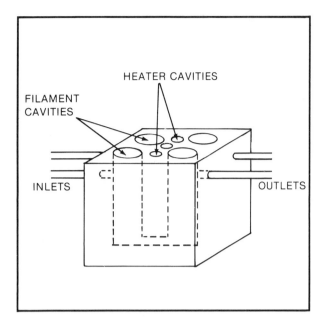

Fig. 4.16—Schematic cell block for thermal conductivity detector (after Rowland[23]).

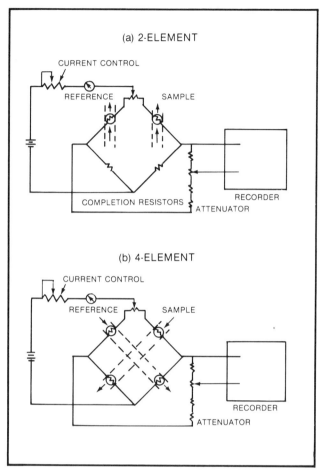

Fig. 4.17—Bridge circuits for thermal conductivity detectors (after David[24]).

The performance of a given thermal conductivity detector depends on many factors. A high-performance system is designed to minimize heat losses caused by (1) mass flow of the gas out of the cell, (2) conduction from the ends of the heat source, (3) radiation, and (4) free convection, thus making the heat transfer primarily conduction through the gas within the cell. The operating temperature affects both the sensitivity and stability. Moreover, the temperature must be low enough to prevent combustion of any hydrocarbon components. Reducing the carrier flow will, up to a point, improve the sensitivity. Exposure to air, always present in samples from drilling muds, will affect some types of filaments. The symmetry of the hot element with respect to the cell walls is important, and some filament designs are more susceptible to vibration than others. David[24] and Grob[25] discuss such performance factors.

The use of thermal conductivity detectors at the wellsite has decreased as better dilution techniques have been introduced for catalytic combustion detection, and as the more sensitive flame ionization method has replaced other detection methods in gas chromatography.

Flame Ionization Detector. Since the 1960's, instruments based on the burning of organic compounds in a hydrogen flame have been recognized as useful to mud logging. Such instruments can be used as either continuous gas-in-mud monitors or as detectors in gas chromatographs.

The burning of most carbon compounds in a hydrogen flame produces charged species that, if collected by suitable electrodes in the proper electric field, produce a current proportional to the amount of organic material present. However, no signal is produced by water vapor, nitrogen, oxygen, sulfur dioxide, carbon dioxide, or hydrogen sulfide. These substances complicate interpretation of responses from catalytic combustion or thermal conductivity detectors. Therefore, insensitivity to such fixed gases can be an advantage—especially when total gas is monitored. Of course, if any nonhydrocarbon gases are to be logged, another detector system must be used. Hydrogen cannot be detected with a flame ionization instrument.

A flame ionization detector is a relatively simple device. It consists of (1) a flame cell containing a burner jet supplied with hydrogen, air, and sample streams; (2) a polarizing field, collector electrodes, and appropriate amplifier circuitry; and (3) a power supply (Fig. 4.19).[26] A typical configuration also has an externally activated ignitor, a source of "purge" gas, and a strip-chart recorder. The required electrical field is maintained by imposing a potential between the collector electrodes. Any ion current from the flame is collected and amplified to drive the recorder. The power can be supplied by a dry cell battery, which is more stable and reliable than some rig site sources.

The detector response is proportional to the number of carbon atoms in the volatile organic content of the sample. Thus, one mole of ethane produces approximately the same response as two moles of methane. However, the chemical nature of the sample also influences the effectiveness of the carbon atom in producing a detector response. For example, an acetylene molecule produces

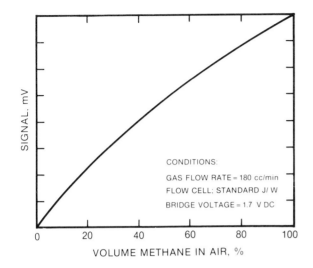

Fig. 4.18—Thermal conductivity detector response as a function of methane concentration (courtesy Delphian Corp.).

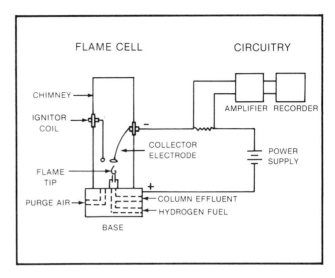

Fig. 4.19—Schematic flame ionization detector (modified after Mercer[26]).

a larger flame response than an ethane molecule, although both have two carbon atoms. Table 4.3 gives the flame responses for some common compounds.

The flame ionization instrument is linear over a wide range of sample concentrations. However, hydrocarbon concentrations encountered in well logging can exceed the linear range, or even the saturation level, of typical instruments. Above the linear range, quantitative analysis requires smaller samples, dilution, or careful calibration.

Wellsite flame detectors are capable of sensing hydrocarbon concentrations in the low parts-per-million range. This is more sensitive than needed to recognize most commercial hydrocarbon accumulations.

Flame ionization instrument response can be calibrated in several ways. One way is to determine the peak height or area produced by a known amount of a compound. Calibration is repeated for each compound of interest. Another way is to determine the calibration factor for one compound and calculate the calibration factors for other components from their carbon numbers, corrected for chemical effects. Table 4.3 gives the corrected carbon numbers for some organic compounds. This requires the use of peak area or an approximation rather than peak height for relating sample responses to calibration responses. As the volume-fraction is the preferred measure for mud logging reports, the recorded signal can be converted to volume-of-compound/ volume-of-total sample by calibrating signal responses with those produced by given volumes of calibration standards with known concentrations. Where proportions of components in a mixture are not known, an equivalent methane response is reported.

The response characteristics for this type of instrumentation will remain constant as long as operating conditions remain generally unchanged. Performance is relatively insensitive to carrier flow rate and external temperature. Once optimized, integrators used to determine peak area, hydrogen flow rate and auxiliary (purge) gas flow have only weak effects on operating stability. The flame cell must always be operated above 100°C to

prevent condensation of water and be kept clean of deposits from difficult-to-burn compounds. Overall, the instrument is robust enough for typical wellsite operation.

Principles and performance of flame ionization instruments are reviewed by Rowland,[23] David,[24] and Grob.[25] Applications to hydrocarbon logging are discussed by Mercer.[26]

Cost and operating convenience aside, flame-ionization detectors are superior to hot-wire and thermal conductivity combinations. Mercer[26] discusses the use of flame-ionization detection for mud logging applications, and Rowland[23] presents an excellent review of principles and performance.

Gas Chromatograph. Since the mid-1950's, gas samples have been analyzed by elution gas chromatography with more accurate and quantitative results than from total gas methods (catalytic combustion, flame ionization, thermal conductivity). The advantages of gas chromatography are partly offset by a requirement of several minutes per analysis, in contrast to the virtually instantaneous total gas response. As a result, the total gas method is preferred for continuous *qualitative* monitoring* of total hydrocarbons in drilling returns. Gas chromatograph methods are preferred for periodic or *batch analysis* of gas in the mud stream. Here the focus on gas chromatography will be as an analyzer rather than as a detector, although the combined total gas and gas chromatography methods do provide some desirable redundancy.

Chromatography, in the context of this discussion, is the separation of components from a mixture. Techniques are available for separating out vapors, liquids, and even some solids. For mud logging purposes, chromatography is primarily restricted to separating mixtures of compounds that are vapors at atmospheric condi-

---

*It is possible to devise a gas chromatograph system with sampling rates that provide virtually continuous monitoring. However, cost and reliability considerations favor the use of hot-wire detectors for continuous detection and a simpler gas chromatograph for batch analysis.

TABLE 4.3—FLAME RESPONSES AND CORRECTED CARBON NUMBERS FOR SOME COMMON GASES
(modified from David[24])

Compound		Number of Carbon Atoms	Response R (C/mole)	Effective Carbon Number
Methane	(1)	1	0.245	1.02
	(2)	1	0.251	1.05
Ethane		2	0.474	1.98
Propane	(1)	3	0.720	3.00
	(2)	3	0.711	2.96
Ethylene		2	0.460	1.92
Acetylene	(1)	2	0.620	2.58
	(2)	2	0.616	2.57
	(3)	2	0.624	2.60
Benzene	(1)	6	1.440	6.00
	(2)	6	1.464	6.10

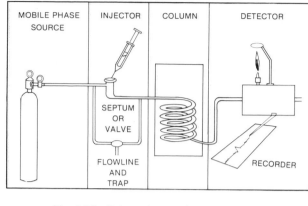

Fig. 4.20—Schematic gas chromatograph.

tions. This is typically achieved by elution development,[24,25] in which individual components are separated by a continuously flowing elutant (or *carrier*) that moves a vapor *sample* through a stationary phase (or *packing*) contained in a tube (or *column*). The components of the sample travel through the column at different rates, which are controlled by retention on the stationary phase. At the end of the separation, only the elutant remains in the column.

Fig. 4.20 shows a schematic of a gas chromatograph. A gas sample of unknown composition is injected into the inlet end of the column and is swept through it by the carrier gas. At the downstream end, the separated components are sensed by the detector (Fig. 4.21), each producing an electrical signal proportional to its volume- or weight-fraction, depending on the detector. This signal, recorded as a function of time, is called a *chromatogram* (Fig. 4.22).

Some general observations about a mixture of gases can be made by inspecting a chromatogram. For example, Fig. 4.22 indicates the following.

1. The mixture contains at least three components.

2. Peak A, with the shortest retention time, represents a compound with a lower molecular weight than Peak C, with the longest retention time.

3. Peak B probably represents the compound with the highest concentration.

4. Individual components are well separated (*resolved*) and do not overlap, which makes quantitative analysis more difficult.

These observations should be considered as "first glance" conclusions, because exceptions are possible to all these statements. A preferred interpretation would be based on injecting known samples and observing the elution times of the peak positions, as shown in Fig. 4.23.

Gas samples are frequently introduced by syringe into the injection port or through a valve programmed to accept the new sample as soon as the column is clear.

Most mud logging operations use one of two types of column. One type consists of a metal or glass tube packed with sized, inert particles coated with a liquid. Gas separation takes place on the coating by a process that can be visualized as a series of partitions as the gas goes into solution in the coating, then is subsequently revaporized by the carrier gas. This type is called a *partition* (or *gas/liquid*) column.

Partitioning columns are used to separate organic gases. Typically, hydrogen, oxygen, nitrogen, and methane are eluted at about the same time. A second common type of column is packed with materials that inherently absorb gas. Such materials include charcoal, silica gel, zeolites, and some polymers. This type is called an *adsorption* (or *gas/solid*) column. They are used primarily to separate oxygen, nitrogen, and methane. Usually the retention times for heavier hydrocarbons (C_{2+}) are prohibitively long when adsorption columns are used. However, it is not necessary to wait for all components to emerge before introducing a new sample, because the heavier components can be backflushed by reverse flow after methane or ethane has been eluted. This allows a new sample to be injected much sooner than if one were to wait for the heavier components to pass through the entire column.

Each eluted component emerging from the column produces an electrical signal from a detection device (catalytic combustion, thermal conductivity, or flame ionization type), assuming it is responsive to that element or compound.

The concentration of each component can be estimated by calibrating the detector response with samples having known hydrocarbon concentrations. Although peak height and the product of peak height and one-half peak width are common measures of response, the area under the response curve is the most reliable measure of concentration. Area under a peak can be automatically computed by electronic integrators or by computer processing. Calibrated response should be reported in volume hydrocarbon/volume air ratios in percent, parts per million, or parts per billion.

The threshold sensitivity of gas chromatographs varies with the carrier/detector/column combination. Systems with a partition column, helium carrier, and thermal conductivity detector can have minimum detectable levels of 50 to 100 ppm of hydrocarbons in air.

Gas chromatography is described by Rowland[23] and Grob,[25] who are good sources for more information.

Infrared Analyzer. Another device for analyzing gases is based on absorption of infrared energy. Infrared analyzers were evaluated for mud logging in the late 1950's. Since then their wellsite applications have been limited; however, infrared-analyzer technology is now

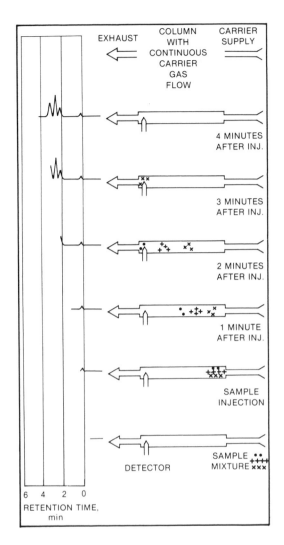

Fig. 4.21—Chromatographic separation of a three-component mixture.

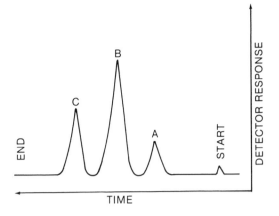

Fig. 4.22—Schematic chromatogram (after Rowland[23]).

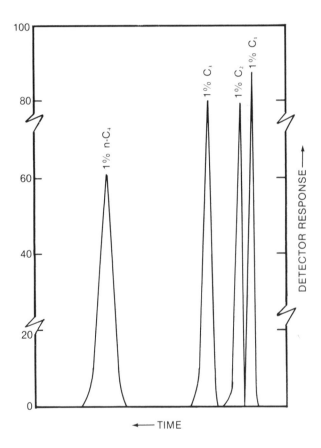

Fig. 4.23—Chromatogram of special calibrating gas (after Jenkins[27]).

routinely used in laboratory analysis—especially of fluids.

Polyatomic gases usually exhibit a unique infrared absorption pattern corresponding to the natural frequencies of their atomic bonding. For example, Fig. 4.24 shows the absorption spectra of methane. These and other spectra can be found in the *Catalog of Infrared Spectral Data* compiled by API Research Project 44 in 1946. If the absorption spectrum of a gas is known, it can be identified, even when present with other compounds, and its concentration can be estimated.

Infrared analysis instrumentation described by Lynch[22] and Jenkins[27] used a single detector, which was sensitive to methane only. Although at that time multiple detectors (sensitized for other hydrocarbons) could have been used as an alternative to catalytic combustion detector/gas chromatograph combinations, considerations of such instrumentation for wellsite hydrocarbon analysis have been limited by cost. Also limiting were problems of compensating for the interference of water vapor and sensitivity to vibration. Under normal operating conditions, the early instruments were reported[27] capable of detecting 100 parts per million of methane in air.

Mass Spectrometer. During the 1950's, mass spectroscopy was evaluated for mud logging purposes. Although an important tool for laboratory applications, mass spectroscopy exhibited a number of limitations that discouraged its use in the field. It is expensive, requires very constant power, and must be operated and maintained by highly qualified personnel.

Oil in Mud

Early mud logging equipment used by Hayward[1] included a device for collecting mud samples, which were ex-

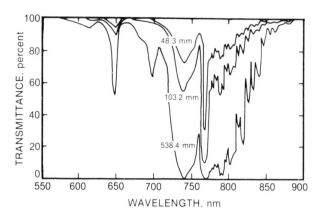

Fig. 4.24—Portion of infrared spectrum (after Lynch[22]).

amined for evidence of oil. If very low gas/oil ratios are present, oil reservoirs cannot always be identified by gas-in-mud analysis. Also, some sandstone reservoirs can disaggregate during drilling so that no composite rock chips are available to show oil staining. When this happens, and the gas/oil ratio is low, oil-in-mud analysis could be the only basis for recognizing oil saturation.

Oil can sometimes be seen in the drilling fluid, especially after the sample is diluted with water, as a color sheen or oil globules on the surface. The diluted mud sample should also be examined under ultraviolet light to see and record the color, intensity, and distribution of any surface fluorescence.

Procedures are also available for distilling out the oil fraction for analysis by a liquid/liquid chromatograph or infrared analyzers.

Gas in Cuttings

Fresh cuttings should be routinely evaluated for gas content. This is done by pulverizing a measured amount of cuttings in a fixed amount of water in a modified food blender. The vapor above the cuttings-fluid surface is analyzed with a total gas detector and/or gas chromatograph. Some pulverizers have a hot-wire detector built into their tops; in others the vapor must be withdrawn and injected into a separate device. The resultant gas readings are called "cuttings gas" or "microgas."

It is also good practice after this analysis to record any signs of oil or escaping gas seen on the surface of the fluid.

Significant amounts of gas in the cuttings are characteristic of gas saturation in low-permeability rocks.

Oil in Cuttings

The importance of evaluating oil in cuttings is stressed by several authors.[20,21,28] This analysis could be the only basis for detecting hydrocarbon saturation with a very low gas/liquid ratio.

Procedures for evaluating oil in cuttings include descriptions of oil staining, ultraviolet fluorescence, and sample appearance after treatment with solvent. The amount and composition of oil in cuttings can also be evaluated by pyrolysis chromatography. The making, recording, and interpreting of these tests are discussed next.

Oil Staining. Oil in cuttings is indicated by coloration called *staining*. The color and intensity of staining depends on the nature of the oil. Low-gravity oils tend to stain dark brown to black; stains from light oils can be virtually colorless. Tests with ultraviolet light and solvents should be made whether or not staining is otherwise visible. These additional tests also help distinguish brown or black oil staining from similar coloration in barren rocks.

Colors of individual cuttings or chips are observed in natural, preferably incandescent, light with the aid of a low-power (10 to 50X) binocular microscope. The use of standard color charts or photographic standards encourages consistency. The sample, as for all oil-in-cuttings tests, should be examined as soon as possible after recovery and while still wet. Distribution of the stain is described and related to interparticle, intercrystal, vug, or fracture surfaces. Estimates of the fraction of stained cuttings should ignore cavings and recirculated chips.

Mud contaminants can interfere with recognizing oil staining. Oil products used for mud additives can often be washed off with water or detergent solutions. However, some detergents can fluoresce and further interfere with recognizing staining. Pipe dope and rig grease are more easily identified in fresh, wet samples because the heat used in drying the sample can disseminate the contamination.

Because description of oil staining is not well standardized, meaningful comparisons are difficult. However, an estimate should be made of the percentage of representative cuttings that exhibit staining.

Hydrocarbon Odor. Sample descriptions should record any hydrocarbon odor in the fresh cuttings as "none," "slight," "fair," or "good." Because the odor can dissipate rapidly, immediate evaluation is best. Very small amounts of some hydrocarbons can be detected by odor under favorable conditions. However, oil or oil-product additives can mask the odors of natural hydrocarbons.

Fluorescence. The fluorescence of samples from drilling returns is useful for detecting crude oil and has been used since the earliest days of mud logging. Almost every complete mud logging operation is routinely equipped to observe the fluorescence of cuttings and mud samples. This useful, long-time, and widespread application encourages further consideration of fluorescence and its application to mud logging.

Many substances emit light after absorbing electromagnetic energy from an external source. This emission of light is called *fluorescence* if the substance stops emitting when the external source is removed, and *phosphorescence* if emission persists after the period of excitation. The fluorescence characteristics of a substance vary with its state, temperature, impurities, and chemical environment. For this review, conditions can be limited to the liquid state, room temperature, contaminants common to drilling fluids, and a crude-oil or hydrocarbon solvent environment.

Considering the absorption characteristics of a substance helps to explain its fluorescence. Absorbing electromagnetic energy disturbs the internal electron

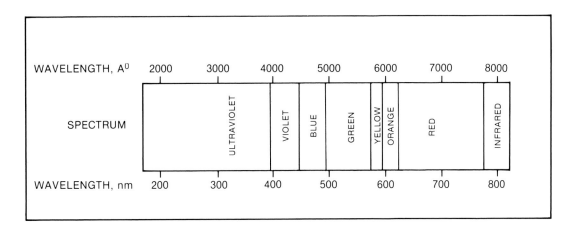

Fig. 4.25—Electromagnetic radiation spectrum (after Lynch[22]).

structure and produces an excited state that can lead to emission of light. The wavelength of the emitted light is usually longer than that which was absorbed. So compounds that absorb in the ultraviolet region (Fig. 4.25) may fluoresce in a longer-wavelength ultraviolet region or in the visible region. For example, Fig. 4.26 shows the fluorescence spectra of three compounds to illustrate emission from ultraviolet excitation that is (1) virtually limited to the ultraviolet range, (2) principally in the ultraviolet but extending into the visible range, and (3) principally in the visible range, where it will appear blue to someone with typical color vision.

Fluorescence in the visible region can be observed without special instrumentation. This is of special interest in keeping wellsite procedures simple, easy to use, and cost-effective.

Fortunately, many compounds commonly found in crude oils exhibit strong absorption in the long-wavelength (300 to 400 nm) ultraviolet region, so that typical wavelength shifts produce visible fluorescence. Table 4.4 lists the absorption/emission spectra of a number of organic compounds found in crude oils.[29] Excitation of the same compounds with shorter-wavelength ultraviolet sources (<200 nm) will produce most or all emission in the ultraviolet. Further, some important longer-wavelength absorption levels are not activated by the shorter wavelengths so do not produce fluorescence. The preferable excitation wavelength for maximum sensitivity is just below the visible region, especially when the strong absorption there by many hydrocarbons and associated compounds is considered.

Some minerals exhibit greater shifts between excitation and emission than organic liquids do, so shorter wavelength sources may be desired for visually observing mineral fluorescence.

Ultraviolet radiation (especially shorter wavelengths) can cause irritation or injury to the eye. Cobalt-nickel glass filters with transmission from 325 to 390 nm help reduce the harmful shorter wavelengths and also reduce the interfering visible contribution from the source. Hercules[30] and Radley and Grant[31] are good sources for more information on fluorescence and its applications.

All crude oils fluoresce. A crude oil could consist of only straight- or branched-chain hydrocarbons, which do

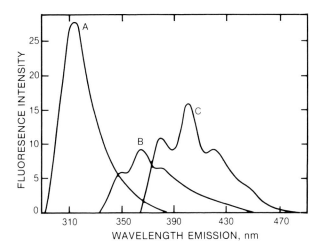

Fig. 4.26—Fluorescence spectra of three aromatic hydrocarbons: A. Fluorene—265 nm excitation; B. Phenanthrene—265 nm excitation; C. Anthracene—365 nm excitation (modified from Ref. 30).

not exhibit true fluorescence. However, most crude oils contain at least some cyclic or polycyclic hydrocarbons or asphaltenes, which do fluoresce. Such compounds are most abundant in aromatic crudes and least abundant in paraffinic ones. Thus, visible fluorescence is typically most intense in aromatic crudes. The apparent intensity varies with concentration, chemical environment, impurities, source strength, and other factors that are not standardized or rigorously controlled. Visual estimates of fluorescence intensity are only qualitative because the eye's sensitivity is not linear throughout the visible region. Regardless, very small amounts of oil can be detected with fluorescence at the wellsite.

The color of crude-oil fluorescence can be used to make rough estimates of oil gravity. Riecker[32] found that emission of the principal fluorescence wavelength increases as the API gravity decreases (Fig. 4.27). This result is consistent with the fluorescence colors of the unsubstituted aromatic compounds (Table 4.5), which fluoresce at longer wavelength as the number of rings

TABLE 4.4—FLUORESCENCE EXCITATION AND FLUORESCENCE EMISSION
SPECTRA OF MODEL COMPOUNDS (after McKay and Latham[29])

Compound	Fluorescence Excitation Spectra Wavelength (nm)								Fluorescence Emission Spectra Wavelength (nm)							
Fluorene	*268*	*275(s)*	*293*	*303*					*303*	310						
Naphthalene	269	*278*	288						*324*	338	350					
Triphenylene	*262*	277	288						*354*	364	373	381(s)	391(s)			
Chrysene	261	*271*	297	308	322				*363*	375	383	404	427			
Phenanthrene	261	278	285	*296*					348	357	*365*	385				
Picene	*287*	304	328						*377*	398	421	449				
Anthracene	*260*	312	325	341	358	377			*380*	401	424	451				
Pyrene	308	322	*337*						374	379	*384*	389	395			
Anthanthrene	260	296	*308*	384	401	407	422	430	*432*	459	494					
Perylene	*255*	370	388	410	438				*440*	466	500	540(s)				
Coronene	292	*303*	324	340					411	422	428	435	*446*	455	475	485 508
Fluoranthene	241	256	266	280	*290*	311	326	344 360	409(s)	418(s)	436	*463*				
Ovalene	314	328	*342*	399	422	448			450	462	475	482	490	*503*	509	514 539

The most intense peak in each spectrum is in italic type.
Shoulders are indicated by (s).

(and molecular weight) increases. The color of fluorescence for a complex crude oil is the cumulative luminescence of a number of compounds.

Because of the large number of possible compounds in oils, those oils with different compositions but the same gravity can have different composite luminescences and colors of fluorescence. Regardless, some qualitative indications of gravity can be interpreted from fluorescence color. One guide is presented in Table 4.6. However, for the reasons just considered, a better guide might be experience in the locality.

Changes in the intensity of fluorescence can sometimes indicate saturation changes. An oil/water transition may display a patchy and progressively duller fluorescence with increasing water saturation (Fig. 4.28). Careful examination of fluorescence distribution can reveal saturation variations between vuggy, fractured, and intergranular/intercrystal pore systems. In general, a gas-saturated interval will fluoresce much less than an oil-saturated interval.

Fluorescence examination with the proper equipment is simple and rapid (Fig. 4.29). Cuttings should be examined as soon as possible after collection and before drying. Special attention should be given to chips previously identified as oil-stained. A solvent-cut test is routinely performed to confirm that any fluorescence observed is caused by hydrocarbons. After observation and testing of the color of fluorescence, its intensity and distribution are recorded with standardized description criteria and nomenclature.

Some minerals and mud additives fluoresce in the visible region and may be misinterpreted as an oil show. Gleason[33] compiled the fluorescence characteristics of minerals. A solvent-cut test helps to distinguish between hydrocarbons, which dissolve, and minerals, which do not. A systematic fluorescence examination of mud additives as they are introduced is good practice. Hydrocarbon products that fluoresce can obscure the difference between legitimate shows and contamination if such products are added to the drilling mud.

Some drilling-fluid additives, particularly in oil-base muds, suppress or even eliminate the fluorescence of entrained hydrocarbons. These additives are anilines, resorcinol, oxygen, the halogens, polyhydroxy phenols,

and amines. The quenching mechanism is often an oxidation-reduction reaction between the excited molecule and the suppressant followed by a regeneration of the original substance.

Fluorescence in cuttings, with appropriate indications from solvent-cut tests, is strong evidence that a prospective interval has been drilled. The method is also applicable for evaluating sidewall or conventional cores. Fig. 4.30, comparing the natural- and ultraviolet-light photos of an oil-stained core, helps illustrate just how effective fluorescence can be for defining the presence and distribution of oil saturation in reservoir rocks.

Cut. An important test that verifies the presence of oil detected by staining and fluorescence involves immersing the sample in a hydrocarbon solvent and observing the color and fluorescence of the resulting solution, called a *cut.* The presence of oil is revealed by the color and fluorescence of the cut.

The color of a cut depends on the oil's characteristics. Low-gravity oils produce dark-colored cuts; high-gravity oils produce amber or straw-colored cuts. A fluorescing cut verifies the presence of oil. Dilute solutions of some hydrocarbons in solvents may exhibit intense fluorescence in the blue region at one concentration but weaker fluorescence in a different region at a lower concentration. The rate of efflorescence of oil from low-permeability chips into the solvent can be accelerated by pulverizing them.

Cut fluorescence can detect very small amounts of crude oil by a simple procedure. A few chips are leached in a clean glass or porcelain dish or nonfluorescent porcelain spot plate. The solvent is then allowed to evaporate and the residue is examined for fluorescence under ultraviolet light.

A solvent to be used for cut tests should effectively dissolve hydrocarbons and be colorless, nonflammable, and nonfluorescent. Chlorothene (1,1,1-trichloroethane) satisfies these requirements and is less toxic than carbon tetrachloride and benzene. Use of acetone or ether as solvents requires more careful interpretation because they also readily dissolve organic compounds other than hydrocarbons. Regular checks of the fluorescence of the

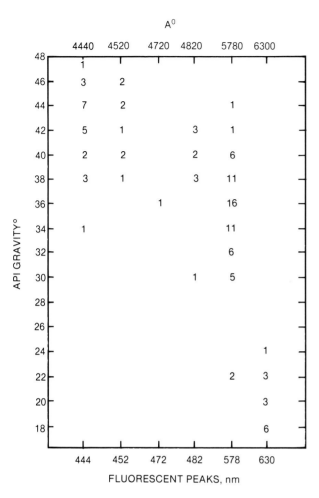

Fig. 4.27—Relation of API gravity to fluorescence peak position for 115 hydrocarbon samples (after Riecker[32]).

TABLE 4.5—EFFECT OF INCREASED COMPLEXITY ON FLUORESCENCE COLORS OF AROMATIC COMPOUNDS

	Number of Rings	Molecular Weight	Fluorescence[30]
Benzene	1	78.11	ultraviolet
Naphthalene	2	128.16	ultraviolet
Anthracene	3	178.22	blue
Pentacene	5	278.33	red

TABLE 4.6—RELATION OF API GRAVITY AND FLUORESCENCE COLORS OF CRUDE OILS

Gravity (°API)	Fluorescence Color
Below 15	brown
15 to 25	orange
25 to 35	yellow to cream
35 to 45	white
Over 45	blue-white to violet

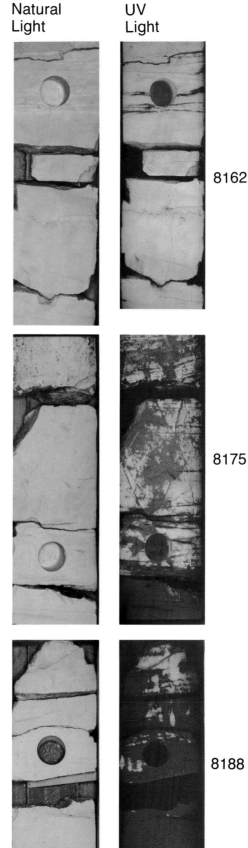

Fig. 4.28—Natural and ultraviolet photographs of slabbed core from an oil/water transition zone.

Fig. 4.29—Equipment needed to examine fluorescence and solvent cut of mud or cuttings samples.

solvent stock is good practice, as contamination will make every test seem positive.

Good ventilation is required when hydrocarbon solvents are used.

Descriptions of odor, staining, fluorescence, and cuts are necessarily qualitative. Good practice requires a consistent method of testing and an organized system of recording visual observations. The system proposed by Wyman and Castano[28] (Table 4.7) provides consistent test procedures and standardized nomenclature.

Acid Test. A test for detecting stain in carbonate or calcareous sandstone is performed by immersing the cuttings in dilute (15%) HCl. The bubbles that usually form will float the chip if it is oil-stained, but an unstained chip will not float.

Pyrolysis. Another method of detecting oil in cuttings is to pyrolyze the samples as discussed by Clementz *et al.*[34]

Hot Water Test. Swanson[35] recommends immersing unwashed cuttings in water 75°C or hotter. This can release oil to float as a film on the surface, detectable with ultraviolet light. An estimate of the amount of oil should be recorded.

Iridescence. Iridescence (lustrous, changing colors) on wet cuttings without apparent staining can indicate the presence of light oil or condensate.

4.3.4 Factors Influencing the Amount of Hydrocarbons in Drilling Returns

The significance of a show depends on the factors that influence the amounts of oil and gas in the drilling returns. Understanding these factors indicates why quantitative interpretation of hydrocarbon log data is beyond present capabilities. However, awareness of the nature and sensitivity of these factors will assist in formulating useful criteria for interpretation. These criteria help answer such questions as the following.

1. Why is correlation so poor between formation productivity and amount of oil and gas in the mud?

2. When can a small gas-in-mud increase be considered an "excellent" show?

3. When can a large gas-in-mud increase be considered a "poor" show?

4. What circumstances might result in little to no gas-in-mud indications after a hydrocarbon-saturated interval is drilled?

5. How effective are attempts to compare, classify, or rank shows through oil-in-mud or gas-in-mud data alone?

To answer these questions one needs to consider the cumulative effects of nearly twenty formation properties, drilling conditions, and sample collection/measurement practices.

Eqs. 4.5 and 4.6 relate the formation properties and drilling conditions that influence oil and gas concentrations in the drilling returns from an oil-saturated interval.

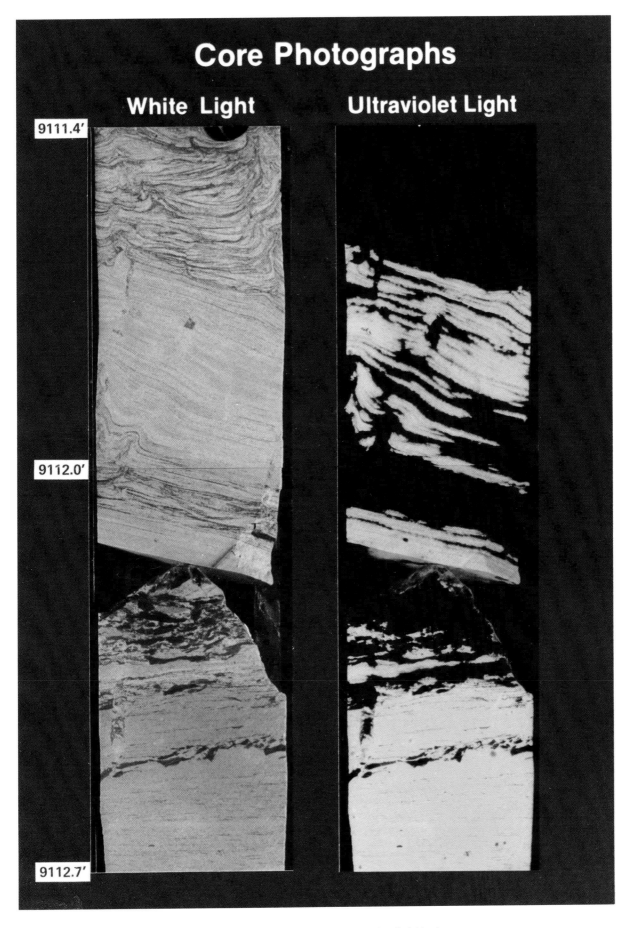

Fig. 4.30—Natural and ultraviolet photographs of slabbed core.

TABLE 4.7—LEGEND FOR OIL SHOWS (after Wyman and Castano[28])

Show Number	Oil Stain (%)	Hydrocarbon Odor	Sample Oil Fluorescence			Trichloroethane Cut		Show Number Average	Show Symbol
			%	Intensity	Color	Color of Cut	Cut Fluorescence		
0	none	none	none	none	none	none	none	0 to 0.5	X
1	>0 to 40	slight	0 to 50	weak	brown (B), orange-brown (OB), brown-gold (BG)	straw	slight (transparent)	0.5 to 1.5 0.5 to 1.5 stain and/or fluorescence over 85%	• X • X̲
2	40 to 85	fair	50 to 90	fair	orange (O), gold (G), yellow-orange (YO), yellow (Y)	light amber	medium (slightly translucent)	1.5 to 2.5	•
3	85 to 100	good	90 to 100	strong	white-yellow (WY), green-yellow (Gn Y), yellow-white (YW), blue-white (Bl W)	dark amber, dark brown	strong (opaque)	2.5 to 3	••

$$C_o = \left(\frac{\pi d_h^2 \cdot h_o}{4 t_h \cdot q_m} \right) \left(\frac{S_o \cdot \phi}{B_o} \right) (1 - F_1)(1 - S_{or})(1 - F_2).$$

$$\dots\dots\dots\dots\dots (4.5)$$

$$C_g = \left(\frac{\pi d_h^2 \cdot h_o}{4 t_h \cdot q_m} \right) \left(\frac{S_o \cdot R \cdot \phi}{B_o} \right) (1 - F_1)$$

$$\cdot (1 - S_{gr})(1 - F_3). \dots\dots\dots\dots (4.6)$$

Or, after a gas-saturated interval is drilled and the returns are circulated to the surface, by Eq. 4.7:

$$C_g = \left(\frac{\pi d_h^2 \cdot h_g}{4 t_h \cdot q_m} \right) \left(S_g \cdot \phi \cdot \frac{p_R \cdot z_s \cdot T_s}{p_s \cdot z_R \cdot T_R} \right) (1 - F_1)$$

$$\cdot (1 - S_{gr})(1 - F_3).$$

$$\dots\dots\dots\dots\dots (4.7)$$

Symbols and units are described in Table 4.8. Calculations can be made with any consistent system of units. These relationships apply to liberated hydrocarbons and ignore any oil or gas coming from previously penetrated intervals.

It is instructive to evaluate the factors in Eqs. 4.5 through 4.7 by calculating examples for representative conditions. This will indicate how much oil and/or gas enters the mud and the significance of relative show sizes.

Formation Oil and Gas Content

The amount of oil and gas available to enter the drilling mud from a hydrocarbon-saturated interval is related to the borehole diameter, d_h, the distance traversed in the interval, h, the porosity, ϕ, and the fraction of the pore volume containing hydrocarbons, S.

Fig. 4.31 shows the quantity of oil in a borehole cylinder 1 ft long for three representative combinations of porosity and saturation. The quantities of oil contained in such a cylinder are usually much less than a gallon per foot. Combinations of large holes, high porosity, and low water saturation yield larger amounts of oil or gas than do small holes with low porosity and high water saturation, if all other factors are constant. Of course, no show is expected when the porosity or hydrocarbon saturation is zero.

Flushing

Drilling fluids tend to displace (or *flush*) formation fluids ahead of the bit. The amount of formation fluid displaced may vary from none to, occasionally, all. Flushing tendencies are greater under the following conditions.

1. The pressure in the borehole is much greater than that in the formation (overbalance) (see Fig. 4.32).
2. The viscosity of the mud filtrate is similar to that of the formation fluid (a mobility ratio close to unity).
3. Formation pore sizes are large (high permeability).
4. Vertical permeability is high (no interlayers).
5. The fluid loss of the mud is high under dynamic conditions (native muds).
6. The drilling bit focuses fluid streams on the formation face (jet bits).
7. Drilling rates are slow.

These conditions are discussed more fully in Sec. 3.1.3.

The influence of flushing is not easily estimated. Gas or oil content can be completely flushed out by whole-mud invasion in fractured or vuggy porosity. Thus, flushing may explain the absence of oil or gas shows after a hydrocarbon-saturated interval is penetrated, as shown by the example in Fig. 4.33, although the low hydrocarbon concentration is partly caused by the decline in the ratio of formation liberated per foot of penetration while coring. Flushing must be considered when oil-in-mud or gas-in-mud data are interpreted, especially under conditions favoring drilling-fluid invasion.

**TABLE 4.8—DEFINITION OF QUANTITATIVE FACTORS THAT INFLUENCE
THE CONCENTRATIONS OF GAS AND OIL IN A DRILLING
FLUID AFTER A SATURATED INTERVAL IS DRILLED**

Symbol	Definition	Units	Comments
C	Hydrocarbon concentration in mud	volume/volume	
d_h	Borehole diameter	length	typically same as bit size
t_h	Drilling time	time	time to drill interval h
q_m	Drilling-fluid circulation	volume/time	
h	Length of well in saturated interval	length	may not be true interval thickness
S	Hydrocarbon saturation	fraction	
ϕ	Porosity	fraction	
B	Formation volume factor	fraction	
R	Gas/oil ratio	volume/volume	at standard conditions
F_1	Flushing factor	fraction	0 = no flushing 1 = total flushing
p	Pressure	force/length²	
z	Compressibility factor		
T	Temperature	degrees	
S_{or}	Oil saturation retained in cuttings at standard conditions	fraction	0 = none retained 1 = all retained
S_{gr}	Gas saturation retained in cuttings at standard conditions	fraction	0 = none retained 1 = all retained
F_2, F_3	Fraction of gas or oil lost from mud in return line	fraction	0 = no loss 1 = total loss
o	Oil		
g	Gas		
R	Reservoir		
s	Surface		
ℓ	Length drilled		
m	Mud		

Mud Volume

The circulating drilling fluid dilutes any liberated hydrocarbons. The dilution factor for a given hydrocarbon volume is determined by the rate of circulation, q_m, and the drilling time, t_h. Typical drilling and circulation rates can result in several hundred to several thousand gallons of mud being mixed with each foot of formation contents (including a fraction of a gallon of oil) drilled. Fig. 4.34 shows the effect of mud flow rate on the bottomhole concentrations of oil and gas. Rates of circulation and drilling can be monitored to account for variations in the hydrocarbon concentrations caused by varying mud volume. Otherwise, fluctuations in the gas or oil content could be caused by changes in drilling or circulation rates rather than formation hydrocarbon content. For example, Fig. 4.35 shows the gas detector responses for different drilling rates in the same formation. Slow drilling tends to reduce the size of a show compared with faster drilling.

Pressure-Volume-Temperature

Oil and gas enter the drilling returns at bottomhole pressure and temperature but are detected and analyzed at surface conditions. The volumetric expansion or shrinkage of the oil and particularly of the gas between bottomhole and surface conditions needs to be considered very carefully. These effects are potentially large compared with those from most other factors influencing the amount of gas in the drilling returns.

A major factor in determining the size of a show is the gas dissolved in the oil. At surface conditions the gas may occupy many times its downhole volume.

The free-gas saturation of a formation is another major factor determining the size of a show. The volume of gas

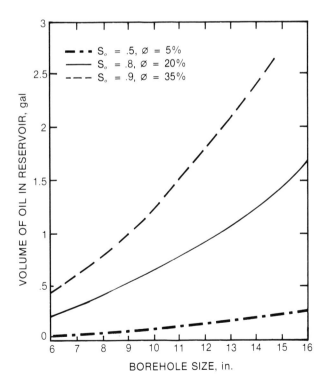

Fig. 4.31—Quantities of oil typically found in a 1-ft borehole cylinder when a hydrocarbon-saturated interval is drilled.

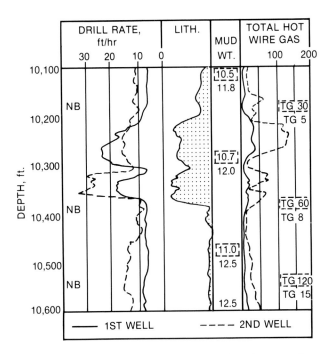

Fig. 4.32—Comparison of hydrocarbon logs from nearby wells drilled with different mud weights (modified from McClure[36]).

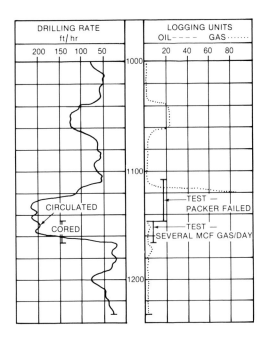

Fig. 4.33—Example mud log illustrating flushing (after Pixler[37]).

observed at the surface after drilling 1 ft of formation containing 0.64 gal of gas-saturated pore volume at various depths is shown in Fig. 4.36. All other formation and drilling factors remaining constant, gas-in-mud shows increase with:

1. gas saturation in the reservoir (minimum oil and water saturations),
2. reservoir pressure (depth),
3. gas compressibility (low molecular weight), and
4. surface temperature (ambient and drilling fluid temperatures).

A warning! Many blowouts can be related to a misunderstanding of show magnitudes from shallow gas reservoirs. Gas at shallow depths appears at the surface in concentrations approximating actual formation volumes since little or no expansion occurs. "Small" shows during shallow drilling can represent the same gas volume as "large" shows from deeper depths. The failure to appreciate the significance of a "small" show at shallow depths can lead to dangerous drilling practices. Another concern is the reduced mud weight at shallow depths from gas cutting as a result of deeper liberated gas. The reduced mud weight can allow inflow of shallow gas. Goldsmith[38] discusses effects of gas on mud weight at shallow depths.

Solution gas in water can also cause a significant gas-in-mud indication at the surface. The amount of gas in water is a function of pressure, temperature, water salinity, and gas composition. Fig. 4.37 shows the possible gas volumes observed at the surface for representative reservoir conditions. The recorded gas-in-mud can be larger from a gas-saturated water reservoir than from an equivalent thickness saturated with oil containing little gas.

Retained Oil Saturation

Some oil and gas will remain in the pores of the cuttings after they reach the surface, reducing the hydrocarbons sensed by the oil-in-mud or gas-in-mud detectors. Quantitative evaluation of these retained hydrocarbons is not usually available. Estimates can be based on representative values for residual-oil saturation after gas expansion and displacement, the primary cause of expulsion. This consideration is more important when oil-in-mud data are evaluated than when gas-in-mud data are interpreted.

Surface Losses

An unknown amount of gas is lost as the mud moves through the flow line. The losses can be significant under conditions shown in Fig. 4.38.

The effectiveness of the gas trap is also a major uncertainty in evaluating gas-in-mud concentration. The trap may extract at best only 25 to 75% of the gas, and at times the trap efficiency may approach zero. Gases with low molecular weights (e.g., methane) are easier to extract than higher-weight gases (e.g., butane).

Measurement and Recording Practices

Methods used to report gas-in-mud readings can affect the interpreting of shows. For instance, the maximum gas-in-mud reading observed during drilling is often used for the entire interval. The example shown by Fig. 4.39 illustrates the possibility that the relative magnitudes of shows can be lost in the recording procedure.

The response of the gas-in-mud detector is a factor in evaluating shows. Frequent calibration of the detector response to the gas concentration is desirable.

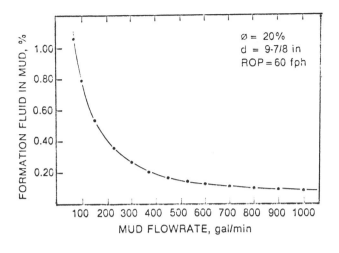

Fig. 4.34—Effect of mud flow rate on bottomhole oil/gas concentration (after Exlog[20]).

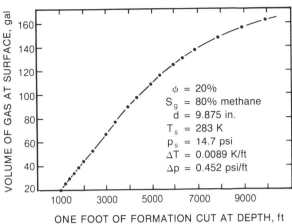

Fig. 4.36—Effect of depth on the amount of gas in the mud (after Exlog[20]).

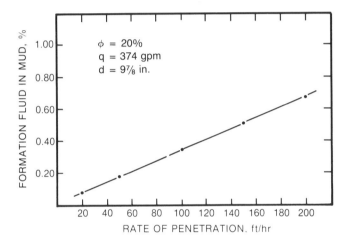

Fig. 4.35—Effect of penetration rate on show magnitude (after Exlog[20]).

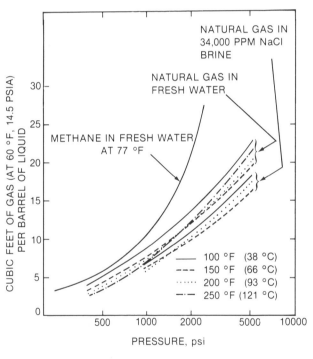

Fig. 4.37—Effect of temperature, pressure, and salinity on the solubility of gas in water (after Exlog[20]).

4.3.5 Comments

Oil and gas in the drilling returns can be related to formation properties and drilling conditions. The small amounts of hydrocarbons entering the mud mix with large quantities of circulating drilling fluid. The size of a show often depends on drilling and sampling factors unrelated to the amount of oil or gas in the reservoir. Consideration of the individual factors and calculated representative values from Eqs. 4.5 through 4.7 indicate the following.

1. The amount of gas in mud can be misleading when the quality of a reservoir is evaluated. A formation that is highly prospective (good saturation, porosity, and thickness) will yield relatively little gas in mud if the gas/oil ratio is low. A less prospective formation with a high gas/oil ratio can produce large gas-in-mud indications. A formation drilled very slowly at a high mud circulation rate can yield a smaller gas-in-mud indication than a poorer interval drilled rapidly.

2. Complete flushing results in no oil or gas in the mud. Mud logging is least effective in deep vuggy or fractured reservoirs saturated with oil but little gas.

3. The uncertainties in the evaluation of flushing, retained saturations, and losses in the return line reduce the possibility of successfully using numerical classification or Eqs. 4.5 through 4.7 to quantify reservoir saturation.

One view, shared by the authors, is that the real value of monitoring hydrocarbons in mud is simply to indicate the presence and extent of a prospective interval. Reservoir quality and oil and gas volumes are better defined by procedures such as sample examination, coring, testing, and wireline logging. Another view is that the value is to

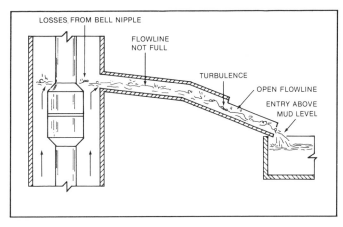

Fig. 4.38—Schematic flowline (after Exlog[20]).

define the thickness and character of the reservoir as well as the composition of the contained hydrocarbons. This definition is aided by a comparison of the configuration of the liberated gas curve to a wireline porosity log.

4.4 Logging Lithology

Lithologic analysis is an important part of mud logging. The significance of a show cannot be evaluated without knowledge of the rock type and porosity; an optimal drilling program requires information about the formation's physical properties, and the detection of abnormal pressures is aided by cuttings analysis—especially for properties reflecting the state of compaction and diagenesis. Lithologic information is useful for well-to-well correlation. To meet these needs, cuttings are

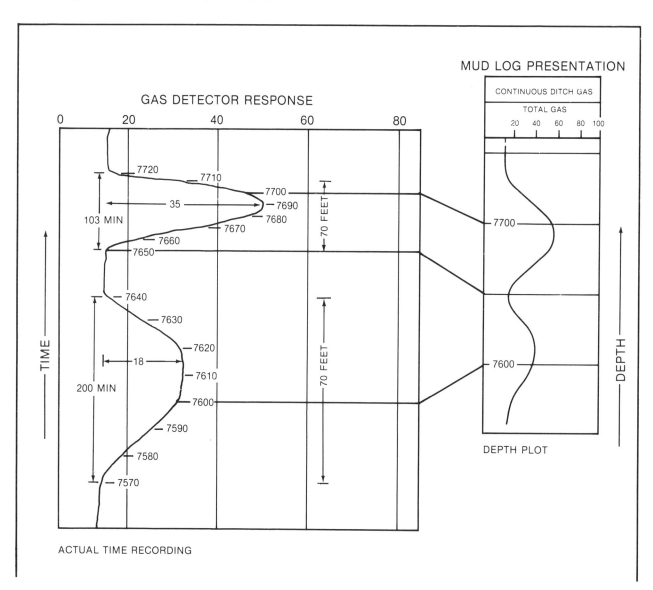

Magnitude of gas-detector response is proportional to area under the time recording. Area of 7,690-ft peak is about 350 units. Area under 7,610-ft peak is about 440 units, hence the larger increase.

Fig. 4.39—Effect of data recording and presentation method on magnitude of reported gas in mud (modified from Exlog[20]).

recovered and examined, and their properties are described. The descriptions are recorded on the mud log, where they are available for interpreting shows, drilling changes, and pressure indications.

4.4.1 Recovering Samples of Cuttings

The importance of obtaining good cuttings samples cannot be overemphasized. Good samples are representative of the interval being drilled and are properly lagged. Representiveness and lag are affected by how the cuttings are transported to the surface and collected for analysis.

Transport Factors

Ideally, cuttings would be recovered in the same order and composition as they were cut. Actually they are not, because the various particles travel at different velocities in the annulus and reach the surface at different times. The different arrival times (or *spread*) of particles is minimized by drilling with muds that have high density and minimum gel strength above the threshold required to keep the cuttings in suspension. Rotating the drillpipe while returns are circulated seems to minimize spread.

Spread is dependent on particle shape, size, and density. Exlog[39] is a good source of more information about cuttings transport in the annulus.

Cuttings tend to become stratified in the flowline. Large sizes are likely to be cavings; small sizes are probably recirculated material; thus, proper location of a diversion line (Fig. 4.40) is important if representative samples are to be obtained.

Collection Factors

Cuttings are collected from the shale shaker screen or a catching site at the foot of the screen, the desilter, and the desander.

Sampling from a shale shaker screen is not always satisfactory. When drilling is slow, the cuttings on the screen represent only a limited drilling interval, perhaps a few inches. To obtain samples from a several-foot interval, the recommended practice is to use a ''board'' (Fig. 4.6) at the base of the shale shaker screen, which allows cuttings to accumulate as the interval is drilled. Another way is to make frequent collections off the screen and combine them into a desired sample interval.

Samples are always taken from the desilter and desander, when they are used. The quantity and appearance of those solids are compared with the ones from the shale shaker. When the quantities of solids emerging from the desilter or desander are larger than those from the shale shaker, disaggregated grains are passing through the shaker screen. When this occurs, a finer-mesh screen should be used. Chart 4.4 relates shaker screen mesh and particle sizes.

Sluice boxes are effective sample-collection devices, providing composite samples and trapping disaggregated grains or small particles that pass through some shaker screens. A mechanical cuttings separator is described by Kennedy.[40]

Sampling Frequency

Sampling intervals are determined by drilling times, evaluation objectives, and presence of shows. When

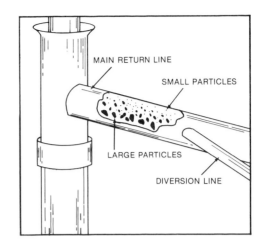

Fig. 4.40—Diversion line for sampling mud and cuttings.

sampling is from the shaker screen, one sample should be collected at least every 15 minutes. When drilling is slower than 25 to 50 ft/hr, a sample should be taken from the base of the shaker or sluice box after a 2-, 5-, or 10-ft interval is drilled unless the sample accumulation exceeds the capacity of the board or box. Samples should be collected after each gas-in-mud change or drilling break.

4.4.2 Preparing Cuttings Samples for Description

Cuttings samples are washed and sieved to remove mud and cavings before lithologic analysis.

Washing

Samples are washed lightly with water to remove drilling mud unless clay components are affected. Overwashing removes clay from the interstices of some sandstones, creating false porosity.

Sieving

The samples can be sieved to remove >5-mm fragments, which are assumed to be cavings.

Periodically, the finer fraction of the returns from the shaker should be sieved through a 170-mesh screen. Both fractions are examined and compared with material collected from the desilter and desander. This helps establish the quantity of solids in the sample and detects unanticipated, unconsolidated fine-grained material.

Bagging

Cuttings for off-site recipients are put in cloth sacks labeled with waterproof markings. Geochemical and palynological samples may require special handling, such as the amount of washing, treating with bactericide, or sealing in airtight packages. It is important that any such requirements be communicated to the logging personnel before logging starts.

4.4.3 Examining Cuttings

Prepared cuttings samples should be examined with a low-power (10 to 50X) binocular microscope. This helps identify cavings, drilling mud, lost-circulation material, cement, recirculated cuttings, and other solids not from the interval being drilled.

Drilling Mud

Drilling mud found in some cuttings samples can be confused with clay or gypsum from the formations. However, drilling mud is not soluble in hot HCl, which will dissolve gypsum. Also, drilling-mud lumps are usually more unstable in water than are most rock fragments. Rock fragments may have internal layering or coloring, while drilling-mud lumps do not. Good sample preparation will usually remove most mud contamination.

Cavings

Cavings are rock fragments that fall from the wall of the hole. The amount of cavings may be more abundant after trips, tests, coring, or a change in mud systems. Large quantities of cavings indicate unstable hole conditions, usually caused by underbalanced drilling or by chemical interaction between the mud and the formation.

Lost-Circulation Material

Mud treated to control circulation problems can contain walnut shells, plant fibers, feathers, cellophane, mica flakes, perlite, or other materials. These can be confused with formation materials. The best way to avoid such confusion is to know what has been put into the mud.

Recirculated Cuttings

Previously drilled rock fragments can recirculate and contaminate samples. According to Goldsmith and Hare,[41] typical muds contain more dispersed formation solids than commonly realized. Recirculated fragments tend to be small and may have an abraded appearance. A set of previous samples should be used for reference to recognize those that are being recirculated. A successful solids-control program may require combinations of mechanical removal and mud dilution or replacement.

Cement

Cement fragments, most often found in the returns after setting casing, are easily mistaken for sandy limestone or calcareous siltstone. Cement tends to discolor in HCl, may have fine black flecks (a "salt and pepper" appearance), and can sometimes be removed with a magnet.

Other

Other mud contaminants include metal fragments from the drillstring, solids added to the mud, powdered rock dust, and pipe dope. Some fine-grain, soft rocks such as shales and chalks, heated and fused by diamond bit drilling, become dark-colored material with smooth, slightly curved surfaces.

Fresh Cuttings

After cavings, contamination, mud solids, and recirculated contents have been identified, the remaining chips are considered fresh cuttings.

There are two common methods of examining and logging samples after eliminating obvious cavings and contamination: (1) the entire sample contents are described and each lithology is plotted as a percentage of the total

contents or (2) only those cuttings interpreted to be representative are described and plotted. The interpretive method works best when sample quality is above average, the examiner is well-trained, logging-while-drilling or wireline log data are available, and the stratigraphic sequence is relatively well known. Actually, both logs are desired and have their place. For instance, cuttings-gas data are qualified by a litho-percent sample log but not by an interpretive log.

The heading of many mud logs has a notation for designating whether the interpretive or percentage method has been used.

4.4.4 Describing Lithology

Lithologic descriptions are prepared in differing amounts of detail. For wellsite purposes the amount of detail is determined by what is needed to determine structural position, drillability, reservoir quality, and rock properties indicative of abnormal pressure. The more-detailed descriptions needed to define the sediment source, transport media, and depositional environment are better prepared at offsite locations, as these require more time, equipment, and specialized expertise. Accordingly, this discussion will focus on the type of lithologic description needed at the wellsite.

A lithologic log useful for mud logging contains descriptions or characterizations of the rock such as:

1. aggregate mass—including color, induration, and (sometimes) density, cation-exchange capacity, and other properties,

2. coarse fraction—especially grain size, shape, sorting, composition, and proportion in the aggregate,

3. fine fraction—such as the cement or matrix color, content, and abundance, and

4. void space—particularly the type, distribution, and amount of porosity.

The style and techniques for describing lithology are considered next.

Composition

Sedimentary rocks are composed of particles from pre-existing rocks, crystals from chemical precipitates or biologic remains, and carbonaceous materials from organic sources. The compositions of the principal constituents are used for defining rock types, predicting reservoir characteristics, and evaluating wireline log responses. This justifies the effort to identify cuttings composition while drilling. However, wellsite analytical facilities are limited to low-power microscopy and simple tests. Offsite facilities, in contrast, can consist of high-resolution electron microscopy with associated elemental spectroscopy, thin section petrography, X-ray diffraction and fluorescence, and sophisticated chemical analysis. Fortunately, the minerals or other materials that constitute the major fraction of a sedimentary rock's coarse-grain components can be identified at the wellsite. Identifying the ultrafine-grain constituents in the field is questionable at best, but sometimes important enough to justify special efforts.

The following criteria are used at the wellsite to identify some common rock-forming minerals.

Quartz is the predominant constituent of sandstones, siltstones, and cherts and may be abundant in shales, limestones, and dolomites. It occurs as particles or grains derived from pre-existing rocks, as overgrowths from chemical precipitation during burial, as crystal mosaics from burial alteration of silica-secreting organisms, and as hydrothermal deposits.

Quartz is commonly white or colorless, but may be pink, red, brown, or black, and is not soluble in HCl. It may have a specular appearance if overgrowths are present. If not, its surface may appear pitted or frosted.

Feldspars, present in many sandstones, are the significant constituents of sediments derived from freshly weathered igneous sources.

Feldspars are colorless, gray, white, or pink. They usually have a more blocky shape than quartz and may be partly resorbed. Overgrowths occur. Staining tests are diagnostic, but require HF acid and are too time-consuming for ordinary mud logging practice.

Kaolinite, *illite*, *montmorillonite*, and *chlorite* clay minerals are common in shales and present in some sandstones, limestones, and dolomite rocks.

Wellsite identification of clay minerals is difficult because of their ultrafine grain size and complex associations. Kaolinite is typically white and chlorite is green. Some tentative mineral identifications may be possible if their behaviors in water are observed and their cation-exchange capacities are measured. Montmorillonite tends to swell and disaggregate in water and has a higher cation-exchange capacity than illite, kaolinite, or chlorite. The cation-exchange capacity may help detect a change from montmorillonite to illite, which sometimes is correlated with a change from normal to supernormal pressure. A wellsite method for evaluating clay content is discussed by Exlog[15].

Calcite, *dolomite*, and *siderite* are abundant in many sedimentary basins as the principal constituents of limestones and dolomite rocks*, and as a cementing material in sandstones, siltstones, and shales.

Calcite and dolomite are usually colorless or white, but limestones and dolomite rocks may be white, yellow, gray, reddish, or black, depending on impurities. Calcite and dolomite tend to occur as well-formed crystals and are more easily scratched than quartz. Effervescence in dilute HCl is diagnostic: calcite reacts instantly and vigorously; dolomite reacts slowly. Effervescence in HCl is diagnostic for identifying either calcite or dolomite alone, but not always for evaluating mixtures of both. For mixtures, versenate analysis[42] or calcimetry[43] can be used to determine proportions.

Anhydrite occurs in beds, inclusions, or cements. It is commonly colorless or tinted red. The occasional dark-colored anhydrite can be distinguished from shale by testing with HCl. Anhydrite is slowly soluble in hot HCl, which will not dissolve most clay minerals.

Good anhydrite cuttings are not recovered with some muds and drilling practices. When this happens, previously drilled material may be more abundant than usual, as changes in mud chemistry (caused by the anhydrite) affect the borehole wall. This can disturb pockets of mud containing old cuttings.

Halite and *sylvite* salts are present in beds, intrusive domes, and cements. These minerals are identified by

solubility in water, taste, and their colorless or white appearance (although impurities produce other colors). Cuttings may show cubic casts where salt has been dissolved.

Salt sections are penetrated rapidly and uniformly unless hole problems are encountered. While salt sections are being drilled, cuttings are sparse or missing unless chloride-saturated muds are used. Monitoring chloride content of the mud helps in recognizing salt penetration.

Opal is present in rocks formed from the remains of diatoms and sponge spicules. Diatomites have a very high porosity, low bulk density, and poor permeability. A dried sample will float on water.

Kerogen, *sapropel*, *solid petroleum*, and *low-viscosity bitumens* are significant constituents of some rocks such as coals, oil shales, and tar sands. Dark color and streaks, combustion in a common flame, and dissolution in petroleum solvents help identify carbonaceous materials.

Phosphatic minerals are common in certain areas, especially in organic-rich rocks. Phosphorites are often dark-green to black, and earthy in appearance. Apatite, commonly green, is a constituent of many phosphorites.

Mica, *glauconite*, *pyrite*, *garnet*, *magnetite*, and *other minerals* occur in minor or *accessory* quantities in sedimentary rocks. Identification aids correlation or helps explain an anomalous log response.

Lithic fragments are pre-existing, multigrained rock particles that were deposited without being broken down into monomineralogic grains. Their presence influences rock classification and therefore should be described.

Color

A rock's color is a combination of visual responses from the grains and matrix or cement. It is affected by staining or coating, as well as by the size of the reflecting particles.

The color of sediments is ordinarily dominated by the siliceous, calcareous, ferruginous, and carbonaceous contents. Yellow, red, and brown colors often derive from limonite or hematite; dark-gray or black, from carbonaceous materials or iron sulfide minerals; and green, from glauconite, chlorite, or epidote.

Colors are best described from wet samples under low magnification and constant illumination from sample to sample. A general description such as "medium brown" or "light gray" is usually adequate; a color chart[44] can be used for more precise designations.

Color distribution is recorded as "uniform," "mottled," "banded," "spotted," or "variegated."

Color can be altered by overheating the samples, oxidation during storage, and by staining from mud or metal contamination.

Color descriptions are often useful in identifying formation boundaries, cavings, and oil staining as well as in interpreting depositional environments.

Texture

Texture is the size, shape, sorting, and arrangement of the particles in a rock.

Grain size is used to classify rock types and to evaluate reservoir quality. To estimate size, Swanson recommends a mounted set of sieved grains or photographs of

---

*The unfortunate but pervasive use of "dolomite" for both mineral and rock names can be confusing. In this discussion, *dolomite* will refer to the mineral and *dolomite rock* to the rock.

TABLE 4.9—
PERMEABILITY ESTIMATES
(md)

>1,000	excellent
100 to 1000	very good
10 to 100	good
1 to 10	fair
<1	tight

these, called comparators. These are available in Appendix III of the AAPG *Sample Examination Manual.*[35]

Grain shape (sphericity and roundness) should be described according to the criteria in Charts 2.4 and 2.5.

When data on grain size distribution are required, the following classification can be used.

Good: 90% of grains are in two class sizes.

Fair: 90% of grains are in three to four class sizes.

Poor: 90% of grains are in five class sizes.

Texture is discussed in more detail in Chap. 2, Sec. 2.1.

Cement or Matrix

Cement is chemically precipitated matter that binds grains together to form a rigid mass. The most common cements are quartz, calcite, dolomite, and clays.

Matrix refers to the fine-grain material that fills the interstices between grains. In siliciclastic rocks this is usually quartz and clay minerals; in calciclastic rocks, carbonate minerals.

The cement or matrix components should be described by color, kind, distribution, and estimated amount.

Porosity

Accurate evaluation of porosity is important in determining whether an interval is prospective. Visual analysis can be supplemented with small-sample measurements made with a microporosimeter or nuclear magnetic resonance instrument.

Porosities are typically described as poor, fair, or good. The porosity ranges for these terms depend on the rock type.

A description of the pore system is useful for differentiating between interparticle, intercrystal, vuggy, and fracture porosities.

Classification of porosities in carbonate rocks can aid in describing and interpreting pore systems. The carbonate classification systems proposed by Choquette and Pray[45] and Archie[46] are discussed in Chap. 2.

Permeability

Permeability is discussed in Sec. 2.2.3. Estimates from cuttings descriptions are at best qualitative. Permeability estimates are described in Table 4.9. Estimates of permeabilities can be obtained from nuclear magnetic resonance measurements.

Density

Shale density is an indicator of the compaction state, which sometimes signals a change from normal to supernormal pressure. A reversal of the normal increase in shale density with depth may indicate abnormal pressure. Any variation from a consistent trend should stimulate the watching of other pressure indicators.

Several methods of measuring cuttings density are discussed by Exlog.[15] They comment on sources of uncertainty—especially possible alteration of the cuttings from contact with the mud. Also, the presence of calcite or pyrite in shales affects their densities and may mask changes caused by compaction.

Other

Factors usually not defined in wellsite descriptions of cuttings include sedimentary structures, fossil content, and precipitation sequences of diagenetic minerals. Accessory minerals should be noted if readily identifiable. Otherwise, the time would be better spent catching and preparing good samples.

4.4.5 Classifying and Naming Rock Types

A simple nomenclature is recommended because it encourages uniformity, aids communication, and takes less time. These objectives are satisfied by Swanson's[35] organization of rock types into siliciclastic, carbonate, and miscellaneous groups, with subdivisions according to composition and texture.

Siliciclastic

Siliciclastic rocks, composed of transported quartz, clay minerals, feldspars, and lithic fragments, are classified and named by grain size and state of lithification. Table 4.10 gives rock type names suitable for mud logging purposes.

Subdivision or classification of siliciclastic rock types is based on composition. Fig. 4.41 contains a classification system for sands and sandstone. Siltstone and shale cannot be classified with a low-power microscope.

The nomenclature of clastic rocks is discussed in more detail in Sec. 2.1.1.

Carbonates

Carbonate rock types are composed of crystals, particles, and/or shell fragments, deposited as detritus or precipitates. The types are defined by mineral composition. Those composed of more than 50% calcite are called limestone, and those with more than 50% dolomite minerals are called dolomite rock. Mixtures are given combination names such as dolomitic limestone or limey dolomite rock.

Classification of carbonate rock types is based on the kinds of particles and the distribution of particles and matrix, using a modification from Dunham[47] (Table 2.7 in Sec. 2.1.2). Subnames for limestones and dolomite rocks are defined by criteria summarized in Fig. 4.42.

A complete carbonate rock classification includes whether the particles are ooids, rock fragments, crystals, or various fossil debris. Fig. 4.43 gives a summary of some particles that can be observed and identified in cuttings. Depending on objectives, this level of description may not be necessary.

Miscellaneous Rocks

Table 4.11 lists a group of miscellaneous sedimentary, igneous, and metamorphic rocks.

4.4.6 Recording Lithologic Descriptions

Descriptions are recorded in two ways, by symbols and

TABLE 4.10—SILICICLASTIC ROCK TYPES

Unconsolidated	Grain Size (mm)	Lithified
Clay or mud	<0.02	shale or mudstone*
Silt	0.02 to 0.062	siltstone
Sand	0.062 to 0.02	sandstone
Pebbles	>2.0	conglomerate

*Depending on fissility. For practical reasons, Wentworth's 0.04-mm boundary has been replaced with the 0.02-mm boundary between clay and silt. [35]

by narrative comments. Symbols record a maximum amount of information in the space provided on a standard mud log form. Written comments should be added only for clarity or emphasis. The recommended standard set of symbols is given in the AAPG *Sample Examination Manual*.

A standard order for comments is also desirable. The recommended order is:

1. rock type: name, subname, and/or classification;
2. color;
3. texture, including grain size, shape, and sorting;
4. cement or matrix composition and abundance;
5. porosity;
6. permeability, if estimated or measured; and
7. stain, fluorescence, and cut.

For example,

Sst: lithic, bu.-wh., f.-med., ang., sli. arg., mica; fx.-bd., fr. intgran. por., gd. Stn., gd. cut Fluor;

Ls: ool. Grst., brn., med.-crs., arg., Brach.-Bry., glauc., gd. intpar. por., gd. Stn., gd. cut Fluor.

The description is written entirely with abbreviations. The abbreviations for nouns always begin with a capital letter. These standard abbreviations are defined in Appendix II of the AAPG *Sample Examination Manual*.

The mud logging recording format (Sec. 4.6) provides

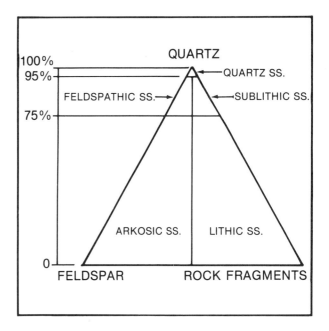

Fig. 4.41—Siliciclastic rock classification. [35]

a column for lithologic plots and porosity estimates. Comments can be written on a supplemental log or on the additional track in the wide format.

4.4.7 Comments

A lithologic log for mud logging does not need to be as comprehensive as logs prepared in an office or laboratory, where more time, special equipment, and specially trained people are available. The wellsite priorities are clearly:

1. recovering representative samples;

Depositional Texture Recognizable					Depositional Texture Not Recognizable
Original Components Not Bound Together During Deposition				Original components were bound together during deposition, as shown by intergrown skeletal matter, lamination contrary to gravity, or sediment — floored cavities that are roofed over by organic or questionably organic matter and are too large to be interstices.	(Subdivide according to classifications designed to bear on physical texture or diagenesis.)
Contains mud (particles of clay and fine silt size, less than 20 microns)		Lacks mud			
Mud-supported		Grain-supported	Grain-supported		
Less than 10 percent grains	More than 10 percent grains	More than 10 percent mud	Less than 10 percent mud		
MUDSTONE	WACKESTONE	PACKSTONE	GRAINSTONE	BOUNDSTONE	CRYSTALLINE CARBONATE

Fig. 4.42—Carbonate rock classification (modified from Dunham [47]).

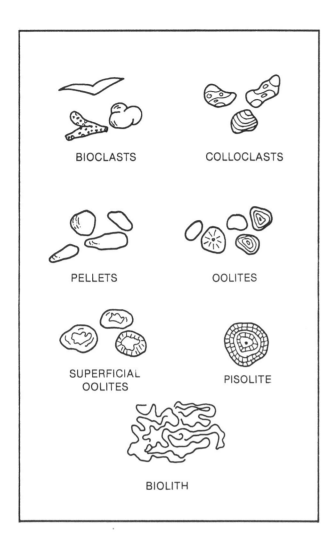

Fig. 4.43—Carbonate particle types (modified from Exlog[39]).

TABLE 4.11—MISCELLANEOUS ROCK TYPES
(after Swanson[35])

Sedimentary
Anhydrite
Chert
Salt
Bentonite
Coal
Phos000pherite

Igneous
Extrusive, acid (rhyolite, granite, diorite, etc.)
Extrusive, basic (basalt, andesite, etc.)
Intrusive, basic (gabbro, diabase, etc.)
Ultrabasic, ultramatic (peridotite, etc.)
Pyroclastic (tuff, ash)

Metamorphic
Quartzite
Slate, phyllite, etc.
Serpentine
Marble
Schist and Gneiss
Greenstone (altered basalt)

2. establishing correct sample depth assignments;

3. preserving the physical integrity of the cuttings;

4. describing characteristics needed to evaluate shows, establish structural position, and define drilling parameters; and

5. recognizing subsurface conditions that could endanger the hole, rig, or wellsite personnel.

Lower priorities can be assigned to (1) making esoteric descriptions and rock classifications, (2) doing geochemical, paleontological, or core analysis, and (3) interpreting sedimentary structures or depositional environments. These tasks require extraordinary resources beyond the normal mud logging complement.

Swanson,[35] Low,[48] and Exlog[39] are good references for more information on cuttings descriptions.

4.5 Interpreting Mud Logging Data

Oil and gas appearances in drilling returns must be carefully evaluated before deciding what follow-up evaluation is needed.

4.5.1 Determining Origins of Hydrocarbon in Drilling Returns

The first interpretation step is to identify the source of the oil and/or gas. As previously discussed, oil or gas observed in the mud can originate in ways that do not require further evaluation. This section covers the criteria for interpreting the origin of such hydrocarbons.

Trip Gas

Gas from previously drilled intervals can enter the mud column. Temporary production is stimulated by the swabbing action of pipe as it is pulled. Saturation gradients between the formation and drilling fluid also result in diffusion of formation gas into the borehole. During trips either process will increase the gas concentration in the mud at depths closely associated with uphole intervals containing gas. Such gas is observed after circulation is resumed and is called *trip gas*.

This source of gas is easily identified if a tracer such as carbide is pumped to the bottom of the hole before drilling is resumed. Trip gas will be circulated to the surface ahead of the tracer. Carbide, put into the drillpipe before circulation and drilling are resumed, is usually a satisfactory tracer. Fig. 4.44 shows this in an example gas-in-mud log. A short period of circulation to pump the carbide to the bottom of the hole before drilling is resumed is good practice.

It is also good practice to ensure that all drilling returns are circulated out before a trip. Returns left in the hole will appear during the trip-gas monitoring period and should be logged after the trip.

Trip gas needs to be reconciled with a previously drilled gas or oil occurrence. If none has been identified, there should be concern that a prospective zone has been missed. The depth of gas entry can be roughly located by a careful analysis of the time or pump-stroke count associated with the trip-gas appearance. The maximum trip gas reading is recorded on the mud log.

Kelly Cut

Air pumped down the pipe after a trip or connection will reappear as a slug of aerated mud called a *kelly cut*. This slug can be mistakenly reported as connection gas.

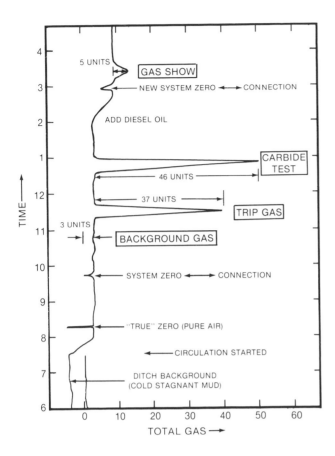

Fig. 4.44—Gas-in-mud recording illustrating relationship between tracer appearance and trip gas indications (modified from Exlog[20]).

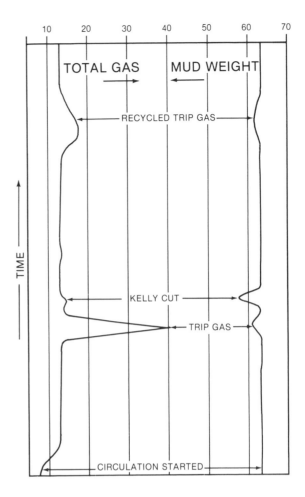

Fig. 4.45—Gas-in-mud recording showing a typical trip gas pattern (after Exlog[20]).

Recycled Trip Gas

Recycled trip gas can be recognized if circulation time through the total mud handling system is known. A "spread-out" gas increase at the time expected for one complete circulation should be interpreted as a recycled trip-gas slug (Fig. 4.45).

Oil Contamination

The oil and gas content of a drilling fluid may abruptly increase after diesel, crude, or bunker fuel is added to the mud. Fig. 4.46 shows an increase in total gas from crude oil added to the mud. Thirty barrels of lease crude were spotted to help free stuck drillpipe during a fishing operation at 914 ft. This slug of oil, especially lease crude, could have been a serious contamination problem for evaluating subsequently drilled intervals. However, the effects of contamination were reduced by circulating the mud system until the total gas was well below the saturation level of the detector and no fluorescent coatings were observed on the cuttings. The residual effect can be treated as background and should not interfere with formation evaluation.

The example shown on Fig. 4.47 illustrates what *not* to do. The abrupt gas increase that occurs at 5,690 ft was caused by the addition of more than 100 bbl of "burner fuel." The original log states that some of the cuttings had surface coatings with gold fluorescence and streaming cuts, presumably from the burner fuel contamination. The high gas-in-mud content and extent of the

fluorescent coating on cuttings would probably obscure any new shows. Because of these problems, the interval affected can be considered unevaluated.

4.5.2 Evaluating Formation Contents

The second step of interpreting a prospective interval is evaluating the formation-fluid contents. Such an interval is indicated when an oil or gas appearance cannot be attributed to a produced, contaminated, or recycled origin.

Criteria for interpreting formation-fluid contents from hydrocarbon logging are illustrated with models on Fig. 4.48.

Dry Gas

Reservoirs saturated with dry gas can be recognized by a hydrocarbon log pattern consisting of (1) gas-in-mud increases; (2) a lack of staining in cuttings; (3) little or no fluorescence; (4) absence of oil in the mud; and (5) high ratios of methane to ethane, butane, and propane ($C_1/C_4 \sim 20$ to 200). Fig. 4.49 is an example mud log acquired while a gas-saturated reservoir was drilled. Sandstone cuttings in the sample recovery associated with a drilling break indicate a reservoir interval at Depths A and B. Gas-in-mud increased at Depth A but decreased at Depth B. The ratio of high voltage to low voltage of the CCD log is consistent with the proportions of methane and propane shown by the GC data. Stain

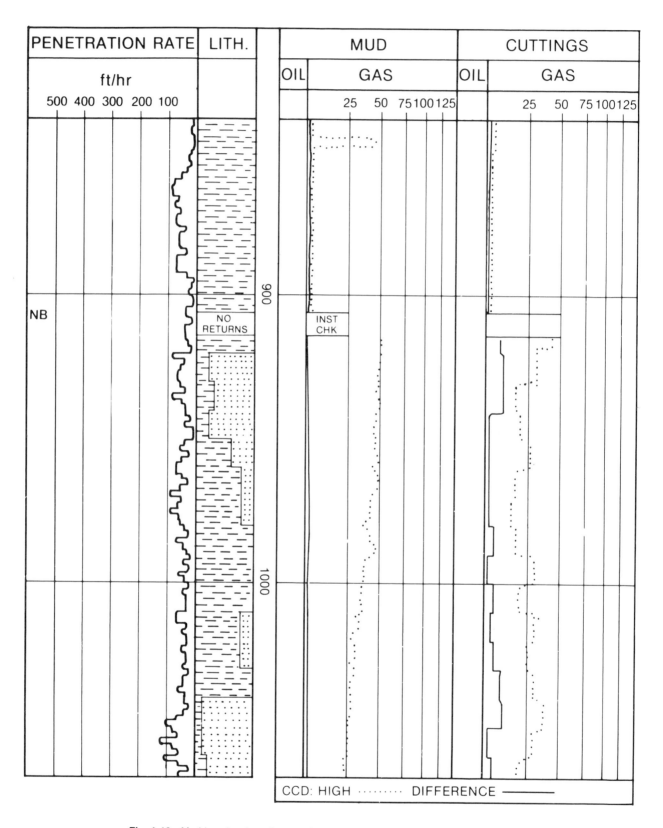

Fig. 4.46—Mud log showing oil contamination that will not interfere with evaluation.

and fluorescence were absent. These criteria support an interpretation that Interval A is saturated with dry gas. Interval B is interpreted to be completely water saturated because of the absence of gas in the mud.

Wet Gas
The presence of wet gas is indicated similarly to dry gas except for more intense fluorescence and an increase in the fraction of heavier compounds. Careful chromatographic analysis is important for distinguishing between wet and dry gas. Conventional mechanical gas traps do not always satisfactorily extract heavier compounds.

Light Oil
Reservoirs containing oil with relatively high gas/oil ratios have a distinctive hydrocarbon log pattern. This consists of (1) a gas-in-mud increase; (2) oil stain on the cuttings; (3) bright blue, white, or yellow fluorescence; and (4) abundant heavier-hydrocarbons indications in the gas analysis ($C_1/C_4 \sim 2$ to 20) as shown by Fig. 4.50. A fine-to-medium grain sand with siltstone in the cuttings accompanied by an erratic drilling break indicates that the reservoir is probably interbedded sand and siltstone. Abundant bright yellow fluorescence and streaming yellow cut were observed in the cuttings. The presence of both oil and gas in the mud and cuttings is characteristic of an oil-saturated interval. The color of the fluorescence and the proportions of the hydrocarbon components are typical for a medium-gravity oil with an intermediate gas/oil ratio. The high cuttings gas and streaming cut are characteristic of low-permeability lithologies.

Heavy Oil
Heavy-oil saturation is indicated by (1) little or no gas-in-mud increases; (2) dark staining; (3) yellow, orange, red, or brown fluorescence (usually not as intense as with light oil); and (4) oil-in-mud indicators. The mud log in Fig. 4.51 illustrates some of these criteria. The sample description (not shown) logged medium to coarse, unconsolidated sand with dark-brown stain and dull, yellow-brown fluorescence. An immediate bright-yellow-to-dark-straw-colored cut was observed. Heavy oil is often associated with poorly consolidated reservoirs. Concerns about not recovering good cuttings samples are warranted. Heavy oil with very little gas can be missed without good cuttings samples.

Water With Dissolved Gas
Aquifers with significant dissolved gas are recognized by (1) gas-in-mud increases, (2) no staining, (3) no fluorescence, (4) absence of oil in the mud, and (5) very high C_1/C_4 ratios (>200). An example mud log is shown in Fig. 4.52. A drillstem test of the interval 4,985 to 5,040 ft recovered 128 thousand cf/D gas and 3,810 ft of water. The mud is often contaminated with gas after a drillstem test. Note the circulation of the mud after testing. This is good practice for reducing gas-in-mud content before resumption of drilling. Otherwise, a new show can be obscured by the residual gas content. Further logging and testing is often needed to differentiate between tight reservoirs saturated with dry gas and higher-quality aquifers containing dissolved gas.

Hydrogen
Hydrogen can be produced by a reaction between the metal of the flow system and some muds. Although hydrogen is highly reactive, some evidence exists that it occurs in the subsurface. The high gas readings shown in Fig. 4.53 are interpreted as being caused by hydrogen because hydrocarbons were not detected by the gas chromatograph. Another interpretation is that the chromatograph was malfunctioning, but the record of a valid methane calibration and carbide lag checks discounts this possibility. It can be directly detected by a gas chromatograph that will resolve hydrogen from carrier gas in the presence of air, although one was not used in logging this well. Flame ionization detectors do not detect hydrogen.

Carbon Dioxide
Gas chromatography can also detect CO_2 through use of an appropriate detector/carrier gas combination. Some types of hot-wire analyzers and thermal conductivity detectors are responsive to CO_2. Other catalytic combustion detectors are less sensitive to low concentrations and brief occurrences of CO_2. Carbon dioxide can be detected by an infrared sensor. Flame ionization detectors and coated-filament hot-wire analyzers do not detect CO_2.

Hydrogen Sulfide
Hydrogen sulfide deserves special respect. Dangerous concentrations in the subsurface can be encountered without H_2S being detected in vapors extracted from mud. Better detection sensitivity is achieved by monitoring soluble sulfide[50] with instrumentation that may not be routinely available from a mud logging company. Selecting this instrumentation and interpreting its response requires expert advice.

4.5.3 Evaluating Reservoir Quality
Reservoir quality is primarily evaluated from the pore description of the pores and estimates of permeability. Gas in cuttings and drilling time are also used in assessing reservoir quality. These criteria are illustrated in the model mud logs shown in Fig. 4.54.

Good Reservoir
A porous and permeable reservoir is usually characterized by a fast drilling break, large pores, low cuttings gas content, and minimum cementation. Some of these criteria are shown by Fig. 4.55. The drillstem test of the interval 5,311 to 5,339 ft flowed gas at a rate of 9.36 million cf/D through a ½-in. choke, indicating high productivity.

Poor Reservoir
A poor-quality reservoir (Fig. 4.56) is usually characterized by high cuttings gas content, low estimated porosity and permeability, and slow or streaming cuts. Fig. 4.56 is an example of what might be observed when a poor-quality reservoir is logged. Note the high cuttings gas. The cuttings description (not shown) recorded pale yellow to white fluorescence and whitish-blue fluorescent cuts in a medium-grain sandstone that was evaluated by Drillstem Test 1. The tested interval produced gas at

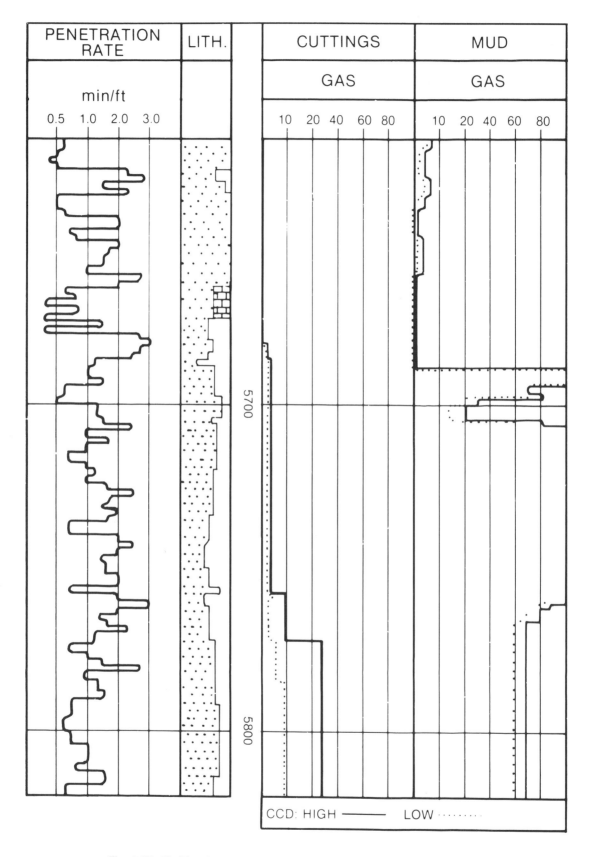

Fig. 4.47—Mud log showing oil contamination that will interfere with evaluation.

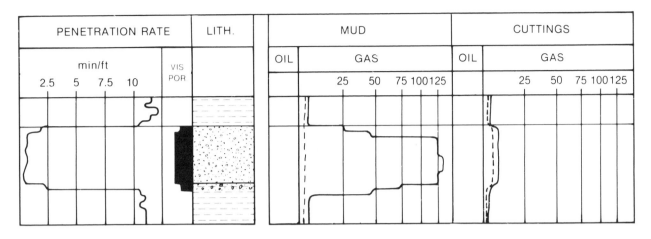

GAS RESERVOIR

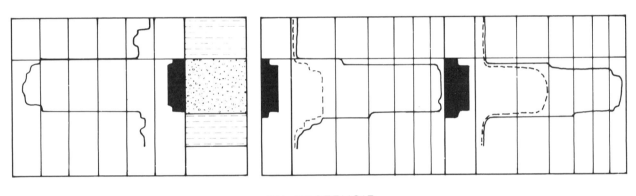

OIL RESERVOIR

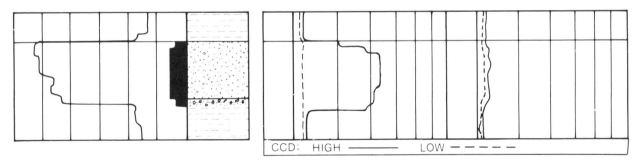

WATER RESERVOIR

Fig. 4.48—Model mud logs illustrating characteristic responses after drilling gas-, oil-, and water-saturated reservoirs (modified from Alfred[49]).

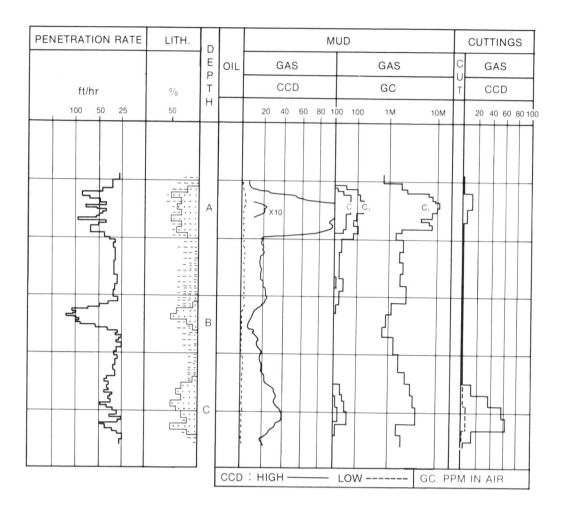

Fig. 4.49—Example mud log—gas-saturation case (after Exlog[20]).

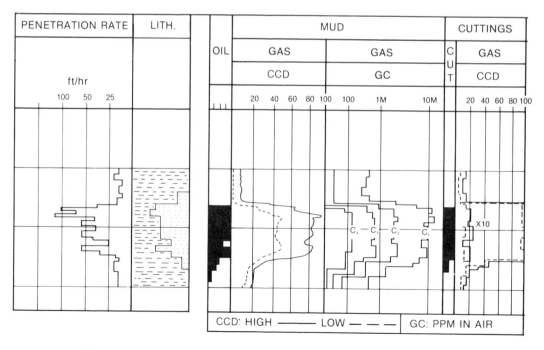

Fig. 4.50—Example mud log—medium-gravity oil-saturation case (after Exlog[20]).

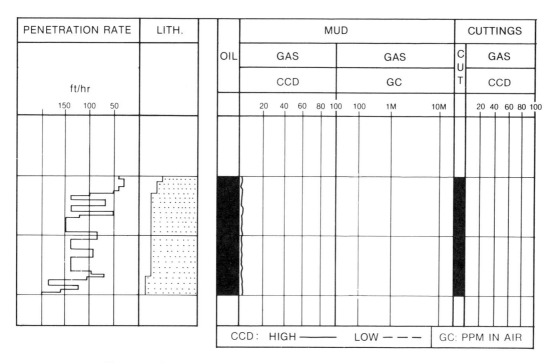

Fig. 4.51—Example mud log—low-gravity oil-saturation case (after Exlog[20]).

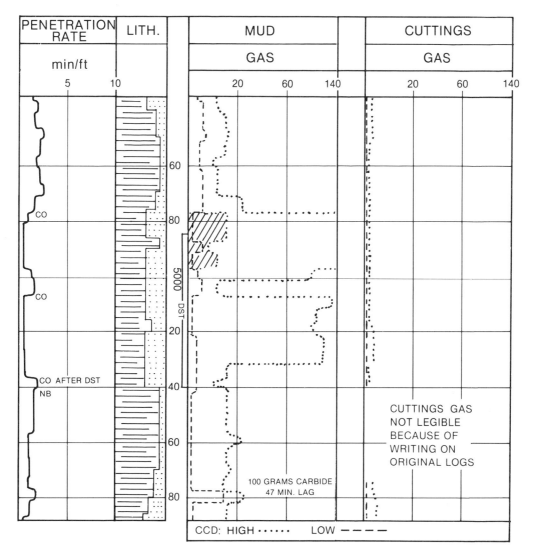

Fig. 4.52—Example mudlog—water-saturated-with-gas case.

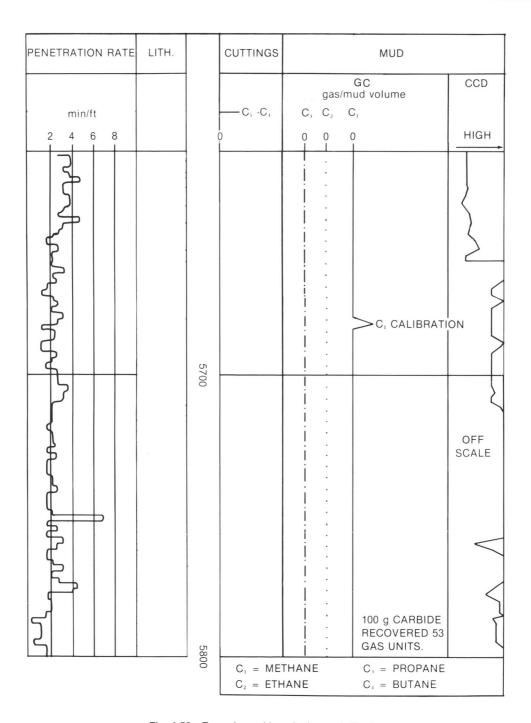

Fig. 4.53—Example mud log—hydrogen indications.

an initial rate of 900 thousand cf/D, declining to 680 thousand cf/D after 2 hours. Also produced during the 2-hour flow period were 375 ft of oil and 180 ft of gas and mud-cut water.

Fractured Reservoir

Models for recognizing a fractured reservoir are not always satisfactory. The criteria for recognizing fractures are combinations of erratic drilling rates, mud gains or losses, the presence of crystalline fracture fillings, slickensided (polished) surfaces on cuttings, and the presence of fine-grain, saturated rocks. Torque, rotary speed, weight on bit, and pit level indicators can be helpful for monitoring erratic drilling characteristics. Gas- or oil-in-mud is not among the recognition criteria, because flushing can be severe in fractured zones if they are drilled with overbalanced conditions. The example shown in Fig. 4.57 illustrates the absence of gas shows. Despite the absence of gas in the mud or cuttings, a drillstem test of the interval 8,450 to 8,617 ft produced gas at the rate of 2.34 million cf/D, decreasing to 1.83 million cf/D after 2 hours. Gas-in-mud may be the best criterion when mud weight is near balance because flushing is reduced.

Unfortunately, some or all of these criteria may not be observed while fractured reservoirs are being drilled,

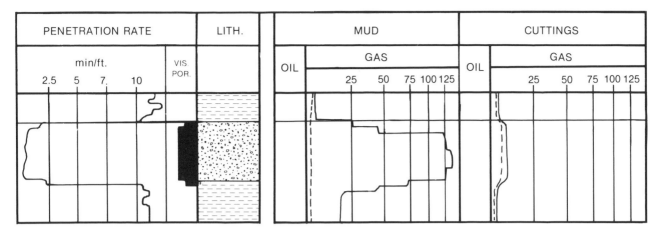

HIGH QUALITY GAS RESERVOIR

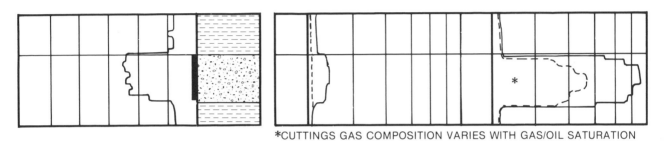

*CUTTINGS GAS COMPOSITION VARIES WITH GAS/OIL SATURATION

LOW QUALITY OIL OR GAS RESERVOIR

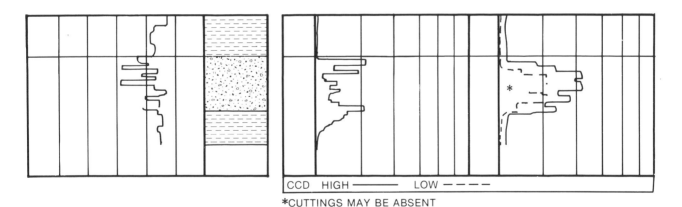

*CUTTINGS MAY BE ABSENT

FRACTURED OIL OR GAS RESERVOIR

Fig. 4.54—Model mud logs illustrating criteria used to interpret reservoir quality (modified from Alfred[49]).

depending on the geologic setting, mud pressure balance, and drilling conditions. Therefore, confirmation by other formation evaluation techniques is recommended.

Coal

Significant gas can occur in coal beds. Fig. 4.58 shows an example of a gas occurrence after a thick coal bed was drilled. Coal and carbonaceous shale were abundant in the cuttings from intervals where high gas was logged in

both the mud and the cuttings. Correct interpretation requires good samples.

4.5.4 Detecting Abnormal Pressure

Successful drilling depends on doing what is needed to operate safely and effectively under abnormal*

_____

*Conventionally, higher-than-normal pore pressure is called "abnormal," which could also mean "below normal." Therefore, "supernormal" and "subnormal" are used here to indicate pressure above and below normal pressures, respectively.

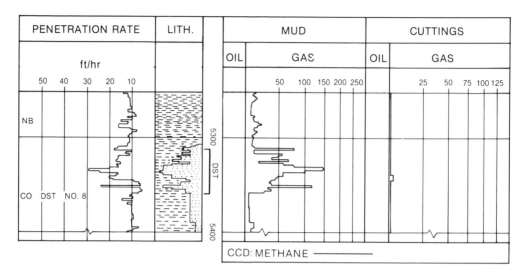

Fig. 4.55—Example mud log—good reservoir quality (after Choate[21]).

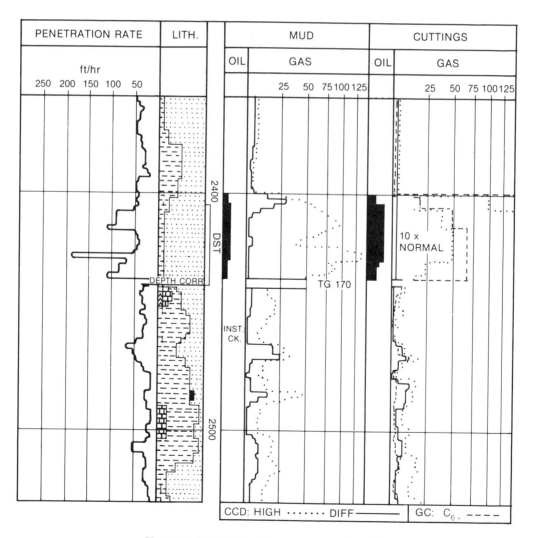

Fig. 4.56—Example mud log—poor reservoir quality.

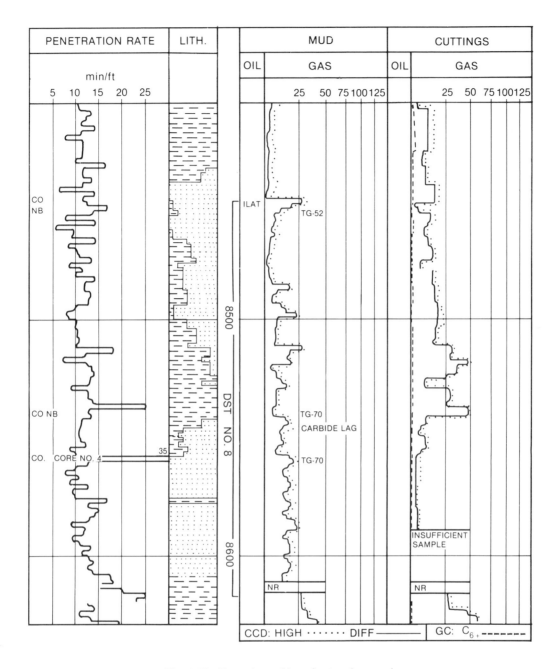

Fig. 4.57—Example mud log—fractured reservoir.

pressures. To do this, it is imperative that such pressures be detected as soon as encountered. Often this can be achieved with monitors available from quality mud logging services. The most important of these are:

1. produced gas in drilling mud,
2. normalized rate of penetration (d exponent),
3. drillstring sensors responsive to the compaction state of the formation,
4. gas in mud after trips and connections,
5. cuttings condition and composition,
6. pit and return flow volumes and standpipe pressure,
7. mud temperature, salinity, and rheology, and
8. weight on bit, torque, and pump pressure.

Examples of these are discussed in Ref. 51. Some pressure indications may be missing or ambiguous, so it is necessary to consider each in terms of the geologic and

drilling conditions—especially the differential pressure between the mud and formation.

Normal Pressure

Normal pressure approximates the hydrostatic pressure of a water column with its head near the surface of the ground and its base at the reference depth. The pressure in such a column is

$$p_f = 0.0519 \cdot \rho_f \cdot h, \quad \ldots \ldots \ldots \ldots \ldots \ldots (4.8)$$

where p_f is pore-fluid pressure (pounds per square inch), ρ_f is fluid density (pounds mass per gallon), and h is true vertical distance from the surface (feet). As the hydrostatic pressure gradient, p_f/h, in a freshwater column is 0.433 psi/ft, and the gradient in a column of

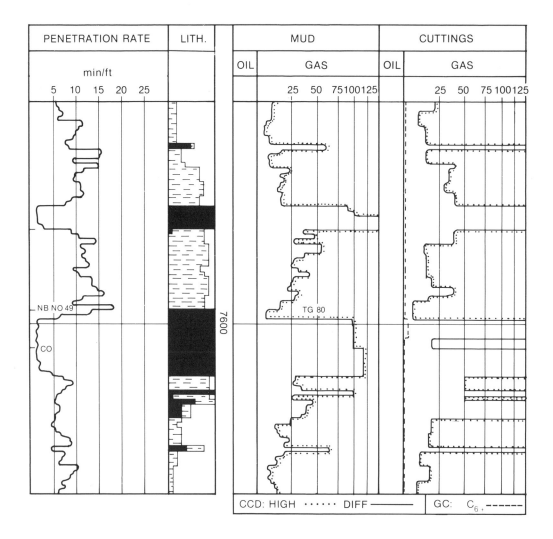

Fig. 4.58—Example mud log—coal.

saturated brine (ignoring temperature and gas effects) is 0.520 psi/ft (relative to the ground water level or sea level), pressures from gradients within that range are considered normal in this discussion.

Supernormal Pressure

A formation pressure exceeding that of the equivalent height of a standing water column is considered supernormal.

Guidelines for detecting supernormal pressure depend on the mud/pore pressure balance. Some or all of the responses diagrammed in Fig. 4.59 can occur while a well is drilled with slightly to moderately overbalanced mud weights. Underbalanced conditions can lead to kicks or fluid flows. Highly overbalanced conditions can mask typical indications and prevent timely detection of supernormal pressure.

Subnormal Pressure

A formation pressure less than that of an equivalent-height standing water column (relative to the surface of the ground) is considered subnormal. This creates an overbalanced pressure differential between the formation and drilling fluids other than foam or air. Severe over-balance, such as with weighted muds, causes flushing

ahead of the bit and reduces the amount of oil and gas entering the returns. This can also cause loss of returns (lost circulation). These problems can seriously affect mud logging results.

Indications of subnormal pressure include:

1. lower-than-expected gas in mud,
2. excessive mud losses,
3. poor cuttings quality,
4. slower-than-expected drilling rates, and
5. sticking and overtorquing of the drillstring.

One or more of these indications should tell the mud log interpreter that prospective intervals may not yield good shows.

4.5.5 Integrating Mud Logging Interpretation Into Overall Formation Evaluation

The final interpretation step is deciding what follow-up action to take after a prospective interval is recognized and evaluated. This decision is supported by planning the formation evaluation program in ways that integrate the mud logging practices into an orderly, systematic, and comprehensive evaluation strategy. This strategy must be consistent with the geologic setting, drilling conditions, prior knowledge of the area, feasibility of

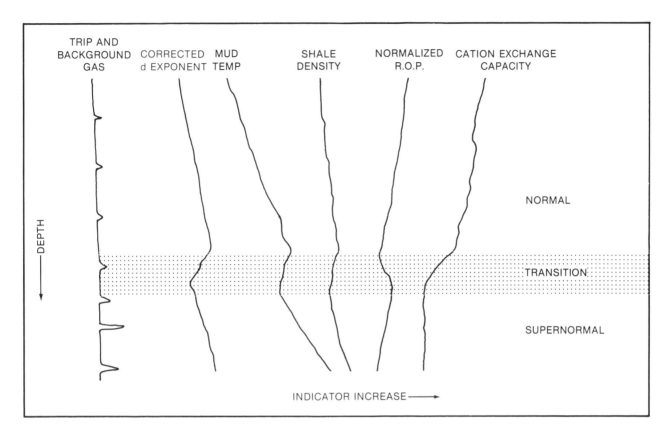

Fig. 4.59—Supernormal-pressure indicators.

testing and coring, and the effectiveness of log analysis.

Although many variations are possible, two basic formation-evaluation programs are considered: one is to test prospective intervals as the well is drilled, with the intent of having a nearly complete evaluation by the time total depth is reached; the other is to test prospective intervals after the well has been drilled and cased. The first program is often used in "hard rock" areas and the second in "soft rock" areas. In either program mud logging data are important.

Hard-Rock Programs

A typical formation-evaluation program for a hard-rock area is described in Table 4.12.* It is applicable to sequences of consolidated sandstones and carbonates with wide ranges of formation-water salinities. In such areas full-hole coring is practical. Openhole testing is possible and diagnostic. Wireline log interpretation is often limited by the presence of fresh waters, low porosities, and shaly reservoirs. These conditions can be successfully evaluated by mud log analysis plus a coordinated followup coring, testing, and wireline logging program. Fig. 4.60 illustrates application of a coordinated program for evaluating a prospective interval as soon as possible. The drilling break between 7,896 and 7,900 ft was circulated out of the hole before it was drilled further. The sample recovery included sandstone with fluorescence, indicating a prospective reservoir. To obtain a more definitive evaluation of saturation and productivity, Core No. 1 was cut and analyzed. The cored interval was tested and produced gas at the rate of 1.4 million cf/D. Porosity, permeability, and saturation data from core analysis and gas recovery from the test provided a more definitive evaluation than could have been made from mud and wireline log combinations in this area. The record of instrument checks and carbide lags indicates component logging practices were used.

Soft-Rock Programs

A typical formation-evaluation program for a soft-rock area is described in Table 4.13.* This program is applicable to sand-shale sequences with predominantly saline interstitial waters. Full-hole coring is not always practical in these areas, but sidewall coring works well. Openhole testing is limited. Wireline logging gives good results. The role of hydrocarbon logging may become secondary for formation evaluation in these areas. However, drilling in many such areas encounters supernormally pressured sections and involves highly deviated wells that require special drilling-fluid monitoring. In these areas, operational problems may be more important than formation evaluation in justifying the cost of mud logging.

4.6 Recommended Practices

Standardization can be good or bad; too much discourages innovation, adds unnecessary costs, and restrains competition; too little contributes to inconsistent performance and unreliable results. Consistent performance, reliable results, and cost-effective operations are most likely when equipment, personnel, and procedures are matched with the operator's drilling and evaluation objectives. With this perspective, factors to

*Tables 4.12 and 4.13 are modified from an unpublished Standard Oil Co. of California manual prepared by J.E. Walstrom.

**TABLE 4.12—COORDINATED FORMATION EVALUATION PROGRAM
FOR TESTING BEFORE CASING IS RUN**

Hard-Rock Areas

General Program*

A	B	C
1. Analyze drilling fluid and cuttings for hydrocarbon content, collect drilling data, and describe lithology and porosity. 2. Circulate out significant drilling breaks and if oil or gas shows: (a) core or drill out of show and (b) test in drillstem off bottom of hole. 3. Run wireline logs and interpret in coordination with core analysis and test results. 4. Take sidewall cores if possible. 5. Run repeat wireline tester if required.	1. Same as A 2. Drill ahead and core if: (a) significant oil or gas shows (b) reaching objective. 3. Test as required to establish productivity or obtain pressure data. 4. Run wireline logs. 5. Take sidewall cores if possible.	1. Drill ahead. 2. Catch and examine samples. 3. Run logs. 4. Take sidewall cores if possible. 5. Formation test as indicated.

General Advantages

1. Bottomhole tests are often more representative because of less invasion and avoidance of water shutoff problems.
2. All intervals are evaluated early in development of field or area.
3. Casting, cementing, and through-pipe testing costs are not incurred before production is evaluated.

General Disadvantages

1. More time is required to reach total depth.
2. Danger of losing hole before reaching total depth is increased.
3. Formation tests are usually limited in duration and pressure data are restricted.
4. Openhole testing can be hazardous.

*Variations are possible depending on evaluation requirements and technology available.

**TABLE 4.13—COORDINATED FORMATION-EVALUATION PROGRAM
FOR TESTING AFTER CASING IS RUN**

Soft-Rock Areas

General Programs*

A	B	C
1. Drill ahead. 2. Collect samples for paleontological analysis. 3. Run wireline logs. 4. Take sidewall cores as indicated. 5. Make wireline formation tests if possible. 6. Run casing and test prospective zones.	1. Analyze drilling fluid and cuttings. 2. Drill ahead without coring. 3. Run wireline logs. 4. Take sidewall cores as indicated from logs. 5. Make wireline formation tests if possible. 6. Run casing and test prospective zones.	1. Same as B. 2. Drill ahead with limited coring if oil or gas shows. 3. Run wireline logs. 4. Take sidewall cores as indicated from logs. 5. Make wireline formation tests if possible. 6. Run casing and test prospective zones.

General Advantages

1. Test intervals can be selected with aid of logs and sample data.
2. Test design and duration can be programmed to obtain large fluid samples and comprehensive pressure data.
3. Total depth is reached in a minimum time, reducing drilling costs and risk of losing hole before reaching total depth.

General Disadvantages

1. Formation exposure to drilling fluid and cement can prevent successful evaluation.
2. Casing costs are incurred before testing.
3. Hole may be lost before any testing is accomplished.
4. Shallow formations may remain unevaluated if deepest objective is commercial.

*Variations are possible depending on evaluation requirements and technology available.

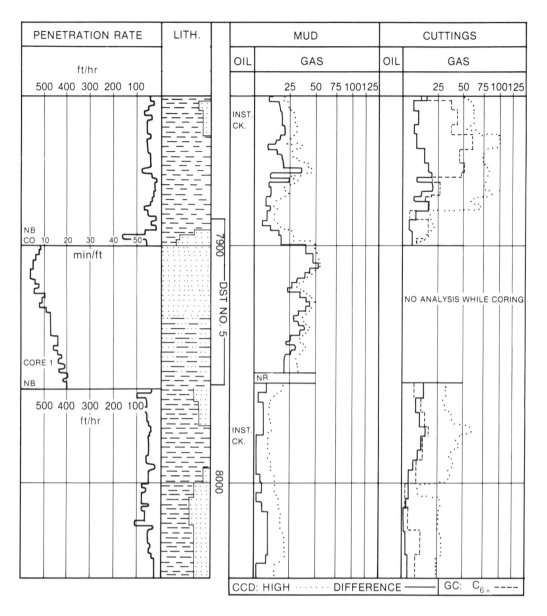

Fig. 4.60—Example mud log of a newly penetrated interval evaluated by a coordinated program of hydrocarbon logging, coring, and openhole testing.

be considered when selecting services, specifying procedures, and recording results are discussed in this section.

4.6.1 Selecting Services

Mud logging services have ranged from an unmanned gas detector and drilling-rate recorder to a multimanned drilling, hydrocarbon, and mud monitoring system supported with specialized analysis and computer facilities. This spectrum of services is becoming broader with the introduction of downhole sensors and computerized data monitoring and interpretation systems. Selecting desired services from such a spectrum depends on the operator's objectives, experience, and risk tolerance after a consideration of the drilling conditions and formation properties that influence how difficult it will be to drill and evaluate the well.

Drilling conditions are considered when wellsite services are selected. For considering service requirements, drilling can be classified in three ways.

Class 1 is deviated drilling where abnormal pressure or unstable hole conditions increase the risk of objectives not being met.

Class 2 includes either straight-hole drilling where abnormal pressure or unstable hole causes problems, or deviated drilling in normally pressured areas, especially if only limited experience for optimizing drilling costs is available.

Class 3 comprises other drilling without special problems, especially if local experience is available for programming bit and mud schedules.

Typical services that might be considered are shown in Table 4.14. Hydrogen sulfide gas or evaporite occurrence generally justifies selecting services that apply to Class 1 or 2 regardless of other factors. Drilling in any new area can be considered Class 1.

Formation properties influence the selection of wellsite services. For considering service requirements, formation properties can be classified in three ways.

TABLE 4.14—GUIDE FOR SELECTING DRILL MONITORING SERVICES

Service	Class 1	Class 2	Class 3
Surface			
Penetration rate	R	R	R
Weight and torque	R	R	R
Rotary speed	R	R	O
Mud weight	R	R	O
Pump pressure and stroke rate	R	R	O
Pit level	R	R	O
Mud pressure and flow	R	O	O
Mud temperature and salinity	R	O	
Downhole			
Formation resistivity	R	R	
Formation gamma ray	R	O	
Weight and torque	R	O	
Mud salinity and temperature	R	O	
Inclination and direction	R	O	

R = recommended.
O = optional.

TABLE 4.15—GUIDE FOR SELECTION, EVALUATION SERVICES

Service	Class A	Class B	Class C
Gas in Mud or Cuttings			
Flame ionization detector	R	O	
Hot wire and thermal detector	O	R	O
Hot wire			R
Gas chromatograph	R	R	O
Oil in Mud Cuttings			
Stain, odor, cut fluorescence	R	R	O
Lithology			
Cuttings description	R	R	O
Porosity and permeability	R	R	O
Trap			
Steam distillation or equivalent	R	O	
Agitator	R	R	R
Baffle			O
Crew			
Trained and experienced	R	R	
Trained or experienced			O
Other			
Density	O	O	
Cation exchange capacity	O	O	
Miscellaneous	O	O	O

R = recommended.
O = optional.

Class A includes fractured, vuggy, or low-porosity reservoirs and any with low gas/oil-ratio fluid content.

Class B contains reservoirs with low to medium porosity and intermediate to high gas/oil-ratio fluid content.

Class C comprises reservoirs with medium to high porosity and high gas/oil-ratio or free-gas saturation.

Typical services that might be considered for each class are shown in Table 4.15. The presence of shallow gas, poor hole conditions, or inadequate rig capacity generally justifies consideration of Class A or B services regardless of drilling conditions.

Formation evaluation becomes more difficult as the well depth and/or the mud-formation pressure overbalance increases. These situations require maximum sensitivity of the gas sampling and detecting equipment and special attention to collecting, describing, and analyzing cuttings. Coals, gas-saturated aquifers, and unconsolidated sections add to the difficulties of evaluating a well. These factors warrant consideration of Class A or Class B services regardless of other formation properties.

Multiple objectives increase the difficulty of meeting formation-evaluation goals, and more comprehensive services are required.

The operator's and service company's experiences in the area are important when services are selected. As experience is gained, the service requirements can be reduced.

4.6.2 Specifying Procedures

Meeting drilling and evaluation objectives requires consistent and dependable hydrocarbon logging. This is partly achieved by using standard practices for:

1. calibrating gas detectors and analyzers,
2. checking gas monitor performance,
3. catching cuttings and mud samples, and
4. describing and analyzing cuttings.

Specifications for operating practices are included in a wellsite program guide provided by the operator to the service company before logging starts. See Chart 4.5 for an example.

Calibration

Calibration relates instruments, service companies, areas, and hydrocarbon data for quality control, comparison, and interpretation.

Any analytical instrument used for mud logging must be capable of calibration in the wellsite environment. This demonstrates the accuracy of instrument response within range of commonly encountered concentrations and perhaps more important, indicates the limits of that range beyond which sensitivity or accuracy of response is lost. Recommended practices are discussed in Ref. 52.

Performance Checks

The performance of the total gas monitor system (trap, vacuum delivery line, filters, regulators, and detectors) should be checked on a regular schedule. Calcium carbide checks are useful. The carbide needs to be introduced into the mud in a way that prevents loss of gas before circulation is resumed.

Sample Collection

Sampling requirements are specified for each well and included in the "wellsite program."

Cuttings Description and Analysis

Techniques for describing cuttings are described in the AAPG *Sample Examination Manual* and Sec. 4.4.1. Sample analysis practices are discussed in Sec. 4.3.

4.6.3 Recording Data

A standard format for recording drilling rate, lithology, and hydrocarbon log data provides important benefits. Standardized data can be interpreted faster: the uniformity makes comparison between wells easier, instructing log users and communicating results are simpler, and direct overlays with wireline logs are possible when standard formats are used for both. According to Mercer and McAdams,[53] many hydrocarbon data are underutilized because of nonstandard recording.

The American Petroleum Institute (API) published[54] standards for hydrocarbon mud logs in 1958. Using the API format as a starting place, the Society of Professional Well Log Analysts (SPWLA) recommended[52] recording practices in 1983. Their recommended format is shown in Chart 4.6 (heading), Chart 4.7 (legend), and Chart 4.8 (log body).

The SPWLA-endorsed format resembles the API standards for wireline logs. Horizontal and vertical scales are chosen by the operator or service company. Symbols and abbreviations conform to the AAPG *Sample Examination Manual*. A binary color system is practical under wellsite limitations. Log content usually should be limited to drilling-rate, hydrocarbon, and lithologic data. Other data are plotted on another log. Marginal notes usually should be limited to bit records, mud properties and drilling history and are not written over trace data.

The SPWLA-recommended log can be directly laid over a wireline log. This permits comparing the SP or gamma ray trace with the penetration rate and the porosity or resistivity logs with the hydrocarbon traces. Direct comparison helps to confirm depth assignments and to identify hydrocarbon containing porous intervals.

4.6.4 Comments

The benefits of using standard operating practices and recording formats clearly justify the efforts that are required. The SPWLA standards[52] and AAPG *Sample Examination Manual*[35] are recommended sources to follow. No recommendation is made concerning standardized instrumentation and types of services.

4.7 Summary Comments

Mud logging can be considered a composite operation for collecting data on drilling operations, hydrocarbon content in returns, and reservoir-rock characteristics. The rate-of-penetration record plus information about drilling-fluid circulation, bit size, type, and history, mud characteristics, and pit levels are important inputs to determining the origin and significance of hydrocarbons in the mud. The gas and oil in the cuttings and drilling fluid are direct and timely indications that an oil and/or gas accumulation has been penetrated. Sample examination provides data and observations that enhance the likelihood of recognizing a prospective oil or gas reservoir and supplies valuable information about rock characteristics needed to evaluate reservoir quality.

The knowledge and experience available from the publications on this subject made this chapter possible. Among the many fine references, Hayward's early paper is a classic and is "must" reading. The service company

manuals are important sources for anyone interested in this subject, and they supplied many of the illustrations and examples used here. Mercer's excellent discussion[19] of the origins of hydrocarbons in drilling fluid provides the basis for a rational interpretation procedure and, although reviewed in this chapter, warrants further careful study. Swanson's *Sample Examination Manual* is a useful reference for sample description.[35] The other references listed provide more information for the interested reader.

References

1. Hayward, J.T.: "Continuous Logging at Rotary-Drilling Wells," *Drill. and Prod. Prac.*, API, New York City (1941) 8–19.
2. Hoberock, L.L.: "Shale-Shaker Selection and Operation," *Oil and Gas J.* (Nov. 23, 1981) 107-13.
3. Hoberock, L.L.: "Shale-Shaker Selection and Operation," *Oil and Gas J.* (Dec. 7, 1981) 130-41.
4. Hoberock, L.L.: "Shale-Shaker Selection and Operation," *Oil and Gas J.* (Dec. 21, 1981) 80-87.
5. Hoberock, L.L.: "Shale-Shaker Selection and Operation," *Oil and Gas J.* (Jan. 4, 1982) 89-100.
6. Hoberock, L.L.: "Shale-Shaker Selection and Operation," *Oil and Gas J.* (Jan. 18, 1982) 92-101.
7. Hoberock, L.L.: "Shale-Shaker Selection and Operation," *Oil and Gas J.* (Feb. 1, 1982) 124-26.
8. Ormsby, G.S.: "Drilling Fluid Solids Removal," *Drilling Practices Manual*, P.L. Moore (ed.), Petroleum Publishing Co., Tulsa (1974) 133-203.
9. Liljestrand, W.E.: "Degassing Mud," *Oil and Gas J.* (Feb. 25, 1980) 112-14, 118, 120.
10. Liljestrand, W.E.: "Degassing Mud," *Oil and Gas J.* (March 3, 1980) 69-70, 72, 74.
11. Bingham, M.G.: *A New Approach to Interpreting Rock Drillability*, Petroleum Publishing Co., Tulsa (1965).
12. Garnier, A.J. and van Lingen, N.H.: "Phenomena Affecting Drilling Rates at Depth," *J. Pet. Tech.* (Sept. 1959) 232-39; *Trans.*, AIME, **216**.
13. Rehm, B. and McClendon, R.: "Measurement of Formation Pressure From Drilling Data," paper SPE 3601 presented at the 1971 SPE Annual Fall Meeting, New Orleans, Oct. 3-6.
14. Zoeller, W.A.: "The Drilling Porosity Log 'DPL'," paper SPE 3066 presented at the 1970 SPE Annual Fall Meeting, Houston, Oct. 5-8.
15. *Theory and Evaluation of Formation Pressures—The Pressure Log Reference Manual*, Applications Manual MS 156, Rev. C, Exploration Logging Inc., Sacramento (1981).
16. Bourgoyne, A.T. Jr. and Young, F.S. Jr.: "The Use of Drillability Logs for Formation Evaluation and Abnormal Pressure Detection," *Trans.*, SPWLA 14th Annual Logging Symposium (1973) paper T.
17. Shepherd, G.F. and Atwater, G.I.: "Geologic Use of Drilling-Time Data," *The Oil Weekly* (July 3, 1944) 17-19, 22, 24, 38, 41-42, 44, 46.
18. Jorden, J.R. and Shirley, O.J.: "Application of Drilling Performance Data to Overpressure Detection," *J. Pet. Tech.* (Nov. 1966) 1387-94.
19. Mercer, R.F.: "Liberated, Produced, Recycled or Contamination?" *Trans.*, SPWLA 15th Annual Logging Symposium (1974) paper T.
20. *Mud Logging: Principles and Interpretations*, Applications Manual MS 196, Exploration Logging Inc., Sacramento (1979).
21. Choate, L.R.: *Mud Analysis Logging*, Baroid Div., National Lead Co., Houston (1963) 1-76.
22. Lynch, E.J.: *Formation Evaluation*, Harper and Row, New York City (1962) 58-82.
23. Rowland, F.W.: *The Practice of Gas Chromatography*, second edition, Hewlett-Packard Co. (1974).

24. David, D.J.: *Gas Chromatograph Detectors*, John Wiley and Sons, New York City (1974) 14–75.

25. Grob, R.L.: *Modern Practice of Gas Chromatography*, John Wiley and Sons, New York City (1977).

26. Mercer, R.F.: "The Use of Flame Ionization Detection in Oil Exploration," *Trans.*, CWLS Symposium (1968) paper F.

27. Jenkins, R.E.: "Three Electronic Methods to Analyze Drilling Fluid Gases," *Pet. Eng.* (Oct. 1959) 75, 80, 82, 85, 88, 90, 96.

28. Wyman, R.E. and Castano, J.R.: "Show Descriptions from Core, Sidewall and Ditch Samples," *Trans.*, SPWLA Annual Symposium (1974) paper W.

29. McKay, J.F. and Latham, D.R.: "Fluorescence Spectrometry in the Characterization of High-Boiling Petroleum Distillates," *Analytical Chem.* (Nov. 1972) **44**, 2132–37.

30. *Fluorescence and Phosphorescence Analysis*, D.M. Hercules (ed.), Interscience Publishers—a Div. of John Wiley and Sons, New York City (1966).

31. Radley, J.A. and Grant, J.: *Fluorescence Analysis in Ultra-Violet Light*, fourth edition revised, D. Van Nostrand Co. Inc., New York City (1954).

32. Riecker, R.E.: "Hydrocarbon Fluorescence and Migration of Petroleum," *Bull.*, AAPG (Jan. 1962) **46**, 60–75.

33. Gleason, S.: *Ultraviolet Guide to Minerals*, Ultraviolet Products, San Gabriel, CA (1962).

34. Clementz, D.M., Demaison, G.J., and Daly, A.R.: "Wellsite Geochemistry by Programmed Pyrolysis," *Proc.*, Offshore Technology Conference (1979) **1**, 465–70.

35. Swanson, R.G.: *Sample Examination Manual*, Methods in Exploration Series, No. 4, AAPG, Tulsa (1981).

36. McClure, L.J.: *Drill Abnormal Pressure Safely*, Houston (1977).

37. Pixler, B.O.: "Some Recent Developments in Mud-Analysis Logging," *Trans.*, AIME (1946) **165**, 268–80.

38. Goldsmith, R.G.: "Why Gas Cut Mud Is Not Always a Serious Problem," *World Oil* (Oct. 1972) 51–52, 54, 101.

39. *Formation Evaluation, Part 1: Geological Procedures*, Applications Manual MS 3017, Exploration Logging Inc., Sacramento, CA (1981).

40. Kennedy, J.L.: "New Device Aimed at Better Sampling," *Oil and Gas J.* (Sept. 27, 1971) 106–07.

41. Goldsmith, R. and Hare, M.: "Solids Analysis Improves Mud Cost Control," *World Oil* (June 1982) 167–70.

42. Weissman, R.C. and Diehl, H.: "A New Method for Utilizing Versene for Determination of the Calcite-Dolomite Ratio in Carbonate Rocks," *Proc.*, Iowa Academy of Sciences (1953) **60**, 433–37.

43. Arnott, D.C.: "Calcimetry in the Field; Theory, Operation, and Uses," *Newsletter*, Pacific Pet. Geol. (March 1982) 1–9.

44. Goddard, E.N. *et al.*: "Rock Color Chart," GSA, Boulder, CO (1948).

45. Choquette, P.W. and Pray, L.C.: "Geologic Nomenclature and Classification of Porosity in Sedimentary Carbonates," *Bull.*, AAPG (Feb. 1970) **54**, 207–50.

46. Archie, G.E.: "Classification of Carbonate Reservoir Rocks and Petrophysical Considerations," *Bull.*, AAPG (Feb. 1952) **36**, 278–98.

47. Dunham, R.J.: "Classification of Carbonate Rocks According to Depositional Texture," *Classification of Carbonate Rocks*, W.E. Ham (ed.), Memoir 1, AAPG, Tulsa (1962) 108–21.

48. Low, J.W.: "Examination of Well Cuttings," *Quarterly*, Colorado School of Mines (Oct. 1951) **46**, 1–48.

49. Alfred, G.H.: "How to Evaluate Mud Logs in the Anadarko Basin," *Oil and Gas J.* (Nov. 26, 1962) 116–19.

50. Hadden, D.M.: "A System for Continuous On-Site Measurement of Sulfides in Water-Base Drilling Muds," paper SPE 6664 presented at the 1977 SPE Sour Gas Symposium, Tyler, TX, Nov. 14–15.

51. *Geological and Mud Logging in Drilling Control—A Catalog of Typical Cases*, Graham & Trotman Ltd., London (1982).

52. *Recommended Practices for Hydrocarbon Logging*, SPWLA, Houston (1983).

53. Mercer, R.F. and McAdams, J.B.: "Standards for Hydrocarbon Well Logging," *Trans.*, SPWLA Annual Symposium (1982) paper LL.

54. "Recommended Practice—Standard Hydrocarbon Mud Log Form," API, New York City (1958).

55. *Field Geologist's Training Guide*, Exploration Logging Inc., Sacramento, CA (1979).

Chapter 5
Temperature Logging

Another physical parameter available inside wells is temperature. Its more than probable practical value has never been doubted, one might say, ever since wells were first drilled...

from Schlumberger, Doll, and Perebinossoff,[1]
who helped introduce the first continuous wireline
temperature survey.

5.0 Introduction. Borehole temperature measurements are used (1) to derive profiles of borehole temperature and formation temperature vs. depth as well as (2) to delineate fluid-inflow zones and to measure inflow rates. Borehole temperature/depth profiles are readily measured. Considerable data reduction is necessary to obtain formation-temperature/depth profiles from these measurements because of their negligible depth of investigation. Also, because borehole temperatures are influenced significantly by downhole fluid flow (hence, heat transfer), their measurement provides considerable information about borehole conditions. Of these, only formation-evaluation problems (e.g., fluid inflow) are discussed in this monograph.

5.1 Heat Flow and Temperature in the Earth and Boreholes

Within the earth or a borehole, heat can be transferred by conduction, convection, or (rarely) radiation.

The equation for the steady-state conduction of heat in one dimension can be written

$$u_h = 10^{-2} k_h (\partial T/\partial D), \quad\dotfill(5.1)$$

where u_h is heat flux (cal/cm^2-sec), k_h is thermal conductivity (cal/cm-sec-°C) and $\partial T/\partial D$ is temperature gradient (°C/m). Because measured heat flow in the earth is often about 10^{-6} cal/cm^2-sec, another convenient term is the *heat flow unit* (hfu), equal to 10^{-6} cal/cm^2-sec.

5.1.1 Earth

An early model of the earth's thermal behavior[2] considered the earth a hot sphere losing heat by conduction through a thin crust, and thence by radiation into space. The heat was considered (1) to originate from a uniform, concentrated radioactive layer near the base of the crust

and (2) to propagate symmetrically so that all the crust received heat at the same rate.

A newer, more sophisticated model[3] (Fig. 5.1) proposes that the heat flow is approximately the same through oceanic and continental shield areas. The heat in the crust is considered to originate from the mantle (transferred by convection) and from radioactive decay of material within the crust. The higher heat-flow rates in continental crust areas other than shields are ascribed to more recent thermal events there. This model says several things about the heat flow.

1. It decreases with geologic time as a result of the decay of the radioactive material involved.

2. It is greatest at the earth's surface and decreases with depth because of the decreasing amount of underlying radioactive material.

3. It varies with geographic position, but is reasonably uniform over large areas (Fig. 5.1).

How do these models affect temperature logging and its interpretation? The following assumptions about heat flow seem reasonable.

1. Heat flow is assumed constant over the "exploitation times" involved in oilwell operations (0 to 100 years).

2. It is assumed constant over the depths involved in oilwell operations (0 to 30,000 ft).

3. It is assumed constant over large areas.

Therefore,

$$g_G \equiv \partial T/\partial D = u_h/k_h = \text{constant}/k_h. \quad\dotfill(5.2)$$

That is, the *geothermal gradient*, g_G, (i.e., the earth's temperature gradient), at any point varies inversely with the thermal conductivity of the rock. Chart 5.1 lists the thermal conductivities of some sedimentary rocks, showing the influences of lithology, porosity, and fluid content.[4,5] The thermal conductivities of most sedimentary rocks decrease as their temperatures increase. Goss *et*

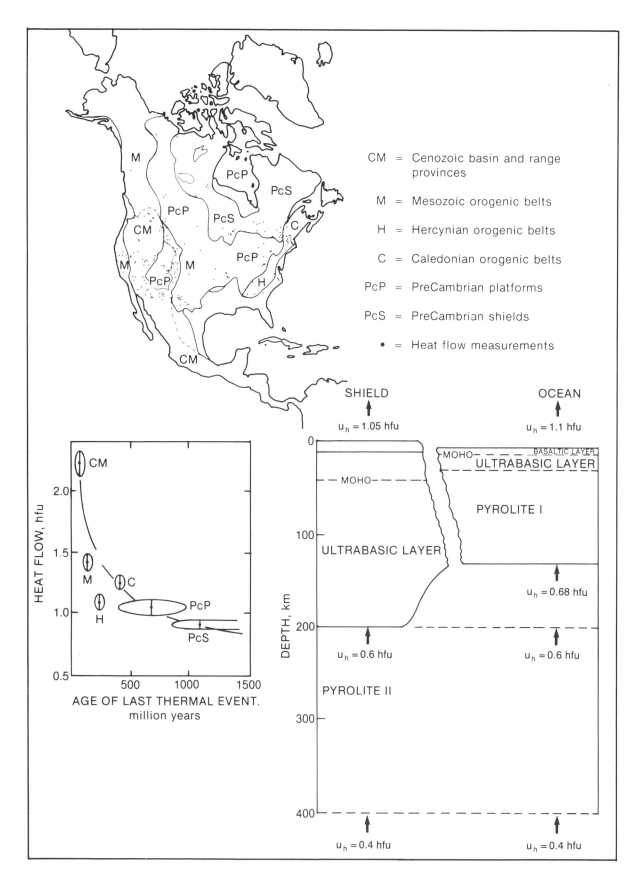

Fig. 5.1—Model of the earth's thermal behavior (modified after Sclater and Francheteau[3]).

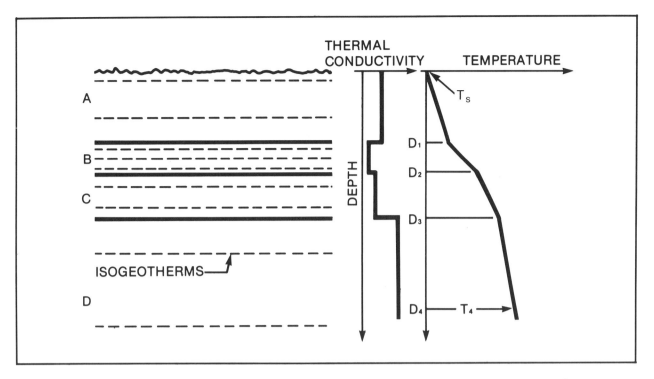

Fig. 5.2—Isogeotherms and formation temperature/depth profile in a hypothetical rock sequence.

al.[6] present a summary of how to predict thermal conductivity from other common well log parameters. Chap. 2 contains data on the thermal conductivities of some rock minerals. Chart 5.2 presents data on the thermal conductivity of water.[7]

If the rocks of the earth's crust were in uniform concentric shells, over reasonable areas this geometry might be approximated by uniform, horizontal layers. In such a geometry, *isogeotherms* (i.e., surfaces of equal temperature) would have the following properties.

1. They would be parallel, horizontal planes.

2. They would be equidistant for a given temperature differential in a given layer.

3. For the given temperature differential, the distance between them would be proportional to the thermal conductivity.

Thus, isogeotherms and formation-temperature profiles through a hypothetical rock sequence would appear as shown in Fig. 5.2. The temperature at Point *n* can be determined from

$$T_n = T_s + \sum_{i=1}^{n} \left[\left(\frac{\Delta T}{\Delta D}\right)_i \left(\Delta D\right)_i \right]$$

$$= T_s + \sum_{i=1}^{n} \left[(g_G)_i (\Delta D)_i \right], \quad \dots \dots \dots (5.3)$$

where T_n is geothermal temperature at depth n, T_s is surface temperature, $(g_G)_i$ is geothermal gradient for the ith layer, and $(\Delta D)_i$ is interval thickness for the ith layer. Thus, accurate determination of subsurface temperature requires knowledge of the surface temperature as well as

of the geometry and geothermal gradient of each layer above the point of interest.

Substituting Eq. 5.2 into Eq. 5.3 develops the following alternative expression for determining subsurface temperature.

$$T_n = T_s + u_h \sum_{i=1}^{n} \left[\left(\frac{1}{k_h}\right)_i \left(\Delta D\right)_i \right]. \quad \dots \dots (5.4)$$

In practice, average surface temperatures and geothermal gradients often are used to obtain subsurface temperatures. Customary units for temperature, geothermal gradient, and depth are degrees Fahrenheit or degrees Celsius, degrees Fahrenheit per 100 feet or degrees Celsius per meter, and feet or meters, respectively. SPE preferred units are degrees Celsius, milliKelvin per meter, and meters, respectively. Figs. 5.3[8,9] and 5.4[10] show the respective mean annual surface temperatures and geothermal gradients for North America and the U.S.

Subsurface rocks are, in fact, not concentric shells of uniform composition. Their spherical and planar symmetries are distorted by natural heterogeneities, facies changes, subsurface faults and structures, salt or igneous intrusions, and topographic relief. Thermal conductivities, isogeotherms, and temperature profiles are similarly distorted.

When using observed temperature profiles to solve geologic or engineering problems, one must infer a unique geologic or subsurface engineering model from borehole temperatures. But one must remember that temperature profiles are determined by the distribution of isogeotherms, which are determined by the subsurface

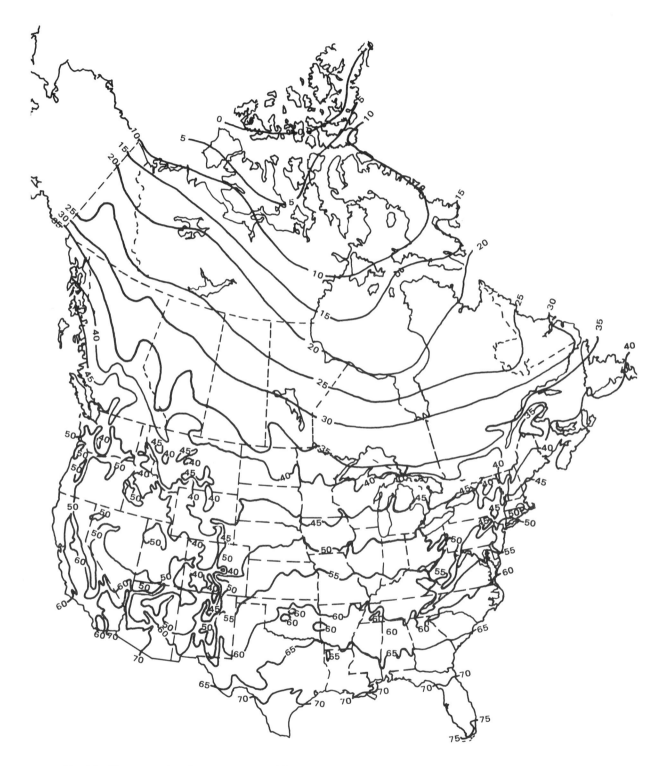

Fig. 5.3—Mean annual surface temperatures (°F) in North America (modified after Connolly[8] and Gearhart-Owen[9]).

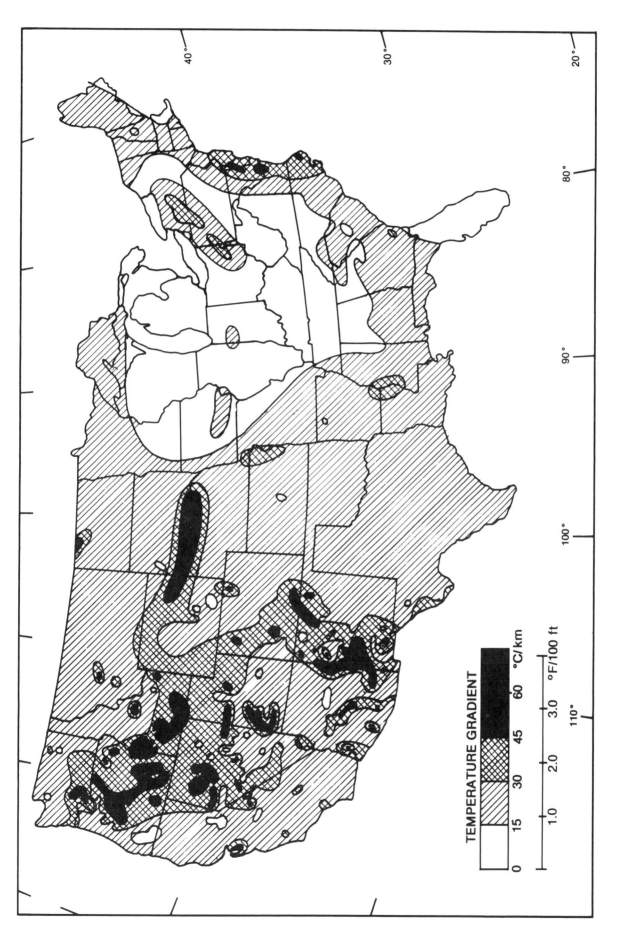

Fig. 5.4—Geothermal gradients in the U.S.A. (modified after Kron and Heiken[10]).

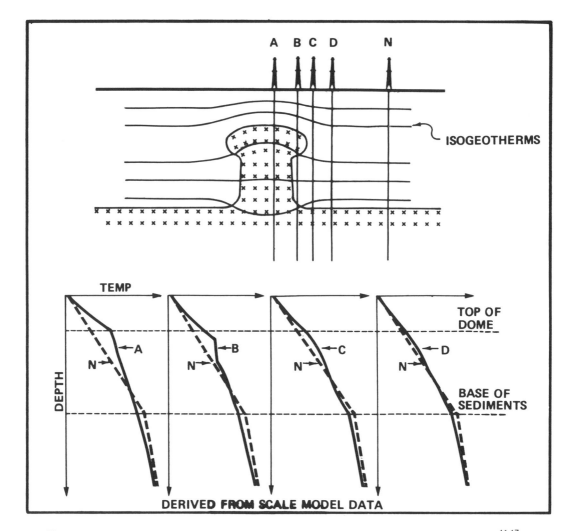

Fig. 5.5—Example of isogeotherms and temperature/depth profiles near a salt dome (after Guyod[11-17]).

geometric distribution of thermal conductivities. Rock properties such as mineralogy, porosity, and fluid content influence thermal conductivity.

For example, Fig. 5.5 shows scale model data of how isogeotherms and temperature/depth profiles would appear near a salt dome of very simple geometry.[11-17] This figure shows the significant effect that salt (with its different thermal conductivity) has on temperature profiles. Fig. 5.6 illustrates, with real subsurface data, how subsurface structure influences isogeotherms and borehole-temperature/depth profiles.[18] A more detailed discussion of the influence of subsurface geologic conditions on isogeotherms and geothermal profiles belongs in a story on geologic prospecting with geothermal data and is beyond the scope of this monograph.

5.1.2 Boreholes

Geothermal measurements are made in boreholes, which have temperature/depth profiles different from the geothermal profile. This is caused by heat transfer resulting from fluid flow (e.g., circulation of drilling mud, upward flow of produced reservoir fluids, and downward flow of injection fluids).

Drilling and Circulation Effects

Fig. 5.7 shows a section of the earth with a given geothermal profile (Curve 1) penetrated by a rotary-drilled borehole.[19] Actual borehole-temperature profiles are approximated by Curves 3a and 3b. As a circulating fluid nears the bottom of the drillpipe, it has gained some heat from the formation and annulus, but not enough to equal the formation temperature. Therefore, as the fluid rises up the borehole/drillpipe annulus, it continues to gain heat from the formation. At some point in the annulus the circulating fluid is hotter than the formation, and heat transfer is from the fluid to the formation.

This heat transfer results in a borehole-temperature/depth profile (Fig. 5.7), which is discussed in more detail in Refs. 19, 20 and 21. One point on that curve, the bottomhole circulating temperature, is plotted in Fig. 5.8 vs. depth from a series of API-sponsored measurements.[22]

During the noncirculation time required to pull pipe and start temperature logging, fluids from the drillpipe and annulus mix, and heat transfer continues between the borehole and the formation. The borehole-temperature profile shown in Fig. 5.7 becomes fairly linear except very near total depth (Fig. 5.9). At Point X the mud col-

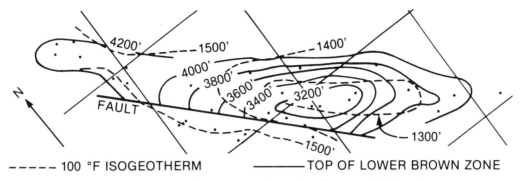

Long Beach Dome, Los Angeles County, California.

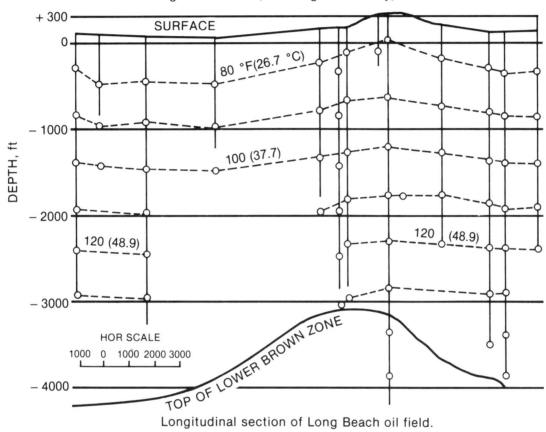

Longitudinal section of Long Beach oil field.

Fig. 5.6—Example of correlation between isogeotherms and subsurface geologic structure (actual data) (modified after van Orstrand[18]).

umn and formation temperatures are equal, so no heat transfer occurs. Eventually the borehole fluid cools above Point X and warms below Point X as both borehole regions approach thermal equilibrium with the formation.

Refs. 23 and 24 discuss natural convection as a heat-transfer mechanism in static boreholes. Convection induced by passage of logging tools can be minimized as described in Secs. 5.2.1 and 5.2.2.

Production Effects

A formation liquid entering a borehole often is at local formation temperature. As the liquid moves up the hole, it heats the overlying (cooler) formations; however, the process is self-limiting. Thus the borehole-temperature/depth profile becomes nearly parallel with the geothermal profile (Fig. 5.10).[25]

A gas entering a borehole often is cooler than the local formation temperature because of the Joule-Thompson effect: lower pressure in the borehole causes the gas to expand and cool. As the gas moves up the hole, it receives heat from the overlying (hotter) formation until at some point the two are equal. At this point (Point A on Fig. 5.11) the borehole-temperature/depth profile must be vertical because the gradient is zero (i.e., $\partial T_{wf}/\partial D = 0$ because no heat flows to or from the formation). As this heat transfer is self-limiting, the borehole-temperature/depth profile becomes nearly parallel to the geothermal profile (Fig. 5.11).

The temperature of the borehole fluid, T_{wf}, in a producing well, as a function of distance, L, above a producing zone and total time of production, t, is given by[26]

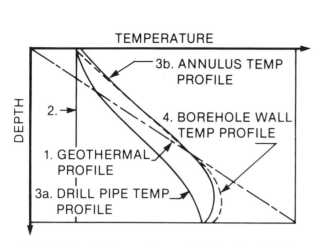

Fig. 5.7—Borehole temperature profile during circulation in a rotary drill borehole (after Raymond [19]).

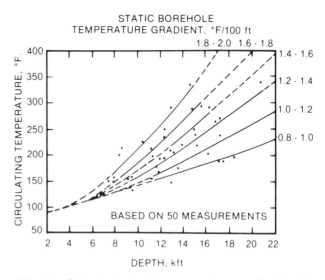

Fig. 5.8—Bottomhole circulating temperature as a function of depth and static borehole temperature gradient (after *Oil and Gas J.* [22]).

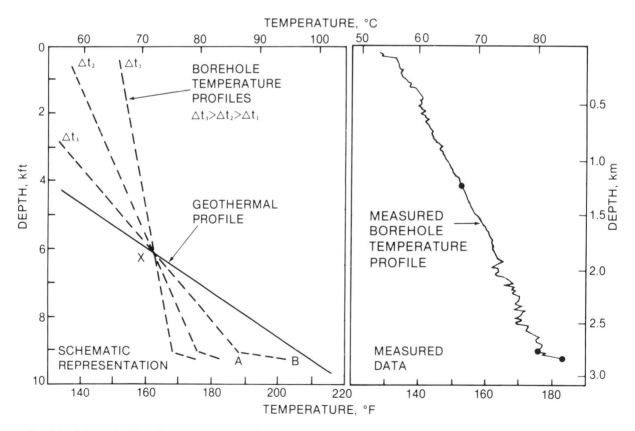

Fig. 5.9—Schematic of borehole temperature profile after circulation ceased and drillpipe pulled from a rotary drill borehole.

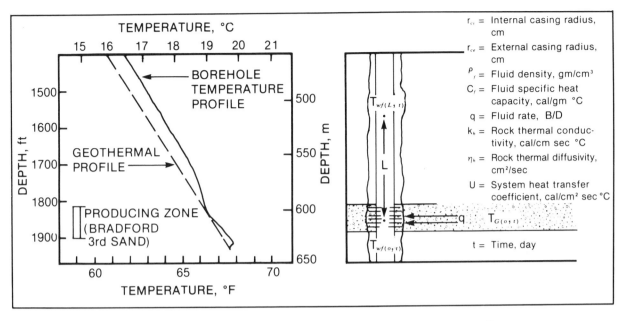

Fig. 5.10—A temperature log in a liquid-producing well (modified after Bird[25]).

$$T_{wf(L,t)} = T_{G(o,t)} - g_G L + g_G A$$

$$+ \left[T_{wf(o,t)} - T_{G(o,t)} - g_G A \right] e^{-L/A} , \quad \ldots \ldots \ldots (5.5)$$

where

$$A \text{ (in meters)} = 0.0184 \frac{q \rho_f C_f \left[k_h + r_{ci} U f(t) \right]}{2\pi r_{ci} U k_h} ,$$

and

$$f(t) \text{(dimensionless)} \approx \ln \left[3.40 \times 10^{-3} \frac{r_{ce}}{(\eta_h t)^{1/2}} \right] - C_1 ,$$

$T_{G(o,t)}$ is geothermal temperature (°C) at the fluid entry point, g_G is geothermal gradient (°C/m), $T_{wf(o,t)}$ is fluid temperature (°C) at the fluid entry point, and C_1 is a constant. Other terms and units are defined in Fig. 5.10.

Eq. 5.5 indicates that the borehole temperature approaches an asymptote given by Terms 1 through 3 of the equation. Terms 1 and 2 define the geothermal profile. Term 3, the asymptotic increase in temperature over the geothermal profile, is governed by mass producing rate, time, and the thermal properties of the rock/fluid/ borehole system. Term 4, the difference in produced fluid and asymptotic temperature (both at entry depth), is influenced by the same factors as Term 3. The rate of decay of Term 4 is governed by distance, of course, as well as mass producing rate, time, and the thermal properties of the rock/fluid/borehole system. The larger the flow rate and the longer the producing time, the more slowly the borehole-temperature profile approaches the asymptote and the larger the displacement of the asymptote from the geothermal profile.[26]

5.2 Description of Temperature-Measuring Devices

Temperature logging devices are of two types: (1) downhole-recording systems and (2) surface-recording systems.

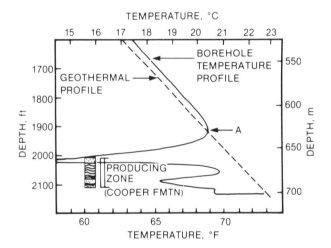

Fig. 5.11—A temperature log in a gas-producing well (after Bird[25]).

5.2.1 Downhole-Recording Systems

The two types within this system are the maximum-recording mercury thermometer and the mechanical recording thermometer (the so-called *temperature bomb*). Neither has a data communications link with the surface; hence, they can be run on any sort of wireline.

Operation of the maximum-recording thermometer needs no explanation. The maximum temperature is assumed to occur at the deepest depth reached, so this device is reliable only where temperature/depth profiles increase monotonically. The tool usually is run with other well logging devices to record bottomhole temperature. When possible, the thermometer should be run successively with a series of logging devices to generate a time/temperature data set for estimating true formation temperature (see Sec. 5.3.1).

When running the maximum-recording thermometer these guidelines should be followed.

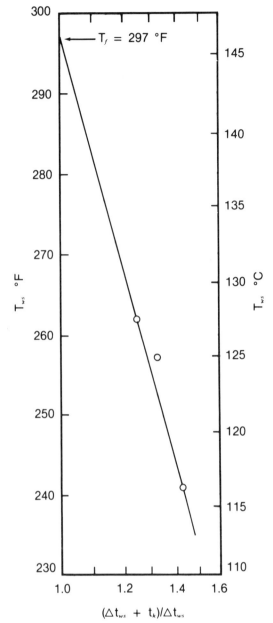

Fig. 5.12—Horner-type plot for estimating formation temperature from maximum-recording thermometer data (modified after Dowdle and Cobb[37]).

1. Ensure that the thermometer is "shaken down" before being run or re-run.

2. Ensure that the thermometer is run in a housing that isolates it from bottomhole pressures, which could produce an erroneous reading. Water in the housing will transmit borehole pressure to the thermometer.

3. Run at least two thermometers, for comparison.

The temperature bomb is a self-contained recording system that produces a basic data record of sensor deflection (proportional to temperature change) vs. time. Chart 5.3 summarizes the various sensor types used and briefly describes the basic physical principles employed in the measuring process. Sensor deflection is calibrated to temperature. While a bomb is in a borehole, a detailed account is kept of time vs. bomb depth. Sensor deflection (i.e., temperature) can be related to depth by comparing both the sensor-deflection/time and depth/time records.

The following guidelines apply when the temperature bomb is run.

1. Choose a clock with sufficient operating time for all required stops.

2. Record the log while going into the hole slowly, to minimize convection.

3. Make stops long enough to allow the sensor to stabilize and to register borehole temperature clearly (e.g., 15-minute stops for a 24-hour clock, 30-minute stops for a 48-hour clock).

4. Run at least two maximum-recording thermometers to produce a calibration point at the highest temperature.

5. Calibrate the tool for each job if maximum accuracy is required, since calibration changes with time and temperature. Calibration is best done in an oil bath, recording temperature corrections against some temperature standard such as a mercury thermometer.

The maximum-recording thermometer yields only one station measurement. The temperature bomb can record at a number of stations or, depending on the skill of the operator and the maximum operating time of the clock, can yield an almost continuous temperature log.

5.2.2 Surface-Recording Systems

These types of systems do, of course, have a data communications cable linking the temperature sensor with the surface. Chart 5.4 summarizes the various sensor types used and briefly describes the basic physical principles employed in the measuring process.

When running the surface-recording systems, follow these guidelines.

1. Record the log while going into the hole slowly, to minimize convection.

2. Run at least two maximum-recording thermometers, to produce a calibration point at the highest temperature.

3. Calibrate the tool for each job.

5.3 Interpretation of Temperature Logs

During the early days of well logging, temperature logging was a major part of the total logging capability. The instrumentation was relatively easy to achieve, so the principles of temperature behavior were adapted creatively to apply borehole temperature data to practical petroleum engineering problems. Table 5.1 summarizes the past and present uses of temperature logs.[1,11-17, 25-36]

TABLE 5.1—SUMMARY OF APPLICATIONS OF
BOREHOLE TEMPERATURE DATA

Application	Significant Reference(s)	Current Use
Determination of geothermal gradient	Schlumberger et al.[1], Nichols,[28] Schoeppel and Gilarranz[30]	high
Determination of lithology	Schlumberger et al.[1], Millikan,[27]	almost none
Delineation of hydrocarbon-bearing rocks	Schlumberger et al.[1], Millikan,[27] Johns[35]	almost none
Location of structural anomalies	Guyod[11-17]	almost none
Location of ore bodies	Guyod[11-17]	almost none
Location of fluid inflow	Schlumberger et al.[1], Guyod[11-17] Bird,[25] Curtis and Witterholt,[26] Millikan,[27] Peacock,[31] Kunz and Tixier[36]	high
Location of fluid injection (or lost circulation) zones	Bird,[25] Millikan,[27] Nowak,[29] Peacock,[31] Smith and Steffensen,[32] Witterholt and Tixier[33]	high
Location of artificially fractured zones	Peacock,[31] Agnew[34]	high
Location of casing leaks and channels	Schlumberger et al.[1], Millikan,[27] Peacock[31]	high
Location of primary cement top	Schlumberger et al.[1], Guyod,[11-17] Millikan,[27] Peacock[31]	moderate
Location of squeeze cement zones	Peacock[31]	low
Determination of hole size changes (caves)	Guyod,[11-17] Peacock[31]	almost none

Borehole temperature data for formation evaluation are now used mainly (1) to determine formation-temperature/depth profiles and (2) to delineate fluid inflow zones and to measure inflow rates. This monograph discusses these two applications. In addition, the bottomhole temperature and the borehole-temperature/depth profile provide support data for many formation-evaluation calculations. Discussion of the use of temperature log data to locate (1) primary cement tops, (2) behind-casing channels and casing leaks, (3) fluid injection (or lost circulation) zones, and (4) artificially fractured zones belongs in a monograph on production logging.

5.3.1 Determination of Bottomhole Temperature, Borehole-Temperature/Depth Profile, and Formation-Temperature/Depth Profile

Bottomhole Temperature

Bottomhole borehole temperature data can be obtained from maximum-recording thermometers, temperature bombs, or surface-recording systems. In wells being drilled, bottomhole temperatures are most likely lower than true formation temperatures.

Dowdle and Cobb[37] demonstrated that Horner-type plots $\{\log [(\Delta t_{ws}+t_k)/\Delta t_{ws}]$ vs. $T_{ws}\}$ of bottomhole borehole temperature data (Fig. 5.12) will yield reliable estimates of true formation temperature. This procedure is most reliable for short circulating times; the method, if at all inaccurate, will yield formation temperatures that are too low.[37] Alternative methods by Middleton[38] and

Roux et al.[39] for estimating bottomhole formation temperature from borehole measurements have not yet been tested extensively in practice.

Borehole-Temperature/Depth Profiles

Data for borehole-temperature/depth profiles can be obtained from temperature bombs or surface-recording systems. Temperatures in wells being drilled usually are not in equilibrium with, nor equal to, true formation temperatures (as discussed in Sec. 5.1.2) except at a single point (Fig. 5.9). Fig. 5.13 illustrates temperature logs in a well being drilled taken at various times after circulation was stopped.

Even in producing wells, borehole and formation temperatures can be significantly different (Sec. 5.1.2). All such data are valid only for the time at which they are taken, because borehole temperatures probably are changing in a process of approaching equilibrium and, even when in equilibrium, probably are not equal to the formation temperature.

Formation-Temperature/Depth Profiles

Formation-temperature/depth profiles can be measured (by use of temperature bombs or surface-recording systems) only when the borehole temperature equals the formation temperature. This seldom occurs.

For use in wells being drilled, Edwardson et al.[40] devised "exact" and "approximate" methods for determining both borehole and formation temperatures at any radial distance as functions of time. Table 5.2 summarizes their model and its assumptions. Mathematical evaluation of this model results in a series of curves of dimensionless temperature disturbance,

TABLE 5.2—MODEL OF TEMPERATURE AROUND A BOREHOLE
(after Edwardson et al.[40])

Basic Mathematical Model

$$\frac{\partial^2 T}{\partial r_D{}^2} + \frac{1}{r_D} \times \frac{\partial T}{\partial r_D} = \frac{\partial T}{\partial t_D},$$

where

$$r_D = \frac{r}{r_w} \text{ and } t_D = \frac{k_h t}{C_h \rho_b r_w{}^2}.$$

Assumptions
1. Borehole is axis of cylindrical symmetry.
2. Heat flow is caused only by conductivity.
3. Vertical heat flow in formation is zero.
4. Formation is radially infinite and homogeneous as concerns heat flow.
5. Mud cake is disregarded.
6. Heat generated by drill bit is disregarded.
7. Rate of radial heat flow at borehole face is zero during noncirculation.

Nomenclature
- T = temperature, °C
- r = radius, cm
- r_w = borehole radius, cm
- k_h = formation thermal conductivity, cal/cm-s-°C
- t = time, seconds
- C_h = formation specific heat capacity, cal/g-°C
- ρ_b = formation bulk density, g/cm^3

$\Delta T(r_D,t)/\Delta T(1,0)$ vs. logarithmic dimensionless shut-in time, $\Delta t_{ws}/(\Delta t_{ws}+t_k)$. Fig. 5.14 shows examples of such curves; Ref. 40 contains a complete set.

"Exact" Method. At any depth in a borehole, the total temperature disturbance caused by any mud-circulation history can be calculated by summing the disturbances caused by each circulation period. The temperature disturbance caused by a circulation period can be calculated (Fig. 5.14). Data required are shut-in time, Δt_{ws}, circulation time, t_k, and borehole temperature disturbance at the start of that circulation period, $\Delta T(1,0)$. Quantities Δt_{ws} and t_k are available from the well-circulation history. The most tedious parameter to determine is $\Delta T(1,0)$, which was influenced by all prior circulation periods. Edwardson *et al.*[40] outline procedures for calculating temperature disturbances at various radii from the borehole, as summarized in Charts 5.5 and 5.6.

"Approximate" Method. At any borehole depth the total temperature disturbance caused by any mud-circulation history can be approximated by treating that history as a single cycle of circulation and shut-in. Edwardson *et al.*[40] outline procedures for approximating temperature disturbances at various radii from the borehole, as summarized in Chart 5.7.

Fig. 5.13 compares borehole temperatures calculated by the "exact" method with temperatures measured at several shut-in times. The difference between the two temperatures is generally less than 5°F. An example shown by Edwardson *et al.*[40] (Fig. 5.15) indicates that

formation-temperature disturbances (calculated by the "exact" method) are not significant at radial distances greater than $10r_w$, even for the briefest noncirculation periods. Fig. 5.16 illustrates borehole temperatures estimated by the "approximate" method as compared with that measured 5 hours after circulation stopped. The difference between the two temperatures is less than 5°F except near the surface. Fig. 5.17 shows the good agreement between the "exact" and "approximate" methods.

5.3.2 Measurement of Fluid Inflow

Two major items of interest in formation evaluation of producing zones are (1) delineation of inflow intervals and (2) measurement of inflow rate.

Gas-Producing Formations

Fig. 5.18 (a theoretical temperature-log response opposite gas-producing zones) illustrates the diagnostic criteria that can be used to delineate gas-producing zones qualitatively.[36] The conditions and assumptions used are itemized on the figure. Fig. 5.19 (an actual log) shows that these same diagnostic criteria are evident in field situations.

Bird[25] presents quantitative methods for evaluating gas-flow rate, q_g, using the expression

$$q_g = C_1 \Delta. \quad \dots\dots\dots\dots\dots\dots\dots\dots (5.6)$$

In the nomenclature of Bird, Δ (*delta*) is defined as $(T_f - T_{wf})/(dT_{wf}/dD)$, and C_1 is a proportionality coefficient.

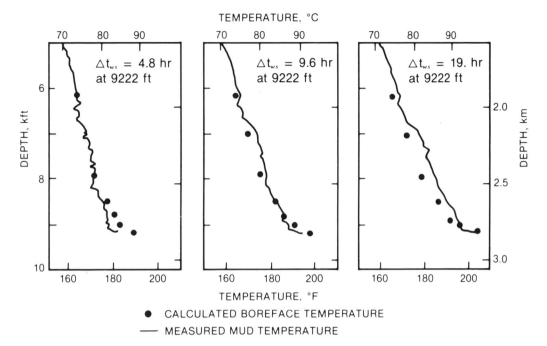

Fig. 5.13—Comparison of calculated ("exact method") with measured temperature logs in a borehole at various times after circulation ceased (after Edwardson *et al.*[40]).

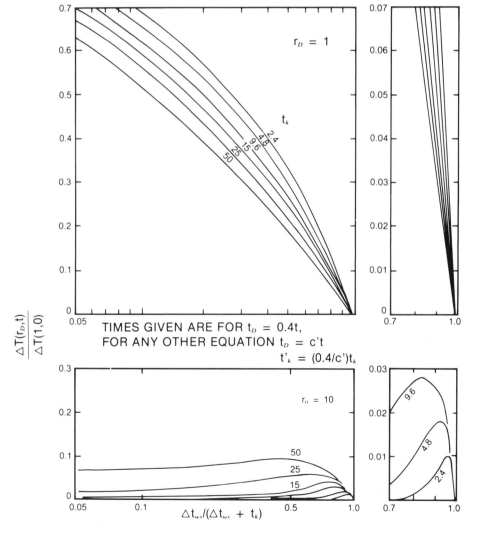

Fig. 5.14—Example curves of dimensionless temperature change as a function of dimensionless shut-in time (modified after Edwardson *et al.*[40]).

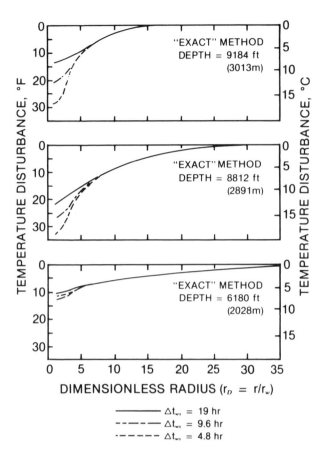

Fig. 5.15—Example of radial temperature disturbances at various depths (after Edwardson *et al.* [40]).

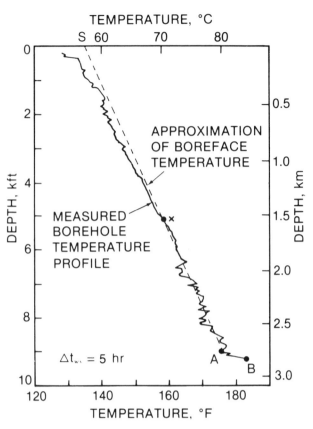

Fig. 5.16—Calculated ("approximate method") temperatures compared with measured temperatures (after Edwardson *et al.* [40]).

Kunz and Tixier[36] present a very similar method by use of the expression

$$q_g = C_2 L. \qquad (5.7)$$

In the nomenclature of Kunz and Tixier, L, the *subtangent*, has the same physical meaning as "delta" in Bird's terminology, and C_2 is a proportionality coefficient. Fig. 5.20 schematically defines the parameters used in these expressions to measure inflow rate.

Fig. 5.21 shows a correlation between gas-flow rate and delta.[41] In regions of laminar flow and in transition from laminar to turbulent flow the slopes are constant (although different), indicating that C_1 in Eq. 5.6 is constant. In regions of high-rate, turbulent flow, the slope is not constant, suggesting that C_1 varies with flow rate. Fig. 5.22 shows that C_2 in Eq. 5.7 is dependent on time as well as on formation thermal conductivity, hole diameter, and the presence or absence of casing. The pertinent assumptions and conditions for this curve are listed on the figure. Similar curves can be calculated using the methods of Ref. 36.

The volumetric gas-flow rate can be estimated from the graph of Fig. 5.21 or from Eq. 5.7, by use of the C_2 from Fig. 5.22 (or a similar one).

Schonblom[42] presents alternate methods for determining delta.

Fig. 5.23 shows the theoretical maximum temperature drop resulting from pressure drop (the Joule-Thompson effect). Bird and Frost[41] present arguments that gas produced from a matrix-permeability system will come closer to the Joule-Thompson expansion temperature than will gas from a fracture-permeability system. Fig. 5.24 supports these arguments, showing temperature logs opposite a gas-producing formation before and after fracturing.

Remember the following points when evaluating gas-producing zones.

1. If the temperature drop seems low for the amount of gas flow, fracturing should be suspected.

2. The presence of fractures will invalidate any empirical relationships between flow rate and delta.

Oil- or Water-Producing Formations
Fig. 5.25 (a theoretical temperature-log response opposite liquid-producing zones) illustrates diagnostic criteria that can be used to delineate such zones.[26] The conditions and assumptions used are itemized on the figure. Fig. 5.26 (an actual log) shows that these same diagnostic criteria are evident in field situations.

Curtis and Witterholt[26] present quantitative methods for evaluating liquid-flow rate using the expressions of Eq. 5.5. Fig. 5.26 illustrates a field application of temperature log data in quantifying the flow profile and flow rate; interpretation is quoted on the figure. The authors concluded: " . . . flow rates from the temperature analysis should only be used as indicating percentage of total flow. . . ."

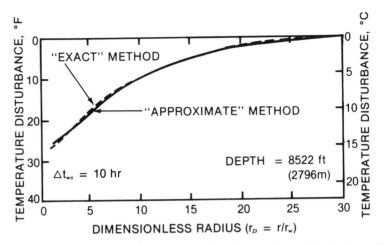

Fig. 5.17—Comparison of temperature disturbances obtained by the "exact" and "approximate" methods (after Edwardson *et al.*[40]).

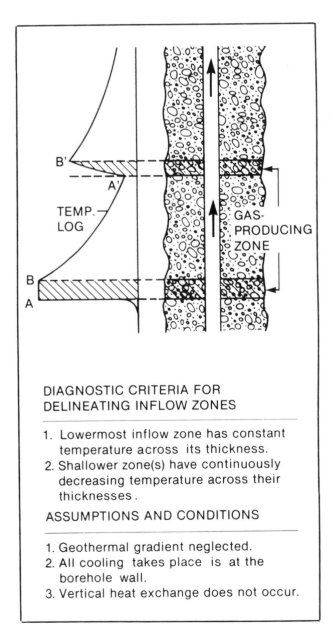

DIAGNOSTIC CRITERIA FOR
DELINEATING INFLOW ZONES

1. Lowermost inflow zone has constant temperature across its thickness.
2. Shallower zone(s) have continuously decreasing temperature across their thicknesses.

ASSUMPTIONS AND CONDITIONS

1. Geothermal gradient neglected.
2. All cooling takes place is at the borehole wall.
3. Vertical heat exchange does not occur.

Fig. 5.18—Typical temperature log response across gas-producing zones (modified after Kunz and Tixier[36]).

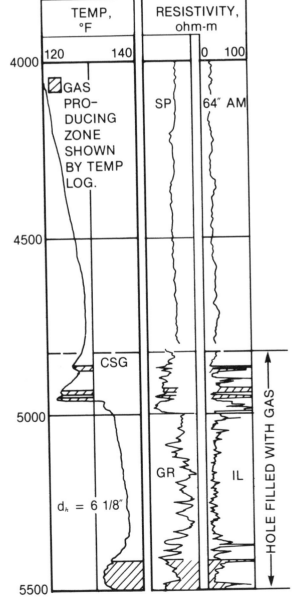

Fig. 5.19—Actual temperature log in a gas-producing well, San Juan basin (modified after Kunz and Tixier[36]).

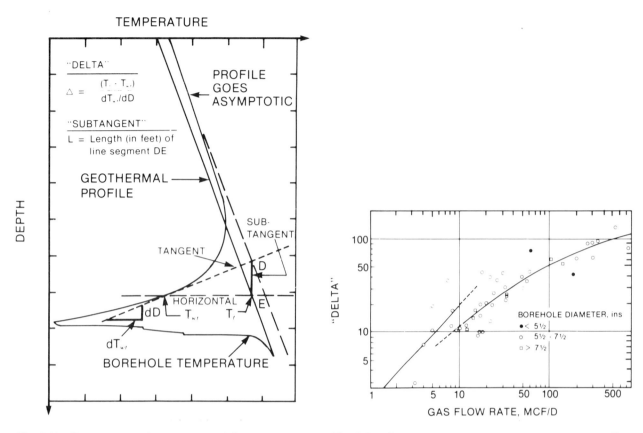

Fig. 5.20—Parameters used to measure gas inflow rate quantitatively from a temperature log.

Fig. 5.21—Correlation between gas flow rate and "delta" (after Bird and Frost[41]).

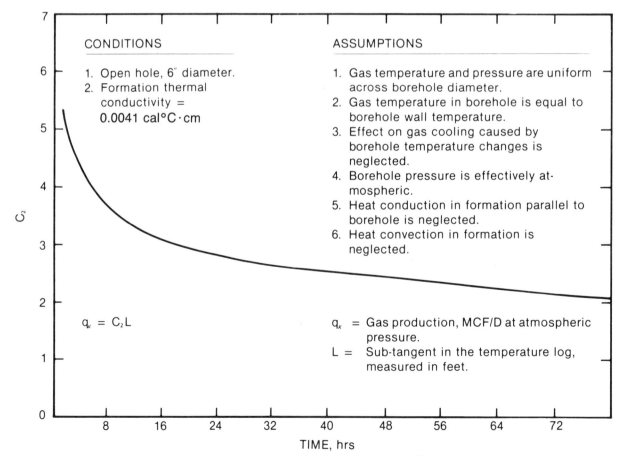

Fig. 5.22—Plot of C_2 vs. time (after Kunz and Tixier[36]).

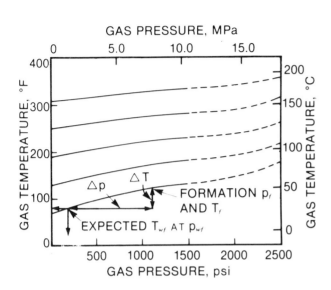

Fig. 5.23—Theoretical maximum temperature drop of gases undergoing Joule-Thompson effect cooling (after Bird and Frost[41]).

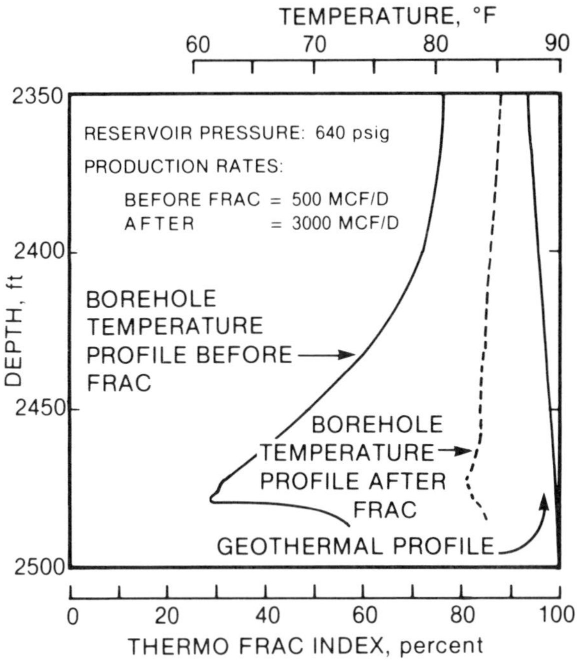

Fig. 5.24—Effect of fracturing on temperature log response opposite a gas-producing zone (after Bird and Frost[41]).

5.4 Summary Comments

Borehole temperature is easily measured by the instruments described in Sec. 5.2. Fig. 5.27 illustrates the various options available to the formation-evaluation specialist in (1) selecting various measuring tools and (2) using various data-reduction procedures to get the desired formation-evaluation information. Detailed study of this figure, in conjunction with the appropriate monograph text, figures, and charts, should lead to a reasonable understanding of the major options and limitations of temperature logging.

References

1. Schlumberger, M., Doll, H.G., and Perebinossoff, A.A.: "Temperature Measurements in Oil Wells," *J. Inst. Pet. Technologists* (Jan. 1937) **23**, 159.
2. Strong, M.W.: "The Significance of Underground Temperatures," *Proc.*, First World Pet. Cong., London (1933) 124–28.
3. Sclater, J.G. and Francheteau, J.: "The Implications of Terrestrial Heat Flow Observations on Current Tectonic and Geochemical Models of the Crust and Upper Mantle of the Earth," *Geophys. J.Royal Astronomical Soc.* (1970) **20**, 509–42.
4. Somerton, W.H.: "Some Thermal Characteristics of Porous Rocks," *J. Pet. Tech.* (May 1958) 61–64; *Trans.*, AIME, **213**, 375–78.
5. Zierfuss, H. and van der Vliet, G.: "Laboratory Measurement of Heat Conductivity of Sedimentary Rocks," *Bull.*, AAPG (1956) **40**, 2475–88.
6. Goss, R., Combs, J., and Timur, A.: "Prediction of Thermal Conductivity in Rocks from Other Physical Parameters and from Standard Geophysical Well Logs," *Trans.*, SPWLA Annual Symposium (1975) paper MM.
7. *Handbook of Physical Constants*, S.P. Clarke Jr. (ed.), Memoir 97, GSA, Boulder, CO (1966) 459–82.
8. Connolly, E.T.: "Geothermal Survey of North America Progress Report and Associated Data-Gathering Problems," *Trans.*, CWLS Symposium (1972) paper F.
9. Gearhart-Owen Industries Inc.: *Formation Evaluation Data Handbook* (1975).
10. Kron, A. and Heiken, G.: "Geothermal Gradient Map of the United States," *Trans.*, Geothermal Resources Council (1980) **4**, 69–71.
11. Guyod, H.: "Temperature Well Logging," *Oil Weekly* (Oct. 21, 1946) 35–39.
12. Guyod, H.: "Temperature Well Logging," *Oil Weekly* (Oct. 28, 1946) 33–42.
13. Guyod, H.: "Temperature Well Logging," *Oil Weekly* (Nov. 4, 1946) 32–39.
14. Guyod, H.: "Temperature Well Logging," *Oil Weekly* (Nov. 11, 1946) 50–54.
15. Guyod, H.: "Temperature Well Logging," *Oil Weekly* (Dec. 2, 1946) 27–34.
16. Guyod, H.: "Temperature Well Logging," *Oil Weekly* (Dec. 9, 1946) 36–40.
17. Guyod, H.: "Temperature Well Logging," *Oil Weekly* (Dec. 16, 1946) 38–40.
18. van Orstrand, C.E.: "On the Correlation of Isogeothermal Surfaces with the Rock Strata," *Physics* (1932) **2**, 139–53.
19. Raymond, L.R.: "Temperature Distribution in a Circulating Drilling Fluid," *J. Pet. Tech.* (March 1969) 333–41.
20. Holmes, C.S. and Swift, S.C.: "Calculation of Circulating Mud Temperatures," *J. Pet. Tech.* (June 1970) 670–74.
21. Keller, H.H., Couch, E.J. and Berry, P.M.: "Temperature Distribution in Circulating Mud Columns," *Soc. Pet. Eng. J.* (Feb. 1973) 23–30.
22. "New Cement Test Schedules Issued," *Oil and Gas J.* (July 25, 1977) 179–81.
23. Gretener, P.E.: "On the Thermal Instability of Large Diameter Wells—An Observational Report," *Geophysics* (Aug. 1967) **32**, 727–38.
24. Sammel, E.A.: "Convective Flow and Its Effect on Temperature Logging in Small-Diameter Wells," *Geophysics* (Dec. 1968) **33**, 1004–12.

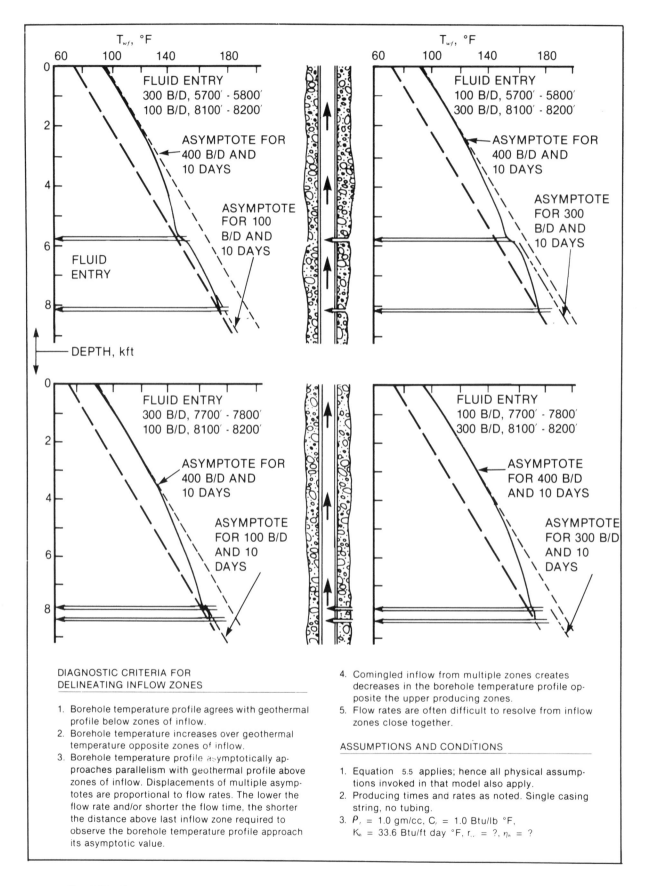

DIAGNOSTIC CRITERIA FOR
DELINEATING INFLOW ZONES

1. Borehole temperature profile agrees with geothermal profile below zones of inflow.
2. Borehole temperature increases over geothermal temperature opposite zones of inflow.
3. Borehole temperature profile asymptotically approaches parallelism with geothermal profile above zones of inflow. Displacements of multiple asymptotes are proportional to flow rates. The lower the flow rate and/or shorter the flow time, the shorter the distance above last inflow zone required to observe the borehole temperature profile approach its asymptotic value.

4. Comingled inflow from multiple zones creates decreases in the borehole temperature profile opposite the upper producing zones.
5. Flow rates are often difficult to resolve from inflow zones close together.

ASSUMPTIONS AND CONDITIONS

1. Equation 5.5 applies; hence all physical assumptions invoked in that model also apply.
2. Producing times and rates as noted. Single casing string, no tubing.
3. P_f = 1.0 gm/cc, C_f = 1.0 Btu/lb °F, K_h = 33.6 Btu/ft day °F, $r_{..}$ = ?, η_h = ?

Fig. 5.25—Temperature log response across a liquid-producing zone (modified after Curtis and Witterholt[26]).

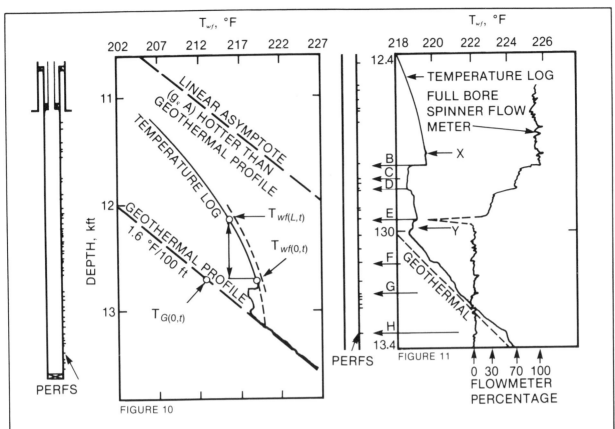

FIGURE 10

FIGURE 11

INTERPRETATION[26]

"Figure 10 shows the temperature curve ... from a well ... producing oil ... no water ... no free gas. The highest level of significant fluid entry is at about 12,755 ft. The temperature profile in the interval from 12,000 to 12,700 ft ... appears to be responding to the mass flow rate ...

The dashed curve aproximately parallel to the temperature curve represents the best fit with Equation 4** except that it has been displaced by 0.5 °F ... This fit corresponds to a value of A equal to 1,599 ft ...

The dashed curve from 12,800 to 13,161 ft. is the extension of the temperature response as predicted by Equation 4** ... The linear asymptote ... is shown ... at the upper right ...

... the volumetric flow rate may be computed ... q ... ≅ 339 BOPD. This value compares with the reported flow rate of approximately 900 BOPD ... Hence, the flow rates from the temperature analysis should only be used as indicating percentages of total flow ...

Figure 11 shows in expanded scale the temperature log ... and Full-Bore Spinner Flowmeter ...

Major zones of oil entry ... are indicated by shifts in the Flowmeter curve ...

Fluid entries are reflected on the Temperature Log by changes in slope and/or abrupt shifts, where fluids of different temperature mix. Zones B, D, and E, shown

by the Flowmeter to be producing, have abrupt shifts on the Temperature Log. Note, however, that the Temperature Log shows a pronounced slope change at Level X and an abrupt shift at Level Y. These levels are probably producing through the liner annulus to the closest set of perforations ... Only the Temperature Log has this ability to detect produced-fluid flow in annulus. Below 13,000 ft. there are three temperature anomalies at F, G, and H that indicate very small amounts of oil production. Also, the Temperature Log suggests a very small amount of productin from Zone C. The production from these zones is too small to be detected by the Flowmeter.

... segments of the Temperature Log have been analyzed by use of Equation 4**

TABLE 1	Flowmeter Results	Temperature Log Results		
INTERVAL	Percent of Total Flow	A	BOPD	Percent of Total Flow
Above Level X	100	1 5 9 9	339	100
Between Zones B and D	70	—		
Between Zones D and E	30	5 9 5	125	37
Between Zones E and F	—	3 3	7	2.1
Between Zones F and G	—	4 4	9	2.7
Between Zones G and H	—	1 8	4	1.1

The results ... are shown in Table 1 . The reliability of ... A and the flow rates ... will depend on the length of the segment and the exponential character it displays. A temperature-computed flow rate is not possible at Zone C because it is too close to adjacent producing zones."

**eqn. 5.5 in this Monograph

Fig. 5.26—Actual temperature log in liquid-producing well, Uinta basin (modified after Curtis and Witterholt[26]).

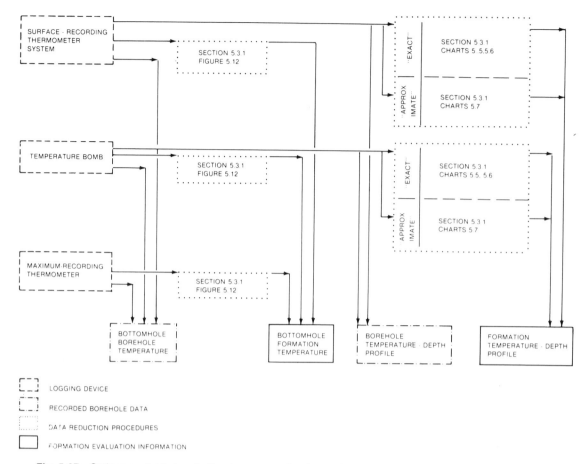

Fig. 5.27—Options available in selecting temperature logging tools and in evaluating formation temperature.

25. Bird, J.M.: "Interpretation of Temperature Logs in Water- and Gas-Injection Wells and Gas-Producing Wells," *Drill. and Prod. Prac.*, API (1954) 187–95.

26. Curtis, M.R. and Witterholt, E.J.: "Use of the Temperature Log for Determining Flow Rates in Producing Wells," paper SPE 4637 presented at the 1973 SPE Annual Fall Meeting, Las Vegas, Oct. 1–3.

27. Millikan, C.V.: "Temperature Surveys in Oil Wells," *Trans.*, AIME (1941) **142**, 15–23.

28. Nichols, E.A.: "Geothermal Gradients in Mid-Continent and Gulf Coast Oil Fields," *Trans.*, AIME (1947) **170**, 44–47.

29. Nowak, T.J.: "The Estimation of Water Injection Profiles from Temperature Surveys," *J. Pet. Tech.* (Aug. 1953) 203–12; *Trans.*, AIME, **198**.

30. Schoeppel, R.J. and Gilarranz, S.: "Use of Well Log Temperatures to Evaluate Regional Geothermal Gradients," *J. Pet. Tech.* (June 1966) 667–73.

31. Peacock, D.R.: "Temperature Logging," *Trans.*, SPWLA Annual Symposium (1965) paper F.

32. Smith, R.C. and Steffensen, R.J.: "Computer Study of Factors Affecting Temperature Profiles in Water Injection Wells," *J. Pet. Tech.* (Nov. 1970) 1447–58; *Trans.*, AIME, **249**.

33. Witterholt, E.J. and Tixier, M.P.: "Temperature Logging in Injection Wells," paper SPE 4022 presented at the 1972 SPE Annual Fall Meeting, San Antonio, Oct. 8–11.

34. Agnew, B.G.: "Evaluation of Fracture Treatments with Temperature Surveys," *J. Pet. Tech.* (July 1966) 892–98; *Trans.*, AIME, **237**.

35. Johns, E.: "Tracing Fluid Movements with a New Temperature Technique," paper SPE 1750 presented at the 1967 SPE Symposium on Mechanical Engineering Aspects of Drilling and Production, Fort Worth, March 5–7.

36. Kunz, K.S. and Tixier, M.P.: "Temperature Surveys in Gas Producing Wells," *J. Pet. Tech.* (July 1955) 111–19; *Trans.*, AIME, **204**.

37. Dowdle, W.L. and Cobb, W.M.: "Static Formation Temperature from Well Logs—An Empirical Method," *J. Pet. Tech.* (Nov. 1975) 1326–30.

38. Middleton, M.F.: "A Model for Bottom-Hole Temperature Stabilization," *Geophysics* (Aug. 1979) **44**, 1458–62.

39. Roux, B., Sanyal, S.K., and Brown, S.L.: "An Improved Approach to Estimating True Reservoir Temperature from Transient Temperature Data," paper SPE 8888 presented at the 1980 SPE California Regional Meeting, Los Angeles, April 9–11.

40. Edwardson, M.J. *et al.*: "Calculation of Formation Temperature Disturbances Caused by Mud Circulation," *J. Pet. Tech.* (April 1962) 416–26; *Trans.*, AIME, **225**.

41. Bird, J.M. and Frost, N.: "Formation Productivity Evaluation from Temperature Logs," *J. Pet. Tech.* (March 1966) 301–05.

42. Schonblom, J.E.: "Quantitative Evaluation of Temperature Logs in Flowing Gas Wells," *Trans.*, SPWLA Annual Symposium (1961) paper 9.

Appendix

Use of SI Units in Well Logging Equations

This Appendix contains the information needed to use the major equations of this monograph in either customary units or SPE-preferred SI metric units.

Customary units are those most commonly used in typical oilfield practice to express the quantity; most often these are English units but sometimes are (cgs or mks) metric. SPE-preferred SI units are fundamental SI units modified by a unit prefix, if any, to achieve convenient unit size.

In the Nomenclature, found on Page 151, both the customary and SPE-preferred SI metric units, as taken from the SPE Metric Standard,* are tabulated for the

*"The SI Metric System of Units and SPE METRIC STANDARD," *Trans.*, AIME (1982) **273**, 1023–59.

quantities used in this monograph. These are the units used in the derivation of the constants found in Table A.1.

The equations of this monograph are developed in the text using units that allow an uncluttered view of the physical/chemical concepts and principles being expressed. Generally speaking, these units are identified in the text; very often they are fundamental SI metric units because this system, being completely self-consistent, eliminates the need for any conversion factors. To apply the major equations to practical problems in either customary or SPE-preferred SI metric units, the constants specified in Table A.1 should be used in the manner indicated.

TABLE A.1—MAJOR EQUATIONS WITH CONSTANT VALUES IN CUSTOMARY AND SPE-PREFERRED SI METRIC UNITS

Equation Number in Text	Equation	Numerical Values of Constants in Order of Appearance $(c_1, c_2, c_3 \ldots)$	
		Customary	SPE-Preferred SI Metric
2.1	$\phi = -\log_2 (c_1 d_{gr})$	10^{-3}	10^{-3}
2.2	$S_O = c_1 \left(\dfrac{d_{25}}{d_{75}} \right)^{1/2}$	1.0	1.0
2.3	$\dfrac{(V_b)_{P_c}}{(V_b)_{P\infty}} = c_1 e^{-G / \log (P_c / P_d)}$	1.0	1.0
2.5	$k = \dfrac{c_1 u \mu}{c_2 \rho g_s - c_3 (\partial p / \partial s)}$	$3.048^* \times 10^4$, $3.008\ 142 \times 10^{-5}$, $2.232\ 471 \times 10^{-3}$	10^{-12}, 1.0, 10^3
2.6	$P_c = c_1 \sigma \cos \theta \left(\dfrac{1}{r_1} + \dfrac{1}{r_2} \right)$	$1.450\ 38 \times 10^{-1}$	1.0
2.9	$P_c = c_1 (\rho_w - \rho_o) g h$	$1.354\ 77^* \times 10^{-2}$	10^{-3}
2.12	$\phi S_w = c_1 C$	1.0	1.0
2.13	$C_{ppm} = C_{mg/L} / c_1 \rho$	1.0	10^{-3}
3.1	$V_{mf} = c_1 c \sqrt{t}$	1.0	1.0

Equation Number in Text	Equation	Numerical Values of Constants in Order of Appearance $(c_1, c_2, c_3 ...)$	
		Customary	SPE-Preferred SI Metric
3.2	$\dfrac{dV_{mf}}{dt} =$	$2.074\ 034 \times 10^{-3}$	10^{-3}
	$c_1\left(\dfrac{2\pi h_f\,(p_w - p_e)}{\dfrac{\mu_{mf}}{k_{mc}}\ln\dfrac{r_w}{r_{mc}} + \dfrac{\mu_{imp}}{k_{imp}}\ln\dfrac{r_{imp}}{r_w} + \dfrac{\mu_{if}}{k_{if}}\ln\dfrac{r_{if}}{r_{imp}} + \dfrac{\mu_f}{k_f}\ln\dfrac{r_e}{r_{if}}}\right)$		
3.3	$\sigma_v = c_1 \bar{\rho}_b h g = \sigma_{zo}$	$1.354\ 77^* \times 10^{-2}$	10^{-3}
3.4	$p_f = c_1 \rho_f h g$	$1.354\ 77^* \times 10^{-2}$	10^{-3}
3.5	$\sigma_e = \sigma_t - c_1 p_f$	1.0	10^{-3}
3.6	$\sigma_{zi} = c_1 \sigma_{zo}$	1.0	1.0
3.7	$\sigma_{\theta i} = \dfrac{2\nu}{1-\nu}\sigma_{zo} - \dfrac{\nu}{1-\nu}\beta c_1 p_f$	1.0	10^{-3}
3.8	$\sigma_{ri} = c_1 p_w = c_2 p_f$	$1.0,\ 1.0$	$10^{-3},\ 10^{-3}$
4.1	$n_\ell = c_1(n_1 - n_2)$	1.0	1.0
4.3	$d_{cs} = c_1 d\left(\dfrac{\rho_{m1}}{\rho_{m2}}\right)$	1.0	1.0
4.5	$C_o = c_1\left(\dfrac{\pi d_h{}^2 \cdot h_o}{4 t_h \cdot q_m}\right)\left(\dfrac{S_o \cdot \phi}{B_o}\right)$ $(1 - F_1)(1 - S_{or})(1 - F_2)$	$8.658\ 006 \times 10^{-4}$	$2.777\ 778 \times 10^{-7}$
4.6	$C_g = c_1\left(\dfrac{\pi d_h{}^2 \cdot h_o}{4 t_h \cdot q_m}\right)\left(\dfrac{S_o \cdot R \cdot \phi}{B_o}\right)$ $(1 - F_1)(1 - S_{gr})(1 - F_3)$	$8.658\ 006 \times 10^{-4}$	$2.777\ 778 \times 10^{-7}$
4.7	$C_g = c_1\left(\dfrac{\pi d_h{}^2 \cdot h_g}{4 t_h \cdot q_m}\right)\left(S_g \cdot \phi \cdot \dfrac{p_R \cdot z_s \cdot T_s}{p_s \cdot z_R \cdot T_R}\right)$ $(1 - F_1)(1 - S_{gr})(1 - F_3)$	$8.658\ 006 \times 10^{-4}$	$2.777\ 778 \times 10^{-7}$
4.8	$p_f = c_1 \rho_f h$	(g/cm^3) $.335\ 264 \times 10^{-1}$ (lbm/gal) $5.194\ 88^* \times 10^{-2}$	$9.8^* \times 10^{-3}$
5.1	$u_h = c_1 k_h (\partial T / \partial D)$	10^{-2}	10^{-6}
5.3	$T_n = T_s + c_1 \displaystyle\sum_{i=1}^{n} [(g_G)_i (\Delta D)_i]$	10^{-2}	10^{-3}

Equation Number in Text	Equation	Numerical Values of Constants in Order of Appearance $(c_1, c_2, c_3 \ldots)$	
		Customary	SPE-Preferred SI Metric
5.4	$T_n = T_s + c_1 \, u_h \sum_{i=1}^{n} \left[\left(\frac{1}{k_h} \right)_i \left(\Delta D \right)_i \right]$	1.0	10^3
5.5	$T_{wf(L,t)} = T_{G(o,t)} - c_1 g_G L + c_2 g_G A$ $+ \left[T_{wf(o,t)} - T_{G(o,t)} - c_3 g_G A \right] e^{-L/A}$ where	$10^{-2}, 10^{-2}, 10^{-2}$	$10^{-3}, 10^{-3}, 10^{-3}$
	$A = c_1 \dfrac{q \rho_f C_f [k_h + c_2 r_{ci} U f(t)]}{2 \pi r_{ci} U k_h}$	$1.752\ 535 \times 10^2$ $8.333\ 333 \times 10^{-2}$	$1.157\ 407 \times 10^{-2}$ 1.0
	and		
	$f(t) \approx \ln \left[c_1 \dfrac{r_{ce}}{(\eta_h t)^{1/2}} \right] - C_1$	$1.388\ 889 \times 10^{-3}$	$1.666\ 667 \times 10^{-2}$

Nomenclature

Symbol	Description	Dimensions	Customary Units	SPE-Preferred SI Metric Units	Customary to Metric Conversion Factors
a	Constant in Eq. 4.2				
A	Constant in Eqs. 2.10 and 2.11; Seevers correlation factor in Table 2.15				
A,B,C	Timur correlation factors in Table 2.15				
A_s	Internal pore surface per unit bulk volume	L^2/L^3	1/cm	1/mm	1.0* E−01
B	Formation volume factor	L^3/L^3	volume fraction	m^3/m^3	1.0* E+00
c	Constant in Eq. 3.1	$L^3/t^{1/2}$	mL/sec$^{1/2}$	cm^3/s$^{1/2}$	1.0* E+00
C	Correlation factor in Eq. 2.12				
C	Hydrocarbon concentration in mud	L^3/L^3	volume fraction	m^3/m^3	1.0* E+00
C	Kozeny constant in Table 2.15				
C_f	Fluid specific heat capacity	L^2/t^2T	Btu/(lbm-°F)	kJ/(kg·K)	4.186 8* E+00
$C_{g/gal}$	Concentration of dissolved solids in water, expressed as grains/gal	m/L^3	grains/U.S. gal	mg/dm^3	1.711 806 E+01
$C_{mg/L}$	Concentration of dissolved solids in water, expressed as mg/L	m/L^3	mg/L	g/m^3	1.0* E−01
C_m	Concentration of dissolved solids in water, expressed as molality	mol/m	g mol/kg	kmol/kg	1.0* E−03
C_M	Concentration of dissolved solids in water, expressed as molarity	mol/L^3	g mol/L	kmol/m^3	1.0* E+00
C_N	Concentration of dissolved solids in water, expressed as normality	eq/L^3	g eq/L	kg eq/m^3	1.0* E+00
C_{ppm}	Concentration of dissolved solids in water, expressed as parts per million	m/m	wt ppm	mg/kg	1.0* E+00
C_W	Concentration of dissolved solids in water, expressed as weight percent	m/m	wt%	kg/kg	1.0* E−02
C_1	Constant in Eq. 5.5				
C_1	Proportionality coefficient in Eq. 5.6				
C_2	Proportionality coefficient in Eq. 5.7				
d	Formation drillability d-exponent				
d_b	Bit diameter	L	in.	mm	2.54* E+01
d_{cs} or d_{xc}	Corrected d-exponent				
d_{gr}	Grain diameter	L	micron	μm	1.0* E+00
d_h	Borehole diameter	L	in.	mm	2.54* E+01
d_i	Diameter of invasion	L	in.	mm	2.54* E+01
d_{25}	Grain diameter, 25 percentile (cumulative weight percent)	L	mm	mm	1.0* E+00
d_{75}	Grain diameter, 75 percentile (cumulative weight percent)	L	mm	mm	1.0* E+00
$\hat{d}_{gr}$	Median grain diameter	L	mm	mm	1.0* E+00
$\tilde{d}_{gr}$	Modal grain diameter	L	mm	mm	1.0* E+00

Symbol	Description	Dimensions	Customary Units	SPE-Preferred SI Metric Units	Customary to Metric Conversion Factors
$\bar{d}_{gr\phi}$	Mean grain diameter, expressed in phi units	L	phi units	phi units	1.0* E+00
$\hat{d}_{gr\phi}$	Median grain diameter, expressed in phi units	L	phi units	phi units	1.0* E+00
$\tilde{d}_{gr\phi}$	Modal grain diameter, expressed in phi units	L	phi units	phi units	1.0* E+00
dL	Incremental distance above an arbitrary datum in a reservoir	L	ft	m	3.048* E−01
$dp_o - dp_w$	Incremental pressure difference	m/Lt^2	lbf/sq in.	kPa	6.894 757 E+00
dV_{mf}/dt	Filtration rate	L^3/t	cm^3/sec	cm^3/s	1.0* E+00
$(\Delta D)_i$	Interval thickness for ith layer	L	ft	m	3.048* E−01
f	Rotary speed	$1/t$	rev/min	rad/s	1.047 198 E−01
F	Purcell correlation factor in Table 2.15				
F_1	Flushing factor in Eq. 4.7				
F_2	Loss factor; oil from mud in return line				
F_3	Loss factor; gas from mud in return line				
g	Acceleration of gravity	L/t^2	ft/sec^2	m/s^2	3.048* E−01
g_G	Geothermal gradient	T/L	°F/100 ft	mK/m	1.822 689 E+01
$(g_G)_i$	Geothermal gradient for ith layer	T/L	°F/100 ft	mK/m	1.822 689 E+01
G	Pore geometrical factor, reflecting the distribution of pore throats and their associated pore volumes				
h	Arbitrary reservoir level; length of well in saturated interval; true vertical distance from surface; true vertical depth	L	ft	m	3.048* E−01
h_f	Height of formation cylinder	L	ft	m	3.048* E−01
h_{mc}	Mudcake thickness	L	in.	mm	2.54* E+01
k	Permeability	L^2	md	μm^2	9.869 233 E−04
k_a	Permeability, air	L^2	md	μm^2	9.869 233 E−04
k_f	Permeability of formation	L^2	md	μm^2	9.869 233 E−04
k_g	Permeability, effective, to gas	L^2	md	μm^2	9.869 233 E−04
k_h	Thermal conductivity	mL/t^3T	Btu/(hr-sq ft-°F/ft)	W/(m·K)	1.730 735 E+00
k_{if}	Permeability of infiltered zone	L^2	md	μm^2	9.869 233 E−04
k_{imp}	Permeability of impregnated zone	L^2	md	μm^2	9.869 233 E−04
k_{mc}	Permeability of mudcake	L^2	md	μm^2	9.869 233 E−04
k_o	Permeability, effective, to oil	L^2	md	μm^2	9.869 233 E−04
k_{rg}	Permeability, relative, to gas	L^2/L^2	fraction	fraction	1.0* E+00
k_{ro}	Permeability, relative, to oil	L^2/L^2	fraction	fraction	1.0* E+00
k_{rw}	Permeability, relative, to water	L^2/L^2	fraction	fraction	1.0* E+00
k_w	Permeability, effective, to water	L^2	md	μm^2	9.869 233 E−04
K	Grain peakedness attribute				
K	Proportionality constant in Eq. 2.4				

Symbol	Description	Dimensions	Customary Units	SPE-Preferred SI Metric Units	Customary to Metric Conversion Factors
K_ϕ	Grain peakedness attribute, expressed in phi units				
L	Distance above a producing zone	L	ft	m	3.048* E−01
L	Length characterizing pore geometry of the rock	L	ft	m	3.048* E−01
L	Length of rock sample	L	cm	mm	1.0* E+01
L_e	Length of tortuous flow path through rock sample	L	cm	mm	1.0* E+01
n_1	Pumpstroke count when sample arrived at the surface				
n_2	Pumpstroke count when sample was drilled				
n_ℓ	Pumpstrokes required to circulate from the bottom to the surface				
p	Pressure	m/Lt^2	lbf/sq in.	kPa	6.894 757 E+00
p_e	Reservoir pressure at drainage boundary	m/Lt^2	lbf/sq in.	kPa	6.894 757 E+00
p_f	Pore-fluid pressure	m/Lt^2	lbf/sq in.	kPa	6.894 757 E+00
p_f/h	Hydrostatic pressure gradient	m/L^2t^2	psi/ft	kPa/m	2.262 059 E+01
p_R	Reservoir pressure	m/Lt^2	lbf/sq in.	kPa	6.894 757 E+00
p_s	Surface pressure	m/Lt^2	lbf/sq in.	kPa	6.894 757 E+00
p_w	Borehole fluid pressure	m/Lt^2	lbf/sq in.	kPa	6.894 757 E+00
P_c	Capillary pressure	m/Lt^2	lbf/sq in.	kPa	6.894 757 E+00
P_d	Extrapolated mercury displacement pressure indicating the pressure required to enter the largest pore throat	m/Lt^2	lbf/sq in.	kPa	6.894 757 E+00
q	Fluid production rate	L^3/t	B/D	m^3/d	1.589 873 E−01
q_g	Gas flow rate	L^3/t	scf/D	std m^3/d	2.831 685 E−02
q_m	Drilling fluid circulation rate	L^3/t	U.S. gal/min	dm^3/s	6.309 020 E−02
r	Radius	L	in.	mm	2.54* E+01
r_{ce}	Casing radius, external	L	in.	mm	2.54* E+01
r_{ci}	Casing radius, internal	L	in.	mm	2.54* E+01
r_e	Radius of drainage zone	L	in.	mm	2.54* E+01
r_{if}	Radius of infiltered zone	L	in.	mm	2.54* E+01
r_{imp}	Radius of impregnated zone	L	in.	mm	2.54* E+01
r_{mc}	Radius of mudcake face	L	in.	mm	2.54* E+01
r_w	Radius of borehole wall	L	in.	mm	2.54* E+01
r_1, r_2	Radii of curvature of fluid interface	L	micron	μm	1.0* E+00
R	Rate of penetration	L/t	ft/hr	mm/s	8.466 667 E−02
R	Gas/oil ratio	L^3/L^3	scf/bbl	std m^3/m^3	1.801 175 E−01
R_{an}	Resistivity of annulus zone	mL^3/tq^2	Ω-m	Ω·m	1.0* E+00
R_m	Resistivity of mud	mL^3/tq^2	Ω-m	Ω·m	1.0* E+00
R_{mc}	Resistivity of mudcake	mL^3/tq^2	Ω-m	Ω·m	1.0* E+00
R_t	True resistivity	mL^3/tq^2	Ω-m	Ω·m	1.0* E+00
R_{xo}	Resistivity of flushed-zone	mL^3/tq^2	Ω-m	Ω·m	1.0* E+00
s	Direction of flow	L	ft	m	3.048* E−01
S	Saturation	L^3/L^3	volume fraction	m^3/m^3	1.0* E+00
S_{gr}	Gas saturation retained in cuttings at standard conditions	L^3/L^3	volume fraction	m^3/m^3	1.0* E+00
S_{iw}	Irreducible water saturation	L^3/L^3	volume fraction	m^3/m^3	1.0* E+00
S_k	Grain symmetry attribute				

Symbol	Description	Dimensions	Customary Units	SPE-Preferred SI Metric Units	Customary to Metric Conversion Factors
$S_{k\phi}$	Grain symmetry attribute, expressed in phi units				
S_O	Trask sorting coefficient				
S_{or}	Oil saturation retained in cuttings at standard conditions	L^3/L^3	volume fraction	m^3/m^3	1.0* E+00
S_w	Water saturation	L^3/L^3	volume fraction	m^3/m^3	1.0* E+00
t	Time; total time of production	t	hr	h	1.0* E+00
t_h	Time to drill interval h	t	hr	h	1.0* E+00
t_k	Circulation time	t	hr	h	1.0* E+00
Δt_{ws}	Shut-in time	t	hr	h	1.0* E+00
T	Temperature	T	°F	°C	(°F−32)/1.8
$\partial T/\partial D$	Temperature gradient	T/L	°F/100 ft	mK/m	1.822 689 E+01
$T_{G(o,t)}$	Geothermal temperature at fluid entry point	T	°F	°C	(°F−32)/1.8
T_n	Geothermal temperature at depth n	T	°F	°C	(°F−32)/1.8
$\Delta T_{(r_D,t)}$	Temperature disturbance at radial distance, r_D, and time, t	T	°F	°C	5/9 E+00
T_R	Reservoir temperature	T	°F	°C	(°F−32)/1.8
T_s	Surface temperature	T	°F	°C	(°F−32)/1.8
T_{wf}	Temperature of borehole fluid	T	°F	°C	(°F−32)/1.8
$T_{wf(L,t)}$	Fluid temperature at distance L above producing zone	T	°F	°C	(°F−32)/1.8
$T_{wf(o,t)}$	Fluid temperature at fluid entry point	T	°F	°C	(°F−32)/1.8
T_{ws}	Static well temperature	T	°F	°C	(°F−32)/1.8
T_1	Nuclear magnetic relaxation time of rock/fluid system	t	seconds	s	1.0* E+00
T_{1b}	Nuclear magnetic relaxation time of bulk fluid	t	seconds	s	1.0* E+00
$\Delta T_{(1,0)}$	Borehole temperature disturbance at start of circulation period	T	°F	°C	5/9 E+00
$\vec{u}$	Volume rate of flow per unit cross-sectional area, a vector quantity	L/t	cu ft/(sec-sq ft)	$m^3/(s{\cdot}m^2)$	3.048* E−01
u_h	Heat flux	m/t^3	Btu/(hr-sq ft)	kW/m^2	3.154 591 E−03
U	System heat-transfer coefficient	m/t^3T	Btu/(hr-sq ft-°F)	$kW/(m^2{\cdot}K)$	5.678 263 E−03
$(V_b)_{P_c}$	Fractional bulk volume occupied by mercury at a capillary pressure, P_c	L^3/L^3	volume fraction	m^3/m^3	1.0* E+00
$(V_b)_{P_\infty}$	Fractional bulk volume occupied by mercury at infinite mercury pressure	L^3/L^3	volume fraction	m^3/m^3	1.0* E+00
V_{gr}	Volume, grain; volume of all formation solids except all shales	L^3	cu ft	m^3	2.831 685 E−02
V_{ig}	Volume, intergranular; volume of fluids and all shales	L^3	cu ft	m^3	2.831 685 E−02
V_{im}	Volume, intermatrix; volume of fluids and dispersed shales	L^3	cu ft	m^3	2.831 685 E−02

Symbol	Description	Dimensions	Customary Units	SPE-Preferred SI Metric Units	Customary to Metric Conversion Factors
V_{ma}	Volume, matrix; volume of all formation solids except dispersed shales	L^3	cu ft	m^3	2.831 685 E−02
V_{mc}	Mudcake volume	L^3	mL	cm^3	1.0* E+00
V_{mf}	Mud filtrate volume	L^3	mL	cm^3	1.0* E+00
V_s	Volume, all formation solids	L^3	cu ft	m^3	2.831 685 E−02
W	Weight on bit	mL/t^2	lbf	N	4.448 222 E+00
X_d	Thickness of diffuse layer	L	micron	μm	1.0* E+00
X_H	Distance from clay surface to outer Helmholtz plane	L	micron	μm	1.0* E+00
z	Gas compressibility factor	L^3/L^3	volume fraction	m^3/m^3	1.0* E+00
z_R	Gas compressibility factor at reservoir conditions	L^3/L^3	volume fraction	m^3/m^3	1.0* E+00
z_s	Gas compressibility factor at surface conditions				
Z	Elevation above an arbitrary datum	L	ft	m	3.048* E−01
β	Difference between unity and the ratio of the bulk compressibility to the rock matrix compressibility	L^3/L^3	volume fraction	m^3/m^3	1.0* E+00
θ	Angle between granular solid surface and fluid interface; angular position around borehole wall		degrees	radians	1.745 329 E−02
η_h	Rock thermal diffusivity	L^2/t	sq ft/sec	mm^2/s	9.290 304* E+04
μ	Viscosity	m/Lt	cp	Pa·s	1.0* E−03
μ_f	Viscosity of formation fluid	m/Lt	cp	Pa·s	1.0* E−03
μ_{if}	Viscosity of fluid in filtered zone	m/Lt	cp	Pa·s	1.0* E−03
μ_{imp}	Viscosity of fluid in impregnated zone	m/Lt	cp	Pa·s	1.0* E−03
μ_{mf}	Viscosity of mud filtrate	m/Lt	cp	Pa·s	1.0* E−03
ν	Poisson's ratio				
ρ	Density	m/L^3	g/cm^3	kg/m^3	1.0* E+03
ρ_b	Bulk density	m/L^3	g/cm^3	kg/m^3	1.0* E+03
$\bar{\rho}_b$	Mean bulk density of formations	m/L^3	g/cm^3	kg/m^3	1.0* E+03
ρ_f	Fluid density	m/L^3	g/cm^3	kg/m^3	1.0* E+03
ρ_f	Fluid density	m/L^3	lbm/gal	kg/m^3	1.198 264 E+02
ρ_{m1}	Normal mud density for area	m/L^3	lbm/gal	kg/m^3	1.198 264 E+02
ρ_{m2}	Equivalent circulating density	m/L^3	lbm/gal	kg/m^3	1.198 264 E+02
ρ_o	Density of oil	m/L^3	g/cm^3	kg/m^3	1.0* E+03
ρ_w	Density of water	m/L^3	g/cm^3	kg/m^3	1.0* E+03
σ	Interfacial tension	m/t^2	dyne/cm	mN/m	1.0* E+00
σ_ϕ	Grain sorting attribute, expressed in phi units		phi units	phi units	1.0* E+00
$\sigma_{ri}, \sigma_{zi}, \sigma_{\theta i}$	Stress components at borehole wall, in cylindrical coordinates	m/Lt^2	lbf/sq in.	MPa	6.894 757 E−03
σ_e	Effective stress	m/Lt^2	lbf/sq in.	MPa	6.894 757 E−03
σ_t	Total stress	m/Lt^2	lbf/sq in.	MPa	6.894 757 E−03
σ_v	Vertical stress	m/Lt^2	lbf/sq in.	MPa	6.894 757 E−03
σ_{zo}	Stress caused by overburden load	m/Lt^2	lbf/sq in.	MPa	6.894 757 E−03
σ_Θ	Effective tangential stress	m/Lt^2	lbf/sq in.	MPa	6.894 757 E−03
τ_r	Shear strength	m/Lt^2	lbf/sq in.	kPa	6.894 757 E+00
ϕ	Porosity; fraction of bulk volume occupied by pore space	L^3/L^3	volume fraction	m^3/m^3	1.0* E+00

Symbol	Description	Dimensions	Customary Units	SPE-Preferred SI Metric Units	Customary to Metric Conversion Factors
ϕ	Grain diameter, expressed in phi units	L	phi units	phi units	1.0* E+00
ϕ_a	Porosity, apparent	L^3/L^3	volume fraction	m^3/m^3	1.0* E+00
ϕ_e	Porosity, effective; fraction of bulk volume occupied by interconnected pore space	L^3/L^3	volume fraction	m^3/m^3	1.0* E+00
ϕ_{ig}	"Porosity," intergranular; fraction of bulk volume occupied by fluids and all shales	L^3/L^3	volume fraction	m^3/m^3	1.0* E+00
ϕ_{im}	"Porosity," intermatrix; fraction of bulk volume occupied by fluids and dispersed shales	L^3/L^3	volume fraction	m^3/m^3	1.0* E+00
ϕ_{ne}	Porosity, noneffective; fraction of bulk volume occupied by noninterconnected pore space	L^3/L^3	volume fraction	m^3/m^3	1.0* E+00

Subscripts

a = apparent
an = annular
b = bit, bulk
cs = corrected (d-exponent)
C = capillary
d = extrapolated displacement pressure, diffuse layer
e = effective, outer boundary
f = formation, fluid, pore-fluid, flowing
g = gas
g/gal = expressed as grains per gallon
gr = grain
G = geothermal
h = hole, thickness drilled, heat
H = Helmholtz plane
i = invasion, ith element, at borehole face
if = infiltered
ig = intergranular
im = intermatrix
imp = impregnated
iw = irreducible water
k = circulating, skewness
l = length drilled
L = distance
m = expressed as molality
m = mud
ma = matrix
mc = mud cake

mf = mud filtrate
mg/L = expressed as milligrams per liter
M = expressed as molarity
n = at depth n, time
ne = noneffective
N = expressed as normality
o = oil
O = Trask sorting coefficient
ppm = expressed as parts per million
P_c = at capillary pressure P_c
r = residual, relative, radial component in cylindrical coordinates, rock
r_D = radial (dimensionless)
R = reservoir
s = surface, solid, static, direction of flow
t = true, total, time
v = vertical
w = wellbore, water
W = expressed as weight percent
xc = corrected (d-exponent)
xo = flushed
z = vertical component in cylindrical coordinates
zo = due to overburden load
θ = azimuthal component in cylindrical coordinates
ϕ = expressed in phi units
∞ = infinite

Selected Reading List

History of Well Logging

Allaud, L. and Martin, M.: *Schlumberger, the History of a Technique*, John Wiley & Sons Inc., New York City (1977).

Archie, G.E.: "Formation Evaluation," *Impact of New Technology on the U.S. Petroleum Industry 1946-1965*, Natl. Pet. Council, Washington, DC (1967) 150-57.

Johnson, H.M.: "A History of Well Logging," *Geophysics* (1962) 27, 507-27.

Leonardon, E.G.: "Logging, Sampling, and Testing," *History of Petroleum Engineering*, API, Dallas (1961) 493-578.

McDonal, F.J.: "Geophysics," *Impact of New Technology on the U.S. Petroleum Industry 1946-1965*, Natl. Pet. Council, Washington, DC (1967) 67-71.

Lithology

Dunham, R.J.: "Classification of Carbonate Rocks According to Depositional Texture," *Classification of Carbonate Rocks*, Memoir 1, AAPG, Tulsa (1962) 108-21.

Grim, R.E.: *Clay Mineralogy*, second edition, McGraw-Hill Book Co. Inc., New York City (1968).

Pettijohn, F.J.: *Sedimentary Rocks*, third edition, Harper & Row Publishers Inc., New York City (1975).

van Olphen, H.: *An Introduction to Clay Colloid Chemistry*, second edition, Interscience Publishers, New York City (1977).

Pore Space Properties

Archie, G.E.: "Classification of Carbonate Reservoir Rocks and Petrophysical Considerations," *Bull.*, AAPG (1952) 36, 278-98.

Beard, D.C. and Weyl, P.K.: "Influence of Texture on Porosity and Permeability of Unconsolidated Sand," *Bull.*, AAPG (1973) 57, 349-69.

Choquette, P.W. and Pray, L.C.' "Geologic Nomenclature and Classification of Porosity in Sedimentary Carbonates," *Bull.*, AAPG (1970) 54, 207-50.

Enos, P. and Sawatsky, L.H.: "Pore Networks in Holocene Carbonate Sediments," *J. Sed. Pet.* (1981) 51, 961-85.

Hubbert, M.K.: "Darcy's Law and the Field Equations of the Flow of Underground Fluids," *Trans.*, AIME (1956) 207, 222-39.

Lucia, F.J.: "Petrophysical Parameters Estimated From Visual Descriptions of Carbonate Rocks: A Field Classification of Carbonate Pore Space," *J. Pet. Tech.* (March 1983) 629-37.

Neasham, J.W.: "The Morphology of Dispersed Clay in Sandstone Reservoirs and Its Effect on Sandstone Shaliness, Pore Space, and Fluid Flow Properties," paper SPE 6858 presented at the 1977 SPE Annual Technical Conference and Exhibition, Denver, Oct. 9-12.

Pittman, E.D.: "Microporosity in Carbonate Rocks," *Bull.*, AAPG (Oct. 1971) 55, 1873.

Pittman, E.D.: "Porosity, Diagenesis and Productive Capability of Sandstone Reservoirs," *Aspects of Diagenesis*, Special Publication 26, Soc. of Economic Paleontologists and Mineralogists, Tulsa (1979) 159-74.

Thomeer, J.H.M.: "Introduction of a Pore Geometrical Factor Defined by the Capillary Pressure Curve," *Trans.*, AIME (1960) 219, 354-58.

Fluid Distribution

Hassler, G.L., Brunner, E., and Deahl, T.J.: "Role of Capillarity in Oil Production," *Trans.*, AIME (1944) 155, 155-74.

Leverett, M.C.: "Capillary Behavior in Porous Solids," *Trans.*, AIME (1941) 142, 152-68.

Pickell, J.J., Swanson, B.F., and Hickman, W.B.: "Application of Air-Mercury and Oil-Air Capillary Pressure Data In the Study of Pore Structure and Fluid Distribution," *Soc. Pet. Eng. J.* (March 1966) 55-61; *Trans.*, AIME, 237.

Petrophysical Relationships Among Fundamental Reservoir Properties

Archie, G.E.: "Introduction to Petrophysics of Reservoir Rocks," *Bull.*, AAPG (1950) 34, 943-61.

Buckles, R.S.: "Correlating and Averaging Connate Water Saturation Data," *J. Cdn. Pet. Tech.* (Jan.-March 1965) 42-52.

Morris, R.L. and Biggs, W.P.: "Using Log-Derived Values of Water Saturation and Porosity," *Trans.*, SPWLA Symposium (1967) paper X.

Timur, A.: "An Investigation of Permeability, Porosity, and Residual Water Saturation Relationships," *Trans.*, SPWLA Symposium (1968) paper J.

Compositions of Formation Waters

"Analysis of Oil-Field Waters," *Recommended Practice 45*, second edition, API, Dallas (1968).

Collins, A.G.: *Geochemistry of Oilfield Waters*, Elsevier Scientific Publishing Co., Amsterdam (1975).

Reistle, C.E. Jr.: "Identification of Oil-Field Waters by Chemical Analysis," Technical Paper 404, USBM (1927).

Stiff, H.A. Jr.: "Interpretation of Chemical Water Analysis by Means of Patterns," *Trans.*, AIME (1951) 192, 376-79.

Washburne, C.W.: "Oil-field Brines," *Trans.*, AIME (1921) 65, 269-89.

Borehole Geometry

Campbell, R.L.: "Borehole Geometry," *Notes*, AAPG Short Course on The Borehole Environment, San Francisco (May 1981).

Hilchie, D.W.: "Caliper Logging—Theory and Practice," *The Log Analyst* (1968) 9, 3-11.

Invasion

Doll, H.G.: "Filtrate Invasion in Highly Permeable Sands," *Pet. Eng.* (Jan. 1955) 53-66.

Ferguson, C.K. and Klotz, J.A.: "Filtration from Mud During Drilling," *Trans.*, AIME (1954) 201, 29-42.

Glenn, E.E., Slusser, M.L., and Huitt, J.L.: "Factors Affecting Well Productivity—I. Drilling Fluid Filtration," *Trans.*, AIME (1957) 210, 126-31.

Glenn, E.E. and Slusser, M.L.: "Factors Affecting Well Productivity—II. Drilling Fluid Particle Invasion into Porous Media," *Trans.*, AIME (1957) 210, 132-39.

Gondouin, M. and Heim, A.: "Experimentally Determined Resistivity Profiles in Invaded Water and Oil Sands for Linear Flows," *J. Pet. Tech.* (1964) 337–48; *Trans.*, AIME, **231**.

Schremp, F.W. and Johnson, V.L.: "Drilling Fluid Filter Loss at High Temperatures and Pressures," *Trans.*, AIME (1952) **195**, 157–62.

von Engelhardt, W.: "Filter Cake Formation and Water Losses in Deep Drilling Muds," Illinois State Geological Survey Circular 191 (1954) 1–24.

Stress and Temperature Disturbance

Bradley, W.B.: "Failure of Inclined Boreholes," *Trans.*, ASME (1979) **101**, 232–39.

Edwardson, M.J. *et al.*: "Calculation of Formation Temperature Disturbances Caused by Mud Circulation," *J. Pet. Tech.* (April 1962) 416–26; *Trans.*, AIME, **225**.

Fertl, W.H.: *Abnormal Formation Pressures*, Elsevier Scientific Publishing Co., Amsterdam/New York City (1976).

Risnes, R., Bratli, R.K., and Horsrud, P.: "Sand Stresses Around a Wellbore," *Soc. Pet. Eng. J.* (Dec. 1982) 883–98.

Tool Performance In Nonideal Environments

Misk, A. *et al.*: "Effects of Hole Conditions on Log Measurements and Formation Evaluation," SAID, Third Annual Logging Symposium (June 1976).

Mud Logging Environment

Field Geologist's Training Guide, Exploration Logging Inc., Sacramento (1980).

Hoberock, L.L.: "Shale Shaker Selection and Operation," *Oil and Gas J.* (Nov. 23, 1981) 107–13.

Hoberock, L.L.: "Shale Shaker Selection and Operation," *Oil and Gas J.* (Dec. 7, 1981) 130–41.

Hoberock, L.L.: "Shale Shaker Selection and Operation," *Oil and Gas J.* (Dec. 21, 1981) 80–87.

Hoberock, L.L.: "Shale Shaker Selection and Operation," *Oil and Gas J.* (Jan. 4, 1982) 89–100.

Hoberock, L.L.: "Shale Shaker Selection and Operation," *Oil and Gas J.* (Feb. 1, 1982) 124–26.

Liljestrand, W.E.: "Degassing Mud," *Oil and Gas J.* (Feb. 25, 1980) 112–14.

Liljestrand, W.E.: "Degassing Mud," *Oil and Gas J.* (March 3, 1980) 69–70, 72, 74.

Ormsby, G.S.: "Drilling Fluid Solids Removal," *Drilling Practices Manual*, P.L. Moore (ed.), The Petroleum Publishing Co., Tulsa (1974) 133–203.

Rate of Penetration

Shepherd, G.F. and Atwater, G.I.: "Geologic Use of Drilling-Time Data," *The Oil Weekly* (July 3, 1944) 17–19, 22, 24, 38, 41–42, 44, 46.

Hydrocarbon Logging

Choate, L.R.: *Mud Analysis Logging*, Baroid Div., National Lead Co., Houston (1963).

David, D.J.: *Gas Chromatograph Detectors*, John Wiley and Sons Inc., New York City (1974) 14–75.

Fluorescence and Phosphorescence Analysis, D.M. Hercules (ed.), Interscience Publishers, Div. of John Wiley and Sons Inc., New York City (1966).

Grob, R.L.: *Modern Practice of Gas Chromatography*, John Wiley and Sons Inc., New York City (1977).

Hayward, J.T.: "Continuous Logging at Rotary-Drilling Wells," *Drill. and Prod. Prac. 1940*, API (1941) 8–19.

Mercer, R.F.: "Liberated, Produced, Recycled, or Contamination?" *Trans.*, SPWLA Symposium (1974) paper T.

Mud Logging: Principles and Interpretations, Applications Manual MS 196, Exploration Logging Inc., Sacramento (1979).

Riecker, R.E.: "Hydrocarbon Fluorescence and Migration of Petroleum," *Bull.*, AAPG (Jan. 1962) **46**, 60–75.

Logging Lithology

Formation Evaluation, Part 1: Geological Procedures, Applications Manual MS 3017, Exploration Logging Inc., Sacramento (1981).

Low, J.W.: "Examination of Well Cuttings," *Quart.*, Colorado School of Mines (1951) **46**, 1–48.

Swanson, R.G.: *Sample Examination Manual*, Methods in Exploration Series, AAPG, Tulsa (1981).

Pressure Detection

Bourgoyne, A.T. Jr., and Young, F.S. Jr.: "The Use of Drillability Logs for Formation Evaluation and Abnormal Pressure Detection," *Trans.*, SPWLA Symposium (1973) paper T.

Goldsmith, R.G.: "Why Gas Cut Mud Is Not Always a Serious Problem," *World Oil* (Oct. 1972) 51–52, 54, 101.

Jorden, J.R. and Shirley, O.J.: "Application of Drilling Performance Data to Overpressure Detection," *J. Pet. Tech.* (Nov. 1966) **18**, 1387–94.

Theory and Evaluation of Formation Pressures—The Pressure Log Reference Manual, Applications Manual MS 156, Rev. C, Exploration Logging Inc., Sacramento (1981).

Recommended Mud Logging Practices

Recommended Practices for Hydrocarbon Logging, SPWLA, Houston (1983).

Heat Flow and Temperature

Handbook of Physical Constants, S.P. Clarke Jr. (ed.), Memoir 97, GSA, Boulder, CO (1966) 459–82.

Ramey, H.J. Jr.: "Wellbore Heat Transmission," *J. Pet. Tech.* (April 1962) 427–35; *Trans.*, AIME, **225**.

Raymond, L.R.: "Temperature Distribution in a Circulating Drilling Fluid," *J. Pet. Tech.* (March 1969) 333–41; *Trans.*, AIME, **246**.

Sclater, J.G. and Francheteau, J.: "The Implications of Terrestrial Heat Flow Observations on Current Tectonic and Geochemical Models of the Crust and Upper Mantle of the Earth," *Geophys. J. Royal Astronomical Soc.* (1970) **20**, 509–42.

Somerton, W.H.: "Some Thermal Characteristics of Porous Rocks," *J. Pet. Tech.* (May 1958) 61–64; *Trans.*, AIME, **213**, 375–78.

van Orstrand, C.E.: "On the Correlation of Isogeothermal Surfaces with the Rock Strata," *Physics* (1932) **2**, 139–53.

Zierfuss, H. and van der Vliet, G.: "Laboratory Measurement of Heat Conductivity of Sedimentary Rocks," *Bull.*, AAPG (1956) **40**, 2475–88.

Interpretation of Temperature Logs

Bird, J.M.: "Interpretation of Temperature Logs in Water- and Gas-Injection Wells and Gas-Producing Wells," *Drill and Prod. Prac.*, API (1954) 187–95.

Curtis, M.R. and Witterholt, E.J.: "Use of the Temperature Log for Determining Flow Rates in Producing Wells," paper SPE 4637 presented at the 1973 SPE Annual Meeting, Las Vegas, Oct. 1–3.

Dowdle, W.L., and Cobb, W.M.: "Static Formation Temperature from Well Logs—An Empirical Method," *J. Pet. Tech.* (Nov. 1975) 1326–30.

Edwardson, M.J. *et al.*: "Calculation of Formation Temperature Disturbances Caused by Mud Circulation," *J. Pet. Tech.* (April 1962) 416–26; *Trans.*, AIME, **225**.

Guyod, H.: "Temperature Well Logging," *Oil Weekly* (Oct. 21, 1946) 35–39.

Guyod, H.: "Temperature Well Logging," *Oil Weekly* (Oct. 28, 1946) 33–42.

Guyod, H.: "Temperature Well Logging," *Oil Weekly* (Nov. 4, 1946) 32–39.

Guyod, H.: "Temperature Well Logging," *Oil Weekly* (Nov. 11, 1946) 50–54.

Guyod, H.: "Temperature Well Logging," *Oil Weekly* (Dec. 2, 1946) 27–34.

Guyod, H.: "Temperature Well Logging," *Oil Weekly* (Dec. 9, 1946) 36–40.

Guyod, H.: "Temperature Well Logging," *Oil Weekly* (Dec. 16, 1946) 38–40.

Kunz, K.S. and Tixier, M.P.: "Temperature Surveys in Gas Producing Wells," *J. Pet. Tech.* (July 1955) 111–19; *Trans.*, AIME, **204**.

Author Index

Subject Index